Paint

- A Boy Soldier's Journey

Simon Hutt

PANIC

PRESS

Visit the author online at www.simonhutt.com

A Panic Press Book

ISBN 978-0-9564831-0-2

Panic Press
The Meridian
4 Copthall Avenue
Station Square
Coventry CV1 2FL
England

This book is also available in **e-book** format, details of which are available at www.panicpressbooks.com

Front Cover Image: Sitting in the front line house in Lijeskovac, Northern Bosnia.

Contents

Introduction

In early 2007 I had another breakdown. I had lost another job and had no money, I started to take it out on my family, and the shouting and the aggression came to the surface. My family had never seen me like that before and for the first time ever I saw fear on their faces. Post Traumatic Stress Disorder is like that; the slightest crack becomes a landslide in minutes, taking over and overwhelming you with the darkness. I immediately saw a counsellor; scared at what I might do to the people I loved the most. We both talked, awkwardly at first until after a few sessions I eventually realised I was talking about the stuff that in the previous weeks had almost made me want to jump in front of a train. He told me to write about my experiences; "it sometimes helps," he said. I started writing and didn't stop.

My initial therapy of a few pages became thousands of emotional words and I realised as I wrote that there is so much to remember that eventually it will be forgotten and my story will no longer exist, so I had to write it all down. Now it is my history, intertwined with events that shaped Europe and the Middle East at the end of the twentieth century, and my children will one day read it, as could their children.

I ought to point out that if you want to read about the ultimate SAS warrior, acts of bravery, tales of "mercenaries" and lurid accounts of killing people then you've got the wrong book. Books that have been written about, or by, foreign volunteers in the former Yugoslavia (we were volunteers not mercenaries) are usually written by the idiot minority; those that went to fight for money (there was none), adventurers, dreamers, psychopaths and criminals. Unfortunately it's stories such as these that grab the headlines. The majority of foreign volunteers fought for a country that was being torn apart by an aggressor whilst the rest of the world looked on, the problem is that a foreign volunteer saying that the arms embargo needs to be lifted so Croatia can defend itself isn't quite as sexy as some idiot telling the world how much he enjoys killing people.

Unfortunately the idiot will always get the headlines, maybe the public's perception is one of the reasons why it's taken me so long to even consider writing this. I hope this book goes some way to redress the balance, and hopefully change peoples opinions.

The other problem with writing a book of this nature is that if you put your head above the parapet, expect to be shot at. At the moment I'm still a nobody, however by the time you read this book I could have been made out by some people to be a neo-nazi killing machine or suicidal maniac just by using a few out of context quotes, these quotes will then themselves be quoted and probably be used as some kind of proof that I am an evil war criminal. The media machine used by all sides during the war in former Yugoslavia is still very much alive and although the physical fighting has stopped the hatred and propaganda war goes on. There's a lot of lies out there and its in a lot of peoples interests for us to be made out as the bad guys or the psychopaths that we are often portrayed as. I've made a point of being as honest as possible throughout this book, there are plenty of things I would like to forget and it would be easy to gloss over the bad bits or not mention them altogether, but like I said; this is the truth.

The 1991 to 1995 Balkan conflict can best be described as "confusing". The shifting alliances of the war and the blaming of war crimes on "the others" makes any clarity difficult, to make it easier I have decided to use the terms Serb, Croat or Bosnian rather than be drawn into the politics of ethnic division. To me, and at the time the Bosnian part of my story takes place, the Serbs were the only enemy, Croatia and Bosnia were allies. Thankfully I had no part in the Croat/Muslim fighting which began soon after I left. The same applies to statistics; rather than be drawn into one version of facts over another I've tried to leave the numbers out unless its relevant or can be objectively verified. Which is why I trust the casualty figures of the Gulf war, but don't mention how many people are still missing after the Serbs took over Srebrenica, for instance. It may however encourage the reader to look a little deeper.

I think a comedian once joked that the UN were organising a special relief convoy for the former Yugoslavia as they urgently needed vowels. Croatian names and places can be hard to read and pronounce but for the sake of accuracy I've left them as they are meant to be. As a quick (and extremely basic) guide however; a "Č" and "Ć" are both usually pronounced –tch, and a "C" -ts, a "J" is usually pronounced –y, therefore the name Crny is pronounced "Tserny" and the towns of Brčko and Osijek would be pronounced "Birchko" and "Osiyek" respectively. A "Ž" as in Županja and Željko is pronounced –zh, and a "Š" as in Orašje is pronounced -sh. The same applies to names; many end in –ić such as Marco Tigrić ("Tigritch"), and Ratko Mladić ("Mladitch"). I've also tried to keep to the military terms that are used, again for accuracy, therefore terms like "Bergen", "'66", and "RPG" are used and for that reason there's a Glossary at the end of the book.

I suppose at this point I have to thank everyone, not just for getting this book out there but also for all the years leading up to it. There are times in the last twenty years when it can't have been easy being one of my friends or family, it's testament to those people that they are still my friends today, as it would have been very easy to walk away. As a parent or sibling it's not possible to walk away, and watching a loved one fall apart must be one of the hardest things to cope with. So this is not only a thank you, but also an apology. I have to thank in particular John Trow; the man who said "Why not write about your experiences?" My friend John Gibbons for reading through this and keeping me motivated right from the start, Pete from the Gulf War as well as Terry and Ivan, fellow volunteers mentioned in the book, these three have helped me with the military accuracy as well as filling in the gaps in my memory. Also all the members of the USDDR (Association of Foreign Volunteers of the Homeland War) whose feedback has made it all worth it, as well as being the nicest bunch of madmen I've ever met!

Most importantly I have to thank my wife, always with me through the bad days as well as the good and if it wasn't for her I probably wouldn't be here at all. A thank you doesn't really seem enough.

Finally I would like to dedicate this book to my late Father –

Bill Hutt.

Maps

The Liberation of Kuwait, Operation Desert Storm. Feb 1991.

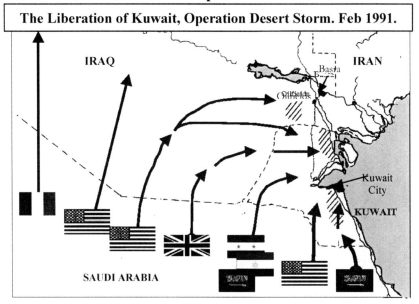

Key to Allied Forces (Left to Right)

*VII US Corps included all other coalition forces

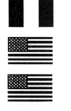 French 6th Light Division

US Airborne and Infantry Divisions

US Armoured Divisions (VII US Corps*)

UK 1st Armoured Division (VII US Corps)

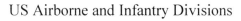 Syrian /Egyptian /Saudi Armoured Divisions

 US Marine Divisions

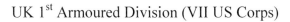 Joint Arab Forces (Including Mujahedeen)

Croatia, Serbia & Bosnia

Maribor □

HUNGARY

■Zagreb

CROATIA

Osijek □   Vukovar □

Belgrade ■

Vinkovci □

SERBIA

REP. SRPSKA

■Sarajevo

FED. BOSNIA HERZEGOVINA

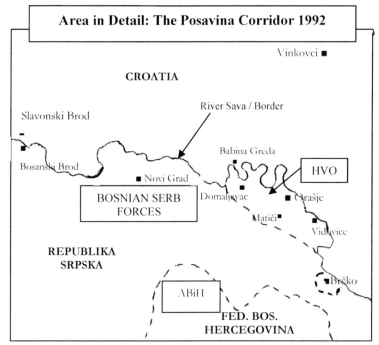

Area in Detail: The Posavina Corridor 1992

Vinkovci ■

CROATIA

River Sava / Border

Slavonski Brod

Babina Greda

Bosanski Brod

HVO

■ Novi Grad

BOSNIAN SERB
FORCES

Domaljevac   ■ Grašje

Matiči ■

Vidovice

REPUBLIKA
SRPSKA

Brčko

ABiH

FED. BOS.
HERCEGOVINA

1. Saturday, November 14th 1992; 10 AM

The house had been left for some time, it might even have once been a shop front as the window was huge, though no glass was left. It was grey and dusty inside and there were no obvious signs that the room had been used for anything in particular. In the middle of the grey floor in stark contrast to its surroundings was a large crimson puddle of liquid.

"Jesus! Look at all that blood!" I said, wondering if whoever owned it was still alive.

Joe had a good look at the pool of red liquid. I noticed now that it had footprints in and smeared marks where someone must have been dragged. There was even the sickly metallic smell of blood.

"That ain't blood," said Farmer Joe confidently.

"What?" I said, not quite understanding what he meant.

The pool had absorbed the dust on the floor and was a greyish-red around the edges; the centre of the puddle was a dark red, almost black.

"It ain't blood, I've seen it before in 'Nam. And that ain't blood."

It was a good couple of pints worth and I was no Doctor but I was sure it was blood. In the warmth of the room flies flew in zigzags above the pool of claret.

"What do you mean it's not blood? Of course it's blood," I said, confused as to what else it could be.

"I'm tellin' ya, that ain't blood!" Joe was adamant.

"We're in the middle of a warzone, it's a derelict house and there's a fucking big red puddle on the floor, what the fuck else can it be?" I said wondering if Joe was just saying it to put me at ease and make me feel better.

"It's paint. Blood don't look like that."

"Paint!"

I didn't believe this. I wasn't sure I heard him properly.

"Paint?"

"Yep, that's paint all right; I know the difference between paint and blood, that's paint."

"Paint?" I repeated, "what's someone doing out here with a pot of red paint?"

"Don't know," he said.

"Were they doing a spot of decorating before being ethnically cleansed?"

"Don't know how or why, I'm just telling ya, it's paint." Joe looked convinced that it was paint, and his face was telling me that he didn't like arguments, he was right and that was the end of it. Here was a Vietnam veteran telling me that the big red pool of liquid on the floor of a derelict house in a front line village of war-torn Northern Bosnia was, in fact, paint. Joe was shaking his head.

"But you can see the boot prints in it, the drag marks…"

The deafening rumble of the armoured personnel carrier stopped any further talking, its tracks squeaking loudly on the paved road, I had been too carried away with my insane conversation with an equally bizarre friend to notice the vehicle was right next to us.

I turned and looked…

2. Boy Soldier

I had always wanted to be in the Army for as long as I could remember, the Falklands War was a strong memory, but it was of the Royal Marines marching with their rifles and Union Jacks and the liberation of the Islands that stuck in my mind, not the sinking of HMS Coventry or Simon Weston's horrific injuries. My toys were all Action Men and small plastic toy soldiers who always ended up spread all over the garden after a summer of epic battles. The posters on my wall were of soldiers and military stuff, I never thought of any other option than joining the Army. At the age of fourteen and a half I had enquired about joining and sat some tests and watched some videos, then at the earliest opportunity, aged fifteen, I took the Queens shilling (eight pounds), swore an oath for God, Queen and Country and signed up. My parents had to give their permission, and also sign the papers, as they were still my legal guardians until I was eighteen. They knew this was always my dream but still didn't want to sign the forms and tried to persuade me to join the Engineers or REME, something where I could learn a trade. Eventually and reluctantly they signed the forms, reasoning that if I didn't do it now I'd only get the hump and do it when I was eighteen anyway. After signing up the rest of school seemed even more of a breeze than usual, I didn't need to worry about exam results or coursework or the careers advice, I just enjoyed my last year. I did study for my exams, the bare minimum as I always did, and cruised through them, getting the average grade, a "C" in absolutely everything.

I had turned sixteen in May and left school in June, and then, on the fourth of July 1989 I was driven by my parents to The Junior Leaders Regiment Royal Artillery based in Bramcote, which coincidentally enough, was just outside my hometown of Nuneaton. I didn't really choose to join the Artillery, the recruitment officer said they wouldn't let me join the Infantry as I had a high score in the intelligence tests, and the Artillery covered loads of different types of jobs that I would be more suited to, or so they said.

That first day was a mad buzz of activity being divided into troops of fifty men, with eight troops per intake, and two intakes per year. So I was amongst around four hundred other sixteen year olds from all over the country. Some of them looked much older than sixteen, there were tattoos, smoke breaks and impenetrable accents, you could tell that a lot of them were hard as fuck. Somehow I found myself in the band troop by virtue of being able to make a sound with the flute, and I had my hair shaved off by the same bloke who did my hair in Nuneaton in his shop above the Bus Station.

The accommodation consisted of three large rooms containing fifteen to twenty men, each man having his own bed and wardrobe. Our equipment was issued over the next few days, everything from helmets to bedding and all of it had a brand new Army smell to it. The first week was mainly kit issue and being measured for clothing, the stuff we did have was meant to be placed in a locker a certain way, pressed and folded, boxed off or rolled up exactly the same as everyone else's. We were woken at five-thirty every morning and bedding was stripped down and made into neat blocks of sheets and blankets topped off with the pillow at the top of the mattress. We were taught how to wash and clean and iron correctly, we were even taught how to shave, for most people, including myself, it was the first time we had done it and from then on it would mean shaving every day. The accommodation was kept spotless, each morning each of us had a certain area of responsibility, and mine was the brass pipes under the sink and urinals, which had to be polished first thing in the morning before all of us would join in to polish the wooden floor by hand with thick, bright yellow floor wax and dusters. Every morning there would be a room inspection followed by a parade whereupon we were inspected. There were two troop Sergeants in charge of our training; there was no "good cop, bad cop" routine, it was purely a very angry and shouty double act, one of them a Geordie and one from Nottingham. We could tell early on the type of people who wouldn't make it, the ones with a bad attitude to discipline or the ones who were simply a bit weedy.

I absolutely loved it. For some reason everything came naturally, and I had no problem with all the bullshit and being shouted at or the Sergeants throwing my bed block everywhere or tipping out the contents of my locker that took hours of painstaking attention to detail, it only happened rarely anyway as, just like school, I could still manage to do the minimum to get by and it was always good enough, but they still had to make sure everyone at some point got a bollocking. A few weeks into my training they must have realised I was cruising. It was a Sunday and everyone had to go to church following a parade and inspection.

"You haven't shaved today have you Hutt?" said the Geordie Sergeant looking at my chin.

"Yes Sergeant!" I shouted, knowing full well this would be a no win situation.

"Are you calling me a liar?"

"No Sergeant!"

"So have you shaved today Hutt?" he shouted in my ear.

"No Sergeant!" I lied, wanting it over with.

"HUTT, GET YOURSELF DOWN THE GUARDROOM AND ASK FOR AN ALMIGHTY BEASTING COURTESY OF SERGEANT HEADLEY. DO YOU UNDERSTAND?" he screamed into my face.

"YES SERGEANT!" I shouted back.

"THEN FUCK OFF!"

I marched out of the ranks of other men seeing their faces, which were a mixture of relief that it wasn't them and of trying not to laugh, before running off to the guardroom. The Regimental Police gave me the required "Beasting," which was marching at double time in a courtyard the size of a large room;

"Leftrightleftrightmarktimeforwardleftturnmarktimeforwardl eftturn." And so it went on for an hour in the drizzle, soaked to the skin with sweat and rain, the steam rising from me. I was happy in the knowledge that I had shaved and therefore it was just "my turn", besides I had missed the weekly trying-not-to-fall-asleep competition of church.

The months went on as more of the recruits left or were weeded out, but there was one soldier from Liverpool in the whole troop that the two Sergeants hated with a passion, purely because he was a Scouser, and were determined to make him leave, this was the only time I have ever seen what would be termed "bullying" in the Army and it was horrible. To everyones amazement and his own credit, he carried on and finished training. We were taught how to use a rifle, infantry tactics, Nuclear Biological and Chemical warfare drills, marching, fitness and plenty of other bullshit required for a Junior Leader in the Royal Artillery including, obviously, leadership skills, all with the minimum amount of sleep. Our troop also had to learn their band instruments and the specialist marching that was required. There were plenty of drummers and buglers, but after several months of training we were left with only three flute players which included myself. We learnt to play Congratulations and the theme tune to Van der Valk, but nobody would be able to hear us anyway which was a shame as one of the other flute players was a brilliant musician who had learnt his skills in a marching band in Portadown, Northern Ireland, so it was decided that we would just march around with the band without playing. I also learned basic signalling, this meant learning how to use a radio and more importantly, send Fire Missions, one of the most important jobs in the Artillery. I enjoyed the radio work, and discovered I was pretty good at it, eventually winning a tankard for getting the highest marks in the test for our class. I also somehow found myself on the Regimental Orienteering Team, probably because I could map-read and run at the same time and, improbable as it sounds, was the Junior Armys (that's every sixteen to seventeen year old soldier in training for that year) Orienteering Champion for 1989-90. My parents were well chuffed. And it's my claim to fame.

The years training passed quickly, the first six months was the shouting and the bullshit of basic training, getting rid of the wasters and wankers and at the same time turning the rest of us from sixteen year old schoolboys into swearing, shouting and shaving soldiers, and, though I didn't realise it until I left the Army, they had turned us into very obedient robots. After the first six months, the Sergeants eased off a bit, focusing now on our training, after all, when we got to our adult Regiments, the Sergeants would be judged on how well we had been trained. In May 1990, with my proud parents watching, the 1989 intake of Junior Gunners marched across the parade ground for the last time before becoming "Gunners" and adult soldiers. And while the other soldiers marched on in polished peak caps and rifles, I was standing in the middle of the ranks of bandsmen with an unplayed flute, wearing the Busby and Artillery uniform of the Napoleonic War, needless to say, I felt a total idiot. My Father was all smiles, and even though I looked a total dick, my family were proud of me.

The Junior Leaders Regiment Royal Artillery Band stayed at Bramcote for another couple of months touring England, playing at country fairs and carnivals, despite the fact that we could only play half a dozen tunes and me and my fellow flautists just marched along doing nothing. We felt like real adult soldiers when we mixed with the civilians at these shows trying to impress the local girls or getting into fights with the local youths. We spent those months enjoying ourselves and when back at Bramcote watched the heartbreak of England in the Italia '90 World Cup on a TV donated by my Dad, lying on beds with duvets instead of sheets and blankets. It was when I was on leave that I noticed the difference in me compared to my friends, they were starting jobs or A-Levels. I had plenty of money in my pocket and felt taller, more grown up. I had a positive attitude to everything and I was following my dreams of being a soldier. I didn't envy them at the time.

There were only two of us going to 39 Heavy Regiment, myself and a guy from Wolverhampton who also stayed behind with the Physical Training Display Team (like the band only without the stupid uniforms). All Army units recruit locally and 39 were then known as the "Birmingham Gunners" even though it recruited people from all over the Midlands. Most people went to their local Regiment although a few tried for the Parachute or Royal Marine Artillery, which sounded like too much effort for me as I had fallen into a "comfort zone" following the intensity of basic training, and 39 Regiment had just been equipped with the brand new Multiple Launch Rocket System.

It was just turning autumn of 1990 when I finally arrived at Dempsey Barracks in Sennelager, West Germany. Playing, or in my case marching, with the band at English Summer shows was now replaced with the reality of being an adult soldier. It was a strange time to be part of British Forces Germany, the Berlin Wall had come down in late 1989, and various quiet revolutions and attitude changes in Eastern Europe meant that our so-called enemy of Communism and the Warsaw Pact no longer existed. World War Three wasn't going to happen here and despite the fact that we no longer had a natural enemy we had just received brand new heavy artillery equipment in the form of the MLRS. An MLRS was a tracked vehicle with a three man crew that could fire twelve rockets at targets 32 kilometres away either one at a time or all twelve in a ripple, each rocket was the size and shape of a long rolled up carpet. The rockets themselves would explode above the target and disperse its load of either anti-personnel mines or more usually six hundred "bomblets" the size of a miniature Coke can, these bomblets would rain down and explode upon contact, and the spread of the bomblets could cover an area about one kilometre square. The MLRS had not long arrived when I first got there, and crews were busy being trained and familiarising themselves with the new push-button technology of modern warfare.

"So your pretty good on the radio then," said the Sergeant Major in charge of the Guardroom that evening, who also happened to be the SMIS, Sergeant Major Instructor in Signals.

"Yes Sir."

"Good, you're in HQ Battery. You had better be a good Signaller, don't let me down," he said, then called out one of the men on guard duty, and a short man in his thirties appeared.

"I've only been here a month myself. I'm Brian by the way."

He was only just over five foot tall, in his early thirties and had "LOVE" and "HATE" tattooed on his knuckles. He talked at a non-stop pace trying to give me as much information as he could in the short walk from the guardroom to the accommodation of HQ Battery, he talked with a confidence of someone who had been here all his life and the attitude of someone who was the hardest man he knew, certainly the hardest man in Carlisle. The buildings were huge seven story blocks; the stairs seemed to go on forever upwards until we reached the living accommodation.

"Lads, this is Simon the NIG," said Brian, dumping my bags on the empty bed. A NIG was a New Intake Gunner.

I said hello to everyone as more and more people entered the room to have a look as beers were opened and passed around. The room was a far cry from the rooms at Bramcote, this place had carpets; nice white wall-to-wall wardrobes with a space for a bed, and there were four beds in the room, a TV and a large sofa sat in the middle of the room. The walls were covered with posters of women and football teams. The introductions were thick and fast, accents from all over the Midlands as well as a Mancunian and a Geordie, each man trying to gauge if I was a complete wanker or not, they were all in there late teens or early twenties as this was the "singleys", or unmarried soldiers quarters.

"Where did you say you were from again?" said a stocky guy sitting on the bed by the window.

"Nuneaton."

"Me too mate, I can't get away from the fucking place can I?" he said laughing, "I'm Pete." Pete was nineteen and had just come to HQ Battery from a Gun Battery. He was shorter than me but had a chest like a barrel, strangely making his head look smaller, and had joined the Army a couple of years ago after working at McDonalds, I didn't know then though that he would become a friend for life.

Over the next few months I gradually got to know them all; Tommo was the slightly overweight Mancunian who also shared our room and was responsible for all the Manchester United posters, he was also known throughout the Battery as a compulsive masturbator, if he had a spare minute Tommo could be seen sloping off to the toilets with a magazine of quality German porn under his arm, for this reason he was often late for absolutely everything but was also one of the funniest men I've ever met. Rob Capewell was from Stoke and was one of those people who could just smile and women would be falling over themselves to get to him, "Smudge" Smith was a tall blonde guy who had to work harder with the ladies due to an impenetrable black country accent. Brian Wade, who had shown me in on the first day was indeed the hardest man in Carlisle. And of course Pete from Nuneaton who was more serious than the rest and spent his time engrossed in books. There were many others in HQ Battery, some worked in administration but most of us were Signallers or Drivers, HQ Battery also contained all the Catering Corps staff, although we never mixed with them. The married soldiers lived away from the barracks in their own quarters, which looked like council estates but without the litter, all grey and hastily built. As the Regiment had been stationed here for the last twenty or so years, some of the married men had settled and married German women and were unlikely ever to go back to the UK. Many of the

British wives found it lonely and difficult to settle and for that reason were always easy prey for the likes of Rob Capewell when their husbands were away on exercise. It was a pretty depressing existence from a single teenagers point of view, but most of the married guys were in the comfort zone, content with their daily duties then home to the wife, even though everything in their life revolved around the Army; their friends, the schools, even the TV station was run by the Forces.

Nightlife in Germany was a handful of bars that soldiers were allowed into, which were full of the same women who went back with a different squaddie every week, those that didn't pull got horrifically drunk on cheap German lager and ended up dancing until four in the morning, the sight of a dance floor full of drunken soldiers raving to Rozallas "Everybody's Free (To Feel Good)" really is a sight to behold. At chucking out time fights would break out between us and the other Regiments based around Sennelager; The Life Guards and 3rd Battalion Light Infantry, or more dangerously, the local Turkish population. This, to us, was what the Army was all about. Getting drunk and trying to score, we didn't need to be super fit or worry about patrolling South Armagh, leave that to the Infantry. We were here for a war that before was always unlikely, but now was never going to happen.

In October 1990 all British soldiers were confined to barracks because the locals were going to have a party, Germany was re-unified, no more East and West. We now felt even more redundant and the hostility we often felt would probably become more open towards us now that we were no longer needed. Germany itself was the cleanest place I had ever seen, not a single piece of litter could be seen on the perfectly paved paths and streets. Germanys post-war reconstruction had been done brilliantly, all neat fences and hedges like a scene built from Lego, a stark contrast to the reconstruction of Coventry and its menacing dark, grey, concrete subways. It was no wonder that the modern Germany didn't want drunken and rowdy British soldiers on its streets or when they weren't drunk, they would be out on exercise, driving in long military convoys down Autobahns before ripping up the countryside in their sixty tonne tracked vehicles churning out diesel fumes.

I hadn't taken much notice of the news up until then, but I was aware that Iraq had invaded Kuwait; it was a long way away and didn't really involve me. Until the rumours started to spread as the political pressure increased on Iraq via the UN, that we would be involved. Eventually the rumours were confirmed and we, as part of 1st Artillery Brigade along with the 3rd and the 7th Armoured Brigades were given the order to prepare for the liberation of Kuwait. Initially the Regiment had been given a year or two to be fully up to speed and operational with the MLRS, now things were starting to speed up, suddenly after fifty years of cold-war inertia broken only by a couple of emergency tours of Northern Ireland, 39 Heavy Regiment finally had a war to get ready for, and only months to do it. There was a brand new enemy, we had the last half-century to learn everything about the Warsaw Pact; from its ration packs to Infantry Battle Tactics, but this new enemy was an unknown quantity. We watched the News with intense concentration focusing on words like "Fundamentalism," and "Religious Extremism." This wasn't a political ideology we were up against, it was a mad dictator and his army of Islamic warriors, at least that's how we interpreted it, or it was interpreted for us.

After we had been told to get ready for the Gulf, November and December 1990 was a constant round of exercises and practise for the real thing, even down to a simulator that blasts out the sound of incoming Artillery as you sat in a box trying to send messages over the radio whilst being shaken by the vibrations and deafened by the noise. The MLRS was test fired and any potential problems were discovered and eliminated. We were briefed in classrooms on how the Iraqi Army was the fifth largest in the world and watched the accompanying video of men shouting and whipping themselves until they drew blood; these were Iraqis. We saw videos of the aftermath of a chemical attack on a Kurdish village, women and children scattered along the street, their mouths frozen open as they died gasping for air. Saddam, we were told, would not hesitate to use this stuff. We were taught about Scorpion stings and Camel Spiders, how to deal with dehydration, nerve gas and biological weapons. We learnt basic first aid and how to put an intravenous drip into an arm, which was actually demonstrated by Sergeant "Chalky" White who was attached to us from the Medical Corps who did it to himself. New faces were brought in from other regiments to bring us up to full strength and we were all on a steep learning curve. We were re-taught infantry skills, went on the ranges and fired our weapons, learnt how to use hand grenades, the General Purpose Machine Gun and the 66mm disposable anti tank weapon. It was all a great laugh even though we were, by now, exhausted. Nobody expected to ever use a hand grenade in anger, it was just boys playing with guns, helped by the fact that it was members of 3rd Light Infantry that were training us and they would be staying here which they weren't happy about. Everyone wanted to be part of the big show, a real war that was never likely to happen again, and any fear we had, especially after seeing the video of Muslim fanatics, was masked by excitement and adrenaline.

There were a few seventeen year olds in the Regiment, another two of which were in HQ Battery along with me. Tim from Hereford was a day older than me and arrived a week after me, he often looked and acted like a twelve year old, bouncing around like an over-excited Labrador, but despite his occasional dizziness he would do any thing for anyone, and as he worked in the stores was extremely useful. Gunner "Noddy" Holder was from Derby and was in the intake after me at Junior Leaders, but somehow was a few months older, he did actually look like a young boy and was immediately voted the man most likely to get screwed in prison due to his youthful looks. He became the Battery Sergeant Majors driver, and nobody envied him that task. Nobody ever said we wouldn't be going because we were so young, but we were pretty sure that you had to be eighteen to serve in Northern Ireland and the general opinion of the other soldiers was that we would be staying behind, that was until everybody realised how under strength the Army would be without any of the seventeen year old new recruits. I was as happy as my parents were distraught.

My job was as a radio operator in the FDC, or Fire Direction Centre. HQ Batterys main job in wartime was to receive the target information from either observers on the ground or Brigade level, interpret it, and send the information in the form of a Fire Mission to the Gun Battery Fire Direction Centre, who in turn would send the Fire Mission on to one or more of the launchers. From the receiving of the target information to the time the launcher fires has to be as quick as possible but at the same time be as accurate as possible, every message is repeated back so that it can be double checked, a single digit sent incorrectly could mean the difference between firing on the enemy and firing on your own troops. The FDC is the operations centre of the Regiment and oversees everything; its callsign is simply "Zero". The FDC was an armoured personnel carrier first in use in the early sixties called an FV432, the inside was cramped due to all the communications equipment, there was a bench along one side and facing it on the other side was a huge Perspex board used to cover a map. Every spare inch of space inside was filled with papers, pens, brew kit, stationery and log books, and whilst on the move we practised how to get the seven man crew complete with rifles and belt kit into the vehicle, we found that one person had to sit in the small area of floor on top of all the belt kit whilst the four others sat on the benches and shelving around the wall with the driver and commander in their own seats at the front, it wasn't for the claustrophobic. On top of the vehicle was a cage welded onto the roof which carried everything we needed; water, rations, spare communications equipment, weaponry we would never use, tents and awnings, camouflage netting, a small cooker and finally strapped to the outside of the cage were our Bergens (Army rucksacks) containing our personal kit; spare clothing, wash kit and the most important thing of all; the sleeping bag and bivvy bag (waterproof outer cover) which would be at the top of the Bergen for quick access.

I knew that being in the FDC was a huge responsibility and didn't want to be there as just a tea boy so made myself known during all the exercises as a man who could use the radio, the only downside to being in the FDC was the constant stream of officers; the Commanding Officer of the Regiment would always be hovering around, even though he probably didn't know how to send a fire mission any more, and every other officer; the Brigadiers, the Commander of Royal Artillery, Generals, for them this would be the main 39 Regiment meeting point. There was a seven-man crew in the FDC, me of course, then Bombardier Dave Sawford and Lance Bombardier "Bugsy" Burrows who were in charge of the vehicle. They were the drivers and made the vehicle run, if there was a problem with the vehicle they would always know how to fix it, both of them were married and in their thirties, examples of soldiers in the comfort zone although they couldn't be more different people; Bugsy had a fantastic sense of humour whereas Dave was a miserable bastard who thought he could motivate people by shouting at them, which worked in basic training but not now. There was also a

Sergeant and a Gunner that had come from another Regiment together, the Gunner was a Scottish lad in his mid twenties who always had a smile on his face. The SMIS that I had seen in the guardroom the first night at the Regiment was also on the crew, he was a short, fat Les Dawson look-alike who never cracked a smile in case his false teeth fell out. Finally, the officer in charge of the FDC and the whole Battery was Captain Lacey; a pipe smoking man in his thirties who always looked half asleep, he would speak quickly, machine-gunning out orders with only a split seconds consideration, he knew exactly how to do the job, and most importantly he had our utter respect. Respect is one of the most important things an officer can have, and strange as it sounds Captain Lacey could have told us to do anything and we would have done it without question.

The desert paint arrived. Tonnes of it were stacked on pallets, floor to ceiling, in one of the large garages. Along with it came spray guns, compressors and thinners. In the Gun Batteries they could paint their own vehicles or the three man crew could paint their launcher, in HQ Battery we had to paint all the support vehicles, the JCB diggers, lorries, medical vehicles, the catering lorries, along with our own vehicles. We worked round the clock painting every single vehicle or trailer as well as Jerry cans, signals equipment and various large containers in a drab beige desert colour. After several exhausting weeks of preparation, the vehicles were ready, the FDC was covered in welded on steel frames for extra Jerry cans of fuel, and boxes were attached to the front of the vehicle containing a cooker and brew kit. Everything was tested one final time before being packed away in the vehicle ready to be shipped off to Saudi Arabia. All it needed now was for us to meet it on the other side of Europe.

We had a weeks leave at the end of December, which was a welcome relief after the past two months of madness of cramming two years worth of training into two months. The single soldiers, as always, were the last to leave. The political discussions were still ongoing in the UN, hoping for an eleventh hour peace deal even though the military build up from the US and Britain seemed too big to stop. Advance parties were already in Saudi Arabia preparing for our arrival and thousands of tonnes worth of newly painted armoured vehicles were in boats on the Mediterranean heading to the Arabian peninsular.

My week off was a blur of goodbyes and good lucks from my friends who only a couple of years ago were at school and getting drunk in the park with me. My parents didn't mention the war, the only reminder was my Father glued to the news, hoping for a peace deal.

"You're too young to go," my Mother said.

"It's my job, I'm a soldier," I said.

My parents were reluctant to sign the papers allowing me to join up in the first place, now that they had signed, all their nightmares were coming true.

"You know that until you're eighteen we're still your legal guardians."

"You can't," I knew they were serious.

"You're not old enough to go into a pub and here you are going off to a war that has nothing to do with us," she said, "It's not right."

"I'm a man, Mum. I've trained to be a soldier, now my country asks me to do something, it's my job to do it," I said with the bravado of a new recruit.

Any patriotic feeling was lost on them; they only saw their little boy going to a war. They also saw the fear in my eyes from the thought of not going, and didn't mention it again. As each day passed the tension at home increased though nothing was said, my parents dread hung in the air as every day I went out with my friends to get drunk and have a good time. People I didn't know would buy me drinks and wish me luck, I was the man of the hour, the soldier going off to war and I revelled in it, mentioning all the training we'd had and how Saddams Army was the fifth largest in the world and what happens in a chemical attack. As the days went on the tension finally hit me and I broke down in tears in front of my brother, a mixture of alcohol and the need to tell somebody how I felt overwhelmed me. The pressure was finally too much after the last couple of months of frantic preparation and all my fears came drunkenly rushing out. The following days sobriety brought with it the discomfort of a man who has displayed his emotions in front of his family. We didn't talk about it. We didn't talk about anything. Christmas day was more strained than usual, though nobody had too much to drink. Every Christmas my Father and I would always find a war film to watch in the afternoon, but this time we watched the film in an uncomfortable silence as my Mother took as much time as she could doing the washing up. They gave me a Walkman and headphones as a present to take with me.

It was Boxing Day and my Father shook my hand at the coach station in Birmingham where we were all being picked up to be taken back to Germany. He wished me luck and told me to be careful before getting back into the car. My Mother and Sister insisted on walking me right up to the coach where many of the others soldiers were already sitting, drinking cans of lager. They embraced me and cried as they said goodbye, I tried my hardest not to fill up as I boarded the coach, then I saw Noddy, my friend and fellow seventeen year old whose eyes were bright red and streaming. It was a long drunken journey to Germany, everybody singing "Bluebirds" as the White Cliffs of Dover vanished out of sight of the ferry. We enjoyed it as much as we could, alcohol masking the tension and fear. In a few days we would be preparing to fly out to Saudi on New Years Eve for what Saddam had called "The Mother of all Battles." Nuneaton already seemed a million miles away.

In Germany all our possessions, apart from the kit we would take with us, were packed in huge boxes and taken to the stores to be opened and unpacked upon our return or forwarded to our next of kin if we didn't. Everyone wrote "the letter", a letter that every soldier writes to be opened by a relative if they didn't come back. I wasn't sure what to write, I wasn't used to "opening up" as our family didn't do that kind of thing. I think I wrote lots of thankyous and don't worries. Everyone else did the same.

3. The Big Machine

The flight over was a noisy and boisterous one, reminding me of a lads holiday to Spain. Soldiers tried to take photos of up the female flight attendants skirts, which they took with patient good humour. They waved us off and wished us good luck when we landed, before flying back to Germany to pick up more soldiers who would also try and take photos of their underpants. It was nighttime when we disembarked and the cold hit us straight away, and despite the lights of the Saudi Arabian airport the sky was clear and thousands of stars could be seen. We entered a large aircraft hangar in single file to be processed by bored looking military clerks; date of birth, blood group, next of kin, a will, check for dog tags. With everything ticked off and confirmed we boarded a civilian bus whose driver managed to take us to Camp Blackadder, as the holding area was called, despite falling asleep at the wheel and veering off road on numerous occasions.

We could hear the strange sound of bagpipes as we approached the Camp. This huge tented area was the place every British soldier would pass through before being reunited with his vehicle and living out in the desert, the vehicle being home during operations. It suddenly dawned on me that it was New Years Eve and the piper belonged to a member of one of the Highland Regiments complete with kilt and Glengarry cap.

Our first night was spent in large twenty man tents, our sleeping bags zipped up around our faces to prevent the non-existent threat of the Camel Spider, and boots covered to prevent Scorpions. It was the first and last time we bothered doing that.

"Shut the fuck up!" shouted Alex the giant Brummie.

It was early morning and the silence had been broken by the Islamic call to prayer that echoed loudly from a nearby minaret.

"I can't be doing with that every fucking day,"

"It's like being back in Birmingham," laughed Alex.

It's strange how we can adapt to every environment, and in a matter of days being covered in a thin film of sand and seeing the night sky with all of its stars in absolute clarity became the norm, I even found the call to prayer beautifully hypnotic. There were no Camel Spiders and nobody could be bothered to worry about Scorpions. There was no heat to speak of either, even though the sun seemed bigger, and the sand wasn't the rolling dunes that we were all expecting but more of a flat, grey surface baked hard like concrete in decades of sunshine. Those first few days were good, you would probably call it a team bonding exercise, the reality of an oncoming war seemed a long way off and we all had a grade "zero" haircut (much to the displeasure of Captain Lacey) and were finally issued with desert camouflage uniforms and floppy hats. The HQ Battery men stayed together in the one tent, the gun crews and their battery support were separate from us.

The time finally came to meet up with our vehicles, and saying goodbye to Camp Blackadder we boarded another civilian bus and another driver who had to be shouted at to stay awake. We were dropped in the middle of nowhere the only sign of life was a small cluster of RAF ground crew awaiting the next helicopter. We sat for an eternity waiting until eventually all the men looked to the sky and watched in awe as the helicopters came in to view, their rotors thumping the air, louder and louder the huge Puma military helicopters came in to land, creating a sandstorm that clogged our eyes and burned our skin. The ground crew waved us into the Pumas, there was a hierarchy of personnel in HQ battery depending on your role and rank, being in the FDC meant I was one of the first on and first off, unlike "Smudge" Smith and our Geordie Lance Bombardier who were in the radio signal rebroadcast Land Rover and had to wait for the helicopters to come back and pick them up. It was a short jump in the Puma before landing and changing to a larger twin rotored Chinook that was already waiting. To me, a seventeen-year-old new recruit, it was like the scene from Apocalypse Now, where the helicopters flew in to the accompaniment of the Sound of the Valkyries. In a few hours we were dropped off at another holding area with yet more buses waiting to take us to our final destination to meet up with our vehicles.

The area around the docks had been turned in to a huge car park, but instead of cars there was a sea of beige-painted armoured vehicles, sixty tonne tanks, heavy artillery, tracked recce vehicles and MLRS sat side by side as if on parade, all neat lines and perfect spacing. The Army consists of a lot of "hurry up and wait" waiting for the helicopters, waiting to get on the bus, waiting to get off the bus and now waiting to find out where our vehicle was. Eventually we found it and eagerly crammed ourselves in the FDC like sardines, before waiting again to see where exactly we were going. Now we had our vehicles, we would be "tactical", and ready for war. Guard duty, standing-to at sunrise and sunset and constantly manning the radios would be our job from now on, twenty-four hours a day.

A long journey in an armoured vehicle isn't particularly pleasant, I didn't smoke but most of the others did, and despite them taking it in turns to smoke the inside of the FDC was a choking fog no matter how high the setting on the fans. Whoever sat on the floor had the best deal even though they had to lay on the rifles and webbing, they could sleep or stretch out as best they could, to the other four men in the back it was a pile inducing nightmare, the radios had to be manned even though the sound of the giant diesel engine was deafening and the vibrations through the lightly padded bench seat would make your backside go numb after twenty minutes, then often have the unfortunate effect of inducing "convoy cock".

The stopping routine was carefully rehearsed, the FDC and its partner vehicle, the TAC HQ, along with Pete and his "Intelligence Wagon" would reverse toward each other until the rear doors were about three metres apart, the back doors were opened and out jumped all the crew who were not manning the radios, a tarpaulin was stretched between the backs of the vehicles creating a covered area, the three vehicles in a "T" shape. The huge camouflage netting was put up and pegged out which made a bubble of sand coloured mesh around the vehicles, then the three radio masts were erected, attached permanently to the vehicles they were telescopic and could reach twenty feet into the air. Once that was done we were operational and after we practised it so much the whole thing took around two minutes. We were now based in a disused quarry, with roads in and out and already made high rubble walls of orange rock around large, flat spaces for the vehicles, it seemed like the perfect ready-made position.

As soon as we were in place the training and practise was ramped up to full intensity, day long exercises of practising fire missions and the guns dry firing to get the turnaround time, the time from receiving the target information to the gun firing on the target, down to as short a space of time as possible, a matter of minutes. All exercises were now done in full Nuclear, Chemical and Biological Warfare suits, sometime with gas masks being worn. The NBC kit is a thick, charcoal lined suit, along with rubber overboots and gloves, wearing it in northern Europe is hard enough, it's thick, bulky and doing the most basic tasks leaves the wearer soaking in sweat. On one hot day we had one of these exercises in full kit, it wasn't long before tempers frayed as sweat slowly filled the gas masks, the disorientation of not knowing who was who, everybody shouting with voices muffled by respirators. Eventually someone threw up in his gas mask due to the heat, the exercise was cancelled and we all hoped to God that Saddam wouldn't use chemical weapons.

We couldn't hear the call to prayer now that we were in the quarry; much to most of the soldiers relief, and the isolation of the desert was brought home to us every morning and evening. At these times all personnel have to stand-to, and have to guard the perimeter, as these are the most likely times of attack. Before it was light we would get into our firing positions along the rocky wall of the quarry and wait for the sun to rise. I could see grown men watch open mouthed as the huge sun could be seen rising, preceded by each colour of the spectrum lighting up the curved horizon in turn, the sun looked so big here as it rose, burning away the cold of the night and bringing a fresh new smell to a new, clean day.

The joys of the sunrise didn't last long though; the rain came. Nobody could believe it could rain, but it did and didn't stop. Those that brought waterproofs, and who were initially laughed at, now walked around smugly with a told-you-so smile. After a couple of days even waterproofs were no use, wet sand got everywhere, in boots, food, underpants and rifles, everything was wet and gritty with sand. The rain was incessant; fat drops of water would change to a constant drizzle and back again. There was nowhere dry to clean our weapons, and when we did manage to find a relatively dry space, the rifle cleaning kit would invariably also be wet and sand filled. The quarry, at first the ideal position, now started to fill with water.

Large pools of water filled the quarry floor, unable to drain away, sleeping bags had to be put on top of the vehicles when not in use so as not to float away. The only dry space I could find was inside my sleeping bag, this came with a bivvy bag, an outer layer that was like a mini tent, waterproof and breathable. I would get in and zip everything up so that only my eyes were exposed and I could hear the patter of rain on the outside, safe in the knowledge that I was warm and dry inside one of the British Army's better inventions.

"Simon, Simon, wake up!" it was the young Scottish member of the crew.

"What!" I said already on full alert, but at the same time not wanting to get out of the sleeping bag unless the Iraqis were on the horizon.

"You're in a fucking puddle mate."

I sat up, still exposing no more than my eyes. The bottom half of the bivvy bag was almost submerged in water from a huge puddle that had been formed when all the other puddles joined to become one. At that moment I wanted to cry.

"Oh," I said as calmly as I could as the jock started to laugh. I wasn't getting out so I shuffled over out of the puddle and went back to sleep.

I had never felt so low as the time the rain came, as professional as I tried to make myself out to be, there was no getting away from the fact that I was seriously pissed off and wanted out. I felt like crying in frustration, and was soaking wet and couldn't even fire my rifle as it was clogged with sand, this, coupled with the constant menial tasks of potato peeling or emptying the toilets which were meant to keep us from getting bored but only served to make things feel so much worse. To top it all the Regimental Sergeant Major insisted on a parade square being created, somehow a flagpole was found and a large square marked out in equally sized stones by half a dozen members of HQ Battery, still the rain came down and the parade square was more of a lake as the 39 Regiment flag hung wet and limp from the flagpole, but the RSM was happy with his little piece of bullshit even if no one else was. Only in the British Army.

On one occasion Tim, Pete and I were outside cleaning our rifles during a break in the rain just before it got dark, the rifle has to be taken to pieces, wiped down, oiled in the right places, then put back together before cocking several times and pulling the trigger with a click. Obviously the cocking should be done with out a magazine full of rounds still attached, otherwise you would be chambering a live round and pulling the trigger. I had finished and I watched Tim and Pete reassemble their rifles, Tim stood up cocking the rifle three times.

I had never heard a gunshot without wearing ear protection; and an ear splitting crack echoed around the stone quarry. Tim screamed and dropped the rifle; Pete lay on his side next to Tim, his hands covering his ears. I felt the blast and the change in air pressure and the bullet kicked up sand and dust as it hammered into the ground a foot in front of me. I sat down and worked my hands down my leg checking for any injury, I must have sat for at least five minutes in the shadows as people started shouting and rushing round whilst Tim continued to scream in panic. Medics arrived and started to check them both over as I stood up in the dark, unnoticed and walked into the large tent, my ears still ringing. The men had been told to stay here and sat inside on high alert.

"Tim's just nearly shot my foot off," I said, clearly in shock.

Petes head was next to Tims rifle when the bullet was fired and was temporarily deafened by the gunshot and the red-hot cartridge case hit him in the face as it was ejected, Tim took an age for the shock to wear off. Statements were taken from Pete, Tim and Myself. We were sure that Tim didn't have a magazine on his weapon and couldn't understand how a round was chambered. Tim was charged for his "negligent discharge", I don't recall what punishment he had but the RSM got his use out of the parade square we had made, making Tim march at the double, splashing around the square for a good half an hour as we had to look on.

Getting out into the desert, even if only briefly, was a relief from the rainwater lake that refused to drain away from the quarry floor, and running around in full NBC kit was less of a sweaty nightmare with the constant drizzle cooling us. Pete and I sat on the canvas deckchairs underneath the cam-net eating tinned cheese.

"What? Kate Adie's coming here?" I said.

Kate Adie, journalist extraordinaire, famous for being on the ground, at the front, with the rest of us.

"You won't get to see her," said Pete, who was a crew member of the "intelligence" wagon, another armoured personnel carrier that followed us around, although there was very little in the way of intelligence going on in there.

"She's here for the live firing, so you can guarantee that every fucking officer in a hundred mile radius will be here to see Miss Adie, and you Gunner Hutt will be getting the brews on."

"And you Gunner Tosspot, will be kissing my arse," I said flicking a piece of cheese at him.

It was true, the FDC was a magnet for officers as it was the operational heart of the Regiment, whereas I was a seventeen-year-old tea boy.

We were non-tactical for the live firing exercise, no NBC kits or running around like headless chickens, just the cam-nets and a desire to see everything we'd trained for since October go without a hitch. The more experienced signallers manned the radios; Dave Sawford, the SMIS that looked like Les Dawson, and a couple of others. I stood outside and out of sight with the vehicle between me and the crowd of public school educated Colonels, Brigadiers and Generals, pumping petrol into the cooker and lighting the small jets that squirted out under pressure, ready to boil several gallons of water. It was a clear day and the rain had been easing off, exposing the endless bright blue skies that we had seen when we first arrived. I could hear the motor of a camera clicking away taking photographs on rapid fire, and the posh voices grew louder as if this was Glyndebourne instead of the Gulf. I looked at the written list they had given me with its multiple permutations of coffee, tea, sugar, if so, how many? Milk? "Just a splash", a fucking "splash", where the fuck do you think you are? "Sweeteners if poss.," Oh, fuck off.

"Dave, have we got sweeteners?" I asked through gritted teeth and silent rage.

"Do they think they're in the fucking Officers Mess?" Dave said, looking up from the radio log on his lap.

"Fifteen fucking brews I've got to make, and I don't even get to meet Kate fucking Adie, wankers!"

"Well, that's what you're here for. Sweeteners in the front box, I'll have one as well," Dave said with his trademark smug bastards grin.

"And stop your fucking swearing, there are ladies present."

I walked away with the realisation that if in the unlikely event of a firefight with the Iraqis, Dave would get one in the back of the head. The thought cheered me up slightly, and at least it wasn't raining.

All the plastic beakers were lined up with their various ingredients, the names of the recipients written in pencil on the side, boiling water added, the perfect brew, Gunner Hutt you deserve a medal. But wait, the magic ingredient was missing. Smiling to myself and making sure there was nobody nearby watching, I cleared my throat as quietly as I could and, hovering over each beaker in turn, made sure each one had a large globule of spit swirling round on the top, oh sweet revenge. I could only manage the first half a dozen before running out of the sufficient amount of saliva, and, searching around as covertly as I could for some kind of substitute, I finally found our can of engine coolant which, although bright blue and potentially dangerous unless you were the diesel engine of an armoured vehicle, would suffice in small quantities. So with saliva or engine coolant added, and in the CO's case both, the junior Lieutenant in charge of Pete's intelligence wagon took the brews away.

"Thank you very much Gunner Hutt," said the quite likeable officer picking up the tray.

"My pleasure Sir. Make sure Miss Adie gets that one, her name is on the side," I said, pointing to the only beaker that didn't have spit or engine coolant in.

Now I could sit back and enjoy the fireworks. The radio traffic had been gradually increasing as the journalists and officers voices became quieter.

"Fire mission Battery," said Dave Sawford in his best radio voice.

"Fire mission on its way, standby," said the SMIS to the crowd outside observing.

Orders and co-ordinates, type of ammunition, number of rounds, a flurry of information and numbers repeated back and forth in minutes, if not seconds.

A pause, the calm before the storm.

The ground shakes and from where I was standing behind the FDC I could see a light brown dust cloud envelop one of the launchers on the horizon in time with the roar of a rocket engine, there's another explosion of dust and sand as the ground shakes again, another launcher turns into beige fog. Then the flash and thick grey smoke bellows from the launchers tubes, the roar is deep and menacing and I watched as the long thin missile emerges as if in slow motion through the cloud of rocket fumes and smoke out of the tube, leaving the launcher and picking up speed in mid-air before accelerating into the sky with the roar of a jet fighter. First one, then others streak into the sky, launchers fire all twelve of their rockets at once in a ripple effect, smoke trails criss-cross each other against the blue background of the sky as the missiles gradually disappear in the distance. The dust clouds dissipate from around the launchers, the rocket smoke drifts away in the light breeze, the MLRS launcher sits, spent and exhausted, its now empty ammunition tubes stained and burnt a dirty black.

"Rounds complete," says Dave loudly into his radio microphone.

The power and violence of two dozen rockets being fired into the desert was almost beautiful, somewhere 15 miles away they were exploding in the sky and raining down smaller bombs, which in turn would fall to earth and explode when they hit something, that would make over one hundred and twenty thousand bomblets. The crowds voices returned, talking in hushed whispers, amazed as I was at the devastation that this weapon could cause.

On January 17th, with all diplomatic routes exhausted, the air war started. The allies had total air dominance, and used their superiority to drop bombs or fire cruise missiles on anything that resembled Iraqi troops or military installations. Wave upon wave of American B-52 bombers streamed northwards, seemingly miles up in the sky, looking like small arrowheads rather than the giant cold war bomber aircraft that they were. British Tornados flew lower and faster, screaming overhead and it was relentless. At night, parts of the horizon would light up with huge orange flashes as Iraqi positions were pounded, it would go on for hours with the ground shaking at each distant explosion. It reminded me of the MLRS and its violence, only now there were real people on the end of the explosions, it is what is known as the "softening up" of targets. The distant positions were supposed to have been the Iraqis Republican Guard Divisions, these troops were the best the Iraqis had, all volunteers rather than the conscripts that made up the bulk of the army, they were disciplined and many had experience of the Iran-Iraq war.

I was supposed to be on guard duty, a two-hour shift patrolling the perimeter of our positions but instead I sat on a large oil pipeline that bisected the desert with the Walkman my parents gave me tuned to the world service. I listened to John Peel playing music by The Wedding Present and Cud as I watched the distant firework display, and the Iraqi position burning, lighting up the horizon like the sun was about to rise.

Music broke the now tedious routine, we were ready to go but now there was no real threat. We spent most of our time writing letters home complaining about the weather, and received hundreds of letters addressed to "A Soldier in the Gulf" these were mostly from people wishing us luck, although there were a lot of single women that included naked photos with their letters, which made our day. Parcels would arrive that include soap, talcum powder along with many other kinds of useless cleaning items such as shampoo, eventually we had so much that unfortunately we had to bury a lot of it in the desert as there was no room for it on the wagon. The "Sunnyside Gulf War Support Group" was a group of families in Nuneaton with relatives in the Gulf, they sent Pete and I plenty of stuff, the most welcome being copies of the local paper, to which we both wrote a letter of thanks and enclosed a picture of the two of us which appeared in print the following week.

"Fucking Tanita Tikaram?" I said as I held up the cassette tape that had been given me.

One of the Sergeants was dishing out items from a parcel addressed to "A Soldier in the Gulf", trying to give out as much of the contents as he could and confining the "bury it" pile to a minimum, as we knew people put effort in to send us this stuff. Magazines and papers were passed around along with music tapes.

"I like Tanita Tikaram," said "Noddy" Holder.

"What? You're admitting to that!" I said to him laughing.

"Yeah…and I've never heard of these," he said holding up the tape that he had been given. My eyes lit up, it was "Carter The Unstoppable Sex Machine - 30 Something" I had heard them on the John Peel show.

"You fucking beauty Noddy, hope you enjoy Tanita Tikaram," I said as we swapped cassette tapes, Carter USM was to be the soundtrack to my Gulf War. I even made Noddy a brew.

With the air war in full swing and everybody else ready for action, it was time to leave the quarry and good fucking riddance to it and its Parade Square and inadequate drainage. We travelled in convoy for hours, the inside of the wagon cramped and smoky. I sat on the bench with the radio headset on and looked out of the six-inch Perspex window in the door. Long lines of armoured vehicles stretched out behind us and trundled along churning up dust and sand, after a few hours the convoy stopped. Brew time. The door was flung open and the guys not on the radio jumped out and immediately stretched, now they were out I stretched my legs out in front of me and looked out the door.

I could see other men getting out of their vehicles and stretching, getting the cups of coffee ready whilst carrying their rifles, there were hundreds of vehicles. It was like the car park at the docks, several long lines of armoured vehicles blocked out the horizon, some carried regimental flags or Scottish saltires, Desert Rats or rams heads painted on the side alongside the large arrowhead that marked us out as allied forces, radio antenna sprouted from every vehicle, infantry Warrior APC and MLRS alongside giant Challenger tanks and 203mm tracked artillery. The sky looked dark and overcast again as the men scurried to fill cups with boiling water, this was half an armoured brigade, thousands of tonnes of rolling, menacing, killing metal, all perfectly organised, almost surgical, every piece interacting and supporting one another as if one single unit with the sole aim of destroying whatever was in the way. A hot plastic beaker of coffee was shoved into my hand and I curled my legs up again as the men got in and attempted to find comfortable space amongst the rifles and webbing whilst not spilling the brews. I pulled the door to with my free hand, and with one final look at the mass of beige armour and men slamming doors closed, I realised I was a small cog in this big machine.

A few hours later and the cam-nets were up and the cooker was heating up a large metal tub containing ration pack menu "F" - chicken curry and rice. This was Area Keys, a space in the middle of the desert in northern Saudi Arabia allocated to ourselves and all that could be seen was a flat grey expanse that stretched to the horizon, the occasional beige lump of a vehicle under its camouflage netting could be seen in the distance. We tried to dig a trench in case of enemy fire but the ground was like concrete, we were told not to bother after the head of the pickaxe bent.

Hurry up and wait again. A day after being there the engineers came bulldozing a high sand berm around our vehicles. We felt less exposed although we were still an obvious focal point in the middle of a moonscape, then the medics came. We had the option of having the vaccinations or not, a couple of injections against Bubonic Plague and Anthrax, two weapons that Saddam Hussein was known to have.

"I'm not having that shit in my arm," said Pete.

"It can't do you any harm, could save your life," I said optimistically.

"Bollocks, it hasn't been tested, I'd rather risk whatever Saddams got."

"Well when there's a global epidemic, I'll be sitting at home with my feet up watching you break out in boils before vomiting your lungs up."

"I'll make sure I puke on your carpet," he said.

"Then I'll say I told you so."

I joined the long line of soldiers being injected and a medic came down the line warning us of potential side effects; vomiting, cramps, diarrhoea, blurred vision. Afterwards, according to Pete, I had all these symptoms, although I can't remember.

"I told you so," said Pete laughing, when I eventually became fully aware of my surroundings.

From now on we had a couple of American soldiers in a Humvee jeep shadowing us. They were an artillery liaison team from 7th U.S Corps as our job was to take out, or "soften up" long range targets for the two British Armoured Brigades and the Americans. We had American troops stationed with us in Sennelager before the MLRS came due to 39 Regiment being a Nuclear Regiment, and apparently only the Americans could handle the nuclear weaponry. They didn't do much except run around in tracksuits and to us they were a bit of a joke, they couldn't march, they had no discipline and we thought they were unprofessional. These two were the same, drinking cans of Coke and throwing the empties on the floor, we didn't even bother trying to be friendly with them. For some reason the Americans had to have cans of Coke and burgers wherever they went. On 30th January we heard that the Iraqis had crossed into Saudi Arabia and attacked the town of Al Khafji, it was the first ground battle of the war and the Americans took casualties, we all knew it was Saddam Husseins show of defiance and needless to say the two Americans with us went all "Rambo" and I even heard the term "kick ass," the wankers.

The routine started again, arse numbing four or six hour shifts on the radio followed by cooking and sleeping as much as possible before starting all over again. I made sure I was always switched on and alert when I manned the radio, and eventually it earned me the respect of the rest of the team who now started calling me by my nickname of "Shed" rather than "Gunner Hutt". I was no longer just the young tea boy, I could be trusted to send fire missions. The tedium was the same, waiting for the word go as we watched enviously the jets flying north doing our job for us, I made a sign from an empty ration box which read: "Holiday Inn - under new management" at the entrance to our position, and even our Commanding Officer saw the funny side.

It was a few weeks of boredom before the Allied aircraft had ran out of targets, and along with the bombs they also dropped leaflets urging the Iraqis to give up and it wasn't long before reports started to come in of small groups of Iraqi soldiers walking south to surrender. We sensed it was almost time. We were to start "night missions", driving miles into Iraq itself before firing everything we had onto enemy targets, and then driving back into Saudi Arabia. Everybody was suddenly switched on and alert, this was what we had been waiting for, and we would be some of the first ground troops into Iraq.

* * * *

We drive for hours in the freezing darkness, tonnes of armour squeaking and rumbling through the desert. The only sign we have entered Iraq is when we went over a large hump of sand, a berm, flattened by the Royal Engineers, which is all that separates Iraq from Saudi Arabia. It is eerie and silent with all the lights off inside and outside the vehicles, nobody speaks, we're on radio silence, all of us are aware that this is the real thing although there is no sign of the enemy. We are refuelled en route, the doors are flung open but no brews are made, only a stretch of the legs and a whispered conversation in the darkness before moving off again. Eventually we stop and wait. The doors are opened and I jump out; rifle and webbing in hand, there is no need for cam nets or tents, we're not here long enough. I'm not on the radio so I'm outside standing guard, helmet, rifle and webbing on.

It suddenly hits me that I'm standing deep in Iraq and I don't wander too far from the wagon, wondering if I should cock my rifle so that I'm ready to fire. The night sky is clear and star-filled and I feel exposed and cold despite wearing my NBC kit, I want this to be over with, I want to be in the FDC on the radio. The telltale sounds of increased radio traffic, this time quieter and more rapid, I stand on one of the few dunes I've seen and await the show.

The ground shakes, launchers positions are lit up by their rockets propellant, I hear the roar of the missile and through the illuminated smoke a cylinder emerges, accelerating upwards. It feels like a continuous earthquake as a battery of launchers expends everything they have on an Iraqi armoured division. I can feel the adrenaline surging through me; it's not an exercise any more. The rockets disappear out of view in the distant night sky, the poor bastards don't know what's going to hit them. As soon as the words "rounds complete" are heard I jump in the wagon closing the door behind me, ready to go. The whole thing lasts twenty minutes. We about turn and drive back, getting refuelled on the way again. The men are still quiet even though the Iraqis know we've been, I feel exhausted, everybody is lost in their own thoughts but happy to have got the job done.

* * * *

The following day the information from drone observation planes and satellite imaging comes through; tanks and armour destroyed and soft skinned vehicles burning. It's a meaningless description of what must be carnage though everyone is in high spirits because we were the ones that made it happen.

We catch as much sleep as we can in preparation for continuous night missions, until we too run out of targets just like the bombers. The next night is the same, pushing deep into Iraq itself before firing then running back over the border, and still there is no retaliation or contact with the enemy, we hear that the few pockets of surrendering Iraqi soldiers has now become a stream. It all seems so easy and feels like target practise instead of a war.

"Go and see them," says Dave

"They're not animals in a fucking zoo," I reply as he takes the radio headset off me and we change places.

I feel sick as I walk around the vehicle to where about ten men in dirty green uniforms sit cross-legged on the floor surrounded by half a dozen of our men, some of whom are taking pictures. The oldest of the Iraqis speaks fluent English, his hair and several days growth of beard are silver, he was in his fifties and the lines on his face said he had seen enough.

"A few months ago I am a teacher, then they tell me to fight, it is madness," he says taking deep gulps of a bottle of water we have given him. "He is only fourteen," he says pointing to one of the others. "No food or water, first the planes, then the little bombs. The officers run away, it is cold," he says staring at the leaflet he had carried with him that had been dropped on his position.

They look like crap; hungry, dirty and clearly at the end of their tether, this isn't the elite Republican Guard we had seen videos of, these are teachers and school kids conscripted to make up the numbers. I watch men take photos of the Iraqi men with disgust before turning away.

"Not up to much are they," says Dave smiling.

"There can't be much fight left in them," I say, hoping that Dave doesn't say something really stupid.

"Brigade says we've got to give them food and water and point them in a southerly direction where they will be picked up eventually," Dave says looking at what he had written in the logbook.

"What? Thanks for giving up, here's some water, now fuck off and keep walking that way and someone will find you. That's shit."

"That's war. Apparently there's so many surrendering that we can't cope."

Another night mission and it's my turn on the radio, it's the same drill, a race into Iraq and being refuelled on the way. The lights are off but the men talk quietly, no longer scared of the previously unseen enemy. We stop and the doors are opened, it must be almost a full moon as everything is illuminated. I'm professional in my job and the fire mission is sent, and repeated back at each stage.

The pause.

It sounds like rolling thunder as the launchers fire their missiles, rippling into the sky.

"Rounds complete. Out." I repeat over the radio. Job done.

The door slams shut and we're off again back to our Holiday Inn. I feel strangely elated at completing a live fire mission, rockets flying towards the enemy thanks to me, the small cog in the big machine. I try not to think about the prisoners we saw; cold, hungry and dirty, and being hammered by artillery. I'm too tired to think too much anyway.

The missions continue, eventually firing in daylight, due to the enemy threat being so low. We sleep as much as we can knowing that when the ground war starts we won't have any.

"What the fuck is that?" asks the SMIS

"This is so everyone in the sky knows were the good guys," says the Quarter Master Sergeant in charge of the stores as he hands over a huge fluorescent orange tarpaulin.

"Strap it to the top so it can be seen from above."

The roof of every vehicle is now covered with a day-glow yellow or orange panel to counter the threat of friendly fire incidents.

Captain Lacey gives us a final briefing outlining the plan to go into Iraq before turning right into Kuwait, cutting off any Iraqi forces attempting to go northwards, then who knows, possibly north into Iraq itself again and getting rid of Mr Hussein. We are to give long range covering fire in support of the British 7th and 3rd Armoured Brigades. I write a letter home, knowing I won't have time from tonight until the end of the war. We pack up and move out as the sun is setting, further north again to a forming up point in the desert, it's like the car park again only this time the vehicles are more spread out, we can feel the tension, it's cold, overcast and trying its hardest to rain. We sit at this start line for hours until there's a flurry of radio communication and Captain Lacey turns and ducks his head into the back of the wagon and smiles to us.

"Gentlemen, start your engines!"

4. Black Rain

We crossed the bulldozed berm that separated the two countries and sped forward behind the advancing British battlegroups of Challenger tanks and Infantry in their Warrior APCs. We drove without a break for hours as the sun rose, being refuelled on the move. Over the radio tanks and infantry were reporting engagements with the enemy, these were short and sharp and even on that first day it was soon evidently clear that nothing the now "softened up" Iraqis had could compete with, or even penetrate the armour of the Challenger tank, or attempt to put up a fight with the highly skilled infantry.

In the back of the FDC the world is viewed through the six-inch Perspex window or via radio reports that are short and to the point, it was disorienting and noisy. Targets came in with brief and meaningless descriptions; troops in open, elements of Republican Guard, enemy armoured vehicles. A fire mission was sent and the launchers would engage within minutes. It was a constant round of target, engage, re-arm, and move forward, always moving forward. On the occasions we stopped on that first day the doors were opened men rushed out to make brews or get food to be eaten cold. The sky was unusually dark and the drizzle was constant, it was as if someone had flicked a switch when we entered Iraq, now everything was black and menacing and real, and the constant state of combat readiness and concentration soon wore us down.

A long line of green clad scruffy men walked towards our vehicle, we had stopped briefly as the tanks and infantry ahead of us ground down some Iraqi resistance. They had the leaflets urging them to surrender in their hands and waved them furiously, there were twenty or thirty of them and more appeared in the distance, we didn't have enough to supply all of them with food and water. Captain Lacey went to talk to them, lighting his pipe as he went.

"He said the bombs were like black rain," said Captain Lacey climbing into the back of the wagon to update the map that covered the one wall of the FDC, things were moving so quickly on the ground that it was out of date in a matter of minutes.

"What bombs?" asked the SMIS.

"The MLRS bomblets, I didn't tell them we did it. We'll soon see some of our handiwork at last." The back of the FDC filled with Captain Laceys pipe smoke; a sweet smell of apple and cinnamon.

The surrendering Iraqis were handed a few bottles of water and some chocolate before being pointed in the direction we had come from. They were cold, wet and hungry. Abandoned by their officers and under constant attack from artillery and aircraft, the thought of now facing tanks and infantry was too much, the fear of what we could do now outweighed any threat that Saddam Hussein had. They walked, beaten and exhausted, south towards Saudi Arabia and further away from home.

We move forward again, aware that we are almost upon the original Iraqi positions. After driving for some time we hear, and feel, a loud metallic bang on the side of the vehicle, we all look at each other nervously as our driver "Bugsy" changes down the gears and comes to a halt.

"Everyone OK?" asks Captain Lacey looking into the back of the vehicle from his position at the front. "I think we just went over a bomblet."

* * * *

I'm lying on the floor on top of the webbing and rifles, suddenly I feel sick and I want to get out of this steel can, I'm overwhelmed by something close to panic as claustrophobia grips me and I open the door and jump out, somebody shouts "WAIT!" but I pretend not to hear in him in my rush to escape.

"Watch where you're walking!" somebody shouts.

"Er…oh yeah," I say gulping in the air.

I walk around the side of the vehicle and see Captain Lacey inspecting a thin, jagged metal shape attached to the vehicle.

"That was lucky it didn't ignite, good job it's diesel, eh?" he says, turning around. "Right, lets go."

A bomblet had been detonated as we drove past, exploding and tearing into a Jerry can of diesel attached to the side of the FDC. I look around me and see in the distance a couple of Iraqi T-55 tanks, one smoulders gently, its steel shell stained black, the other sits like a headless doll, its detached turret is upside down fifty feet away. On the horizon plumes of dirty black smoke rise from burning vehicles, making the sky even more unnaturally dark. It's as if an evil storm has passed through, and I wonder which is worse, being out here and witnessing this or the claustrophobia of the FDC. I realise I'm not just a witness, this is all 39 Regiments handiwork, and with heart racing I dive on top of the rifles and webbing in the wagon, and the door is shut behind me.

* * * *

We stop in darkness, the first day is behind us. Reports come in of initial token resistance before mass surrenders, there is no fight left in them. Now it's a matter of destroying as much as we can to make our passage to Baghdad easier if necessary, before Saddam finally knows it's over and uses what is remaining of his Army to crush the likely revolt or civil war that would follow. The night is spent moving forward, stopping occasionally for fuel, coffee or cold food. Long-range targets given to us by reconnaissance troops of the 16/5th Lancers or Queens Dragoon Guards are fired upon in minutes. We stop more often as our supply lines are stretched as we have moved so far so quickly. Everybody is now running on adrenaline and coffee, nobody has slept for over 24 hours and we are robots, knowing what we have to do and doing it without question. We all started to feel dirty and grimy, our sweat mixing with the charcoal lining of our NBC suits.

Sunrise on day two, though sunlight is blocked out by the black smoke of burning oil wells, the landscape is illuminated by burning vehicles. It's a different sunrise to the ones we saw at the quarry; there is no spectrum of colours or glowing disc of the sun, there isn't that "new day" smell of the dawn. There is no colour, only the black sky and the violent red and yellow oil fires. Shattered vehicles litter the ground, tanks and armour upended and thrown like toys, tyres melted, vehicles burnt.

* * * *

It is some kind of jeep, its tyres melted into black sand, the outer shell blistered and black, it has no roof or windscreen. There is a silhouette of a figure in the drivers seat.

He reminds me of a sculpture, his left hand frozen trying to cover his face, the now thin black fingers open, his right hand joined to the steering wheel. But there is no hand to speak of, the steering wheel and hand had melted into each other, an extension of one another, the same as the seat he was in, melted and joined to the rest of his body. I can't tell where one ends and the other begins. His clothes and a layer of flesh are burnt off making him look unnaturally skinny, his body like a shadow, black and empty and his skin uneven and cracked. In contrast to the charred black body are his teeth, bright white in a mouth frozen open mid scream. I don't know how long I stared at him and there were others nearby, body parts black and burnt. I had never seen a dead body before, but my mind took it all in impassively, my brain incapable of making sense of it and the surrounding fires and the daytime looking like night time. For a moment I wonder what his name is.

"Shed, lets go," it was Dave, his hand on my shoulder.

"Yeah...sure...lets go."

* * * *

We drove forward in short hops, stopping and occasionally firing. There was no time for sleep, and nowhere to sleep if you could. We had all got into the habit of sitting semi-conscious whilst on the radio, eyes half closed, dozing until we heard a voice on the radio at which point eyes would flick open and the brain would engage. Time stopped mattering; there was no sleep, no day or night. We tried not to stop when we saw the now huge columns of surrendering Iraqis, Captain Lacey would throw a bottle of water from his vantage point at the front and point them southwards. We couldn't stop for them, there were too many.

"Whatever you do don't touch one of these," said Dave pointing out one of the MLRS bomblets that lay unexploded on the desert floor.

"I know, we saw them in training," I was hardly in the habit of playing football with shiny cylinders of steel that I find in war

46

zones. As if on cue there was a sound of a small, sharp, explosion, and we both turned in time to see what was left of the windscreen in one of the support lorries spray out onto the ground a hundred metres away. From the vehicle someone started screaming.

"Get Sergeant White, I'll go over there," Dave said as he ran over to the truck.

A call was put out for our Medical Corps Sergeant, and he's there in minutes. He gave emergency first aid to the Royal Corps of Transport soldier who thought one of the shiny cylinders of metal that were scattered around would make a nice souvenir, the bomblet detonated on his dashboard, thankfully only shattering his arm.

"What a twat!" says Sergeant White later.

The day turns into night, though it's hard to tell them apart, a lot of the oil well smoke seems to have cleared but it's cold, and the drizzle continues. I felt dirtier with every passing hour. The night passes with more fire missions and moving forward and I'm not sure what day it is, the third day of this shit? Still without sleep, I'm not sure if I'm even tired, my body has passed that hurdle. According to the map on the wall we have just turned eastwards and are on our way into Kuwait.

The radio communication suddenly becomes frantic, serious tones of voice are heard, someone, somewhere has had contact with the enemy and there are injuries. The overwhelming fatigue suddenly evaporates as everyones brain switches to a combat ready mode. Nobody can quite believe it; they're supposed to be running away, there are lots of casualties. Information trickles through, everyone wants to know the details and if there are more enemy putting up a fight. The news that it's 3rd Battalion the Royal Fusiliers that have been hit just ahead of us makes it especially painful, 3 RRF, like 39 Artillery, is the local midlands regiment for the infantry. One of their Warrior armoured personnel carriers had been hit.

"Jesus, I can see the smoke. It's just over the horizon. The helicopters are coming in," someone says from outside.

We sit silently, awaiting further news, I know Pete's brother is in the Fusiliers. First it's six casualties, then we hear there are nine. Eventually we hear the words "K.I.A"- killed in action, no longer just the vague term "casualty". They're dead. We sit in black silence, fatigue replaced by sadness and the knowledge that it could have been us. We hear more helicopters coming in. Nobody wants to make eye contact. Information comes through from the Brigade radio, I sit manning the Regimental radio, passing the information down the chain.

"Hello all stations this is Zero. Sitrep; now confirmed nine Kilo-India-Alpha, from 3 Romeo-Romeo-Foxtrot. Wait out."

The short message saying that nine men have been killed is passed down from me to the two Gun Batteries HQs and from the Battery HQs to the launchers, in the space of a few minutes everybody will know and feel exactly as we do. Other soldiers are gathered around the rear door of the FDC, listening in. Time passes; Captain Lacey is speaking furiously with a furrowed brow into what we call the "Batphone", a secure telephone that only the officer in charge can use. I can hear him sighing as he looks down rubbing his forehead.

"OK. Roger. Confirm we have blue on blue, I repeat blue on blue. Over," he says, his voice losing its usual sharp, crystal clear authority. He hears the confirmation.

"OK. Roger out."

There is a collective disbelief when we hear the words "blue on blue".

"The fucking wankers! Useless cunts!" one of the guys by the door says before walking off.

"I bet it's the Americans, always the fucking Americans!"

I can see tears of anger, the disbelief turning to rage. The American pilots had been responsible for a couple of friendly fire incidents during the last few days, but nothing on this scale.

"Those two dickheads soon fucked off when they heard the news," someone says referring to the two American soldiers we had shadowing us but not actually doing anything.

Captain Lacey dictates a message to me, the bearer of bad news.

"Hello all stations this is Zero," I can sense them all listening, awaiting the further information.

"Sitrep; Romeo-Romeo-Foxtrot casualties a result of a blue on blue situation. I repeat blue on blue situation. All stations must ensure colour identification sheets are correctly displayed on top of vehicles...."

I can sense their anger now, a desire for revenge. Everyone can understand being killed by the enemy in a war, but not by your own side. We all know that accidents happen in the fog of war but nobody can understand why and it certainly doesn't make us feel any better. The silence continues, everyone struggling with their own thoughts. I imagine the Fusiliers families receiving the letters they would have written and put with their belongings in storage, just as we all had. Letters that aren't meant to be read, letters that are meant to be ripped up upon your return and never spoken about. For the first time I think about the dead Iraqi welded to his jeep and I'm hit by a wave of anger and it suddenly seems all such a fucking waste. I'm trying to be strong when all I want to do is scream, I don't want to be here anymore. I'm exhausted, is it three days without sleep? I hope I wrote something nice and thoughtful in the letter I left behind, I can't remember. I can't remember anything, Nuneaton seems to belong to someone elses life.

"Sometimes good men die for no good reason," says Captain Lacey quietly.

The war carries on and we drive through a constant landscape of black, twisted steel and the debris of destroyed Iraqi positions along with a background of burning oil wells shooting flames high into the black sky, the night comes and I can't take any more. I'm not sure if I'm falling asleep and dreaming or awake and hallucinating.

"Sir, I have to sleep," I say to Captain Lacey. It's not a request, it's a statement. "I can't go on."

I think I've performed well for the last few days, and showed myself to be a man to be relied upon, professional despite my age, but although I've tried in my effort to keep up with the others I'm now running on empty.

"OK, Shed, go," he says without even looking at me. I can do nothing other than admire this officer, he has had no sleep either but is still in charge, responsible for the lives of so many men.

I've been awake for the last three nights, around seventy-two hours, with my brain on overdrive taking in things that some people will never even dream of. I collapsed into sleep and dreamt of burning oil wells.

"Lets go!" someone shouts and gives me a kick.

My eyes flick open and I'm up and ready, my body aches and my eyes are sore. I look around and the black sun is rising, I've slept for less than an hour.

We rumble on eastwards, further into Kuwait, over the radio we are informed that the Iraqis are pulling out of Kuwait, but have not agreed to surrender. It's a race to cut the Iraqi army off from making its escape northwards, everybody can sense it's almost over. There are fewer targets now, they have all been obliterated already or simply abandoned, turning the landscape into a giant junkyard. Black lakes of oil form in the desert, Iraqi armour is littered everywhere, smashed into smouldering steel pieces or left, inoperable, its insides destroyed by an infantryman's grenade just in case. Dead Iraqi soldiers lay covered in a thin film of sand and dried, dark bloodstains surround the bodies, ownerless torn and ragged limbs are spread everywhere at random. What's left of the occupying Iraqi Army races northwards on the only main road out of Kuwait that leads to Basra, southern Iraq. It becomes choked with fleeing vehicles. Allied aircraft drop everything they have on the escaping Iraqis, making the road even more clogged, thousands die as the Allied pilots have a field day.

I'm awake and alert, and looking at the abandoned Iraqi vehicles I catch myself smiling. I realise I'm enjoying this and I'm good at it, I hope we go all the way to Baghdad. I feel clear and focused, maybe only in witnessing death is when you can feel truly alive. We move on again and head towards the road to Basra north of Kuwait city, the going is slow and laboured, there are no targets left and no real space to manoeuvre the brigades. People take it in turns to sleep and we even manage some hot food.

It's late in the evening on day four and I'm on the radio when I hear the message. Saddam Hussein has given up, agreeing to the conditions of the surrender, the cease-fire will begin be in effect from 0500 hours the following morning. It's a long meandering message and I write everything down in abbreviations, the meanings of which I later forget. We wake up Captain Lacey who deciphers the crap I've written in the logbook. I don't feel any elation that it's over, just an anger that Saddam could have surrendered earlier and saved thousands of lives. There's also a disappointment that it's finished, and by the tone of the message, the cease-fire is final, we won't be heading to Baghdad and finishing the job by getting the man responsible for all this shit. Allied aircraft continue to destroy anything that dares to move on the road to Basra right up until the cease-fire. We can hear cheering in the distance, word has spread that we can go home now, it's over. Everyone smiles at each other in the wagon.

"Gentlemen, well done," Captain Lacey says lighting his pipe, and then shakes us all by the hand. We had advanced 350km in 97 hours of constant firing and moving, and now sat north west of Kuwait city.

At 0500 we immediately become non-tactical, the NBC suits finally come off exposing grimy grey skin and dirty, stinking desert combat uniforms, the stench is disgusting. We change clothes, washing our armpits and groin as we strip, then have a shave in warm water and all have a crap after four days of holding it in. Sleeping in sleeping bags, now clean and grime free, at first we sleep in short bursts unable to totally switch off. I dream of the man burnt into his jeep. After a day or two it's as if the FDC, now that it stands still, is taking root. Tents and awnings attached to the vehicle which hadn't been used for the last few days are now put up, sleeping and bivvy bags are rolled up neatly outside, all the equipment we hadn't needed for the last four days is taken out of the cage on top, all the tables, chairs, cookers and rations spread out and used. It looks like the FDC has been burgled and its contents strewn outside, much like the rest of Kuwait.

I feel clean and fresh again but inside I'm empty and deflated. All the build up and training, the painting of vehicles in the early hours, watching videos about Islamic fundamentalism and chemical warfare. I was all geared up to plough on into Baghdad, the fire missions and cold food, the dirt and the darkness started to feel like what I was meant for. Saddam Hussein was getting away with it and we all knew that the best of his Army had escaped and the ones left behind, the conscripts who didn't want to be there, were the ones whose bodies were spread all over the desert. The whole machine had now ground to a halt, it was too good at its job and the momentum it had built up had now gone, hundreds of armoured vehicles and their crews sat, spent and exhausted like a launcher after firing all its missiles. The war machine without the war.

"I'm fucked if I'm cleaning this mess up," said Pete.

We both sat on army issue foldaway chairs eating a packet of Chewits that I had found in an unopened parcel. In front of us in the distance burning oil jetted in to the black sky, silhouetted against the bubbling fire was the outline of an Iraqi APC, its rear doors open, mattresses and blankets spilling out onto the desert floor.

"The RSM will have the brushes out in a minute," I laughed.

"Right lads, here's the binbags, get sweeping!"

"I don't want to be burying all the stiffs," I said, for once being serious.

"Nah," said Pete hesitating, "they'll use the bulldozers for that."

After a few days we were packed up and ordered south to another holding area in the middle of the desert. The area was "clean" and would be our semi-permanent base until we left Kuwait. Engineers and other units moved into the zone we had left and started the long process of making sure enemy ammunition was destroyed or disarmed, left behind bomblets detonated and the dead bodies bulldozed into large pits before they became a health hazard.

Again the FDC took root with its awnings and tents coming off the wagon at all angles, this time HQ battery were all together as it was when we were in the quarry. It was a chance to catch up with Smudge, Tommo and Rob and all the others swapping stories and generally taking the piss out of each other. Nobody talked about the bad stuff like the charred bodies and devastation, soldiers don't do that, and we dealt with it by making a joke out of it all. The RSM was on the case again, imposing some discipline on men who had just finished fighting a war and were now left with nothing to do and wondering what happens next. Again the parade square was built, this time captured Iraqi anti-aircraft guns pointed skywards at each corner of the square, monuments to the RSM's Napoleon complex rather than any impressive display of Military bullshit. The 39 Regimental flag was hoisted on the flagpole, even Captain Lacey wondered what the point of it was and the RSM's idea of the guard being inspected on the parade ground was a step too far for the officers. Maybe the RSM wasn't aware of the short sharp intensity of the war, I wasn't even sure of the RSM's role during wartime, but it wasn't long before men sat around sunbathing under black, oil filled skies in shorts, vests, boots and carrying a rifle.

We were now centrally fed, meaning the soldiers from the Catering Corps were on site cooking for hundreds at a time. The downside to this was that they needed extra men everyday for spud-peeling and pot-washing, despite the hassle of cooking just for yourself and the crew as we had during the war, at least there was the freedom to cook something extra and not worry about giant metal tubs encrusted with burnt on meat or a jumped up "sloppo" insisting that only one large ladleful of whatever was on display was allowed. Several crates of non-alcoholic San Miguel Lager was given us which not only tasted like shit but also, as we had no fridges, was always warm. So the warm, alcohol-free fizzy crap was quietly buried or used as seating. Around the vehicles of HQs base men lazed around in shorts, although at mealtimes or when on duty, as the radios still had to be manned, uniform had to be worn. We also had to wear uniform when we left the area which we did to scrounge anything from the Americans, their rations were dehydrated powder "Meals Ready to Eat" and were vile compared to the stuff in British rations, so we tried to tempt them with the delights of Lancashire Hotpot and Mixed Fruit pudding in the hope that we would get a few cans of Coke out of them. The few Americans we could find were usually truck drivers, sitting on their own in huge sixteen-wheel wagons. They were mostly the U.S. National Guard - part time soldiers, and being alone in those trucks seemed to have made them a little stir crazy.

The only other time we had any reason to leave the camp was to get some souvenirs and have a closer look at what the Iraqis left behind. Pete and I were in our element. There was an abandoned position nearby which covered at least a square mile, nothing had been damaged by the allies, the place had been completely abandoned and untouched. Huge tracked Iraqi anti -aircraft guns sat lifeless, their guns still pointing skywards but placed around and on top of the vehicles were mines that had been armed and left in plain sight. Jeeps and other wheeled vehicles had their batteries removed and electrics ripped out by fleeing Iraqis intent on a little revenge. In some of the vehicles looted mattresses and other home furnishings could be found, there was even a suitcase full of ladies clothes. Huge untouched bunkers were burrowed deep into the ground, in one a gigantic map filled the wall and on a table in the middle of the floor a three dimensional map of the Saudi/Kuwait/Iraq borders had been made with sand and coloured wooden blocks representing Brigades and Divisions, our advance was marked with huge red arrows that stopped at the border of Kuwait, at which point the position must have been abandoned. In some of the bunkers the souvenirs that the Iraqis had were more chilling, Kuwaiti passports were found along with driving licenses and other forms of identification with anti-Allied propaganda. This position didn't belong to the rag tag and starving conscripts that surrendered eagerly, it was clearly the base of a Republican Guard unit who had fled north into Iraq before the Allied forces could cut them off. We reported back anything that would be useful like the strange missile shaped object with some kind of camera in the nose cone and handed in the passports and identification in the hope they would be reunited with their owners.

We found helmets and equipment, cap badges and badges of rank, and weaponry by the boxload. We eagerly fired Kalashnikovs on full automatic into the abandoned bunkers as well as throwing in a few hand grenades to the cries of "fire in the hole!" as if we were in a bad American war film. Some took Kalashnikovs as souvenirs, which would be de-activated courtesy of the British Army; some just took the Kalashnikovs and hid them in the vehicles until they got home. It wasn't long before the Iraqi position was stripped of anything useful and soon it became out of bounds until the Engineers and Intelligence people had finished with it.

"Sir...I can still leave the Army can't I?" I said to Captain Lacey.

I had been thinking for some time that technically I could just leave as the Army don't "own" my services until I sign up at eighteen for three, six or nine years service. The thought of that amount of time stretching out in front of me was daunting and depressing. I thought there could never be another war on this scale ever again, so it would be back to a unified Germany and the bullshit routine of everyday Army life. I had tasted the excitement and intensity of a war, I had something to tell my grandkids about, and nothing in my Army career would ever come close.

"In theory, yes. You haven't signed your contract have you?" he said surprised at my question.

"No, I'm eighteen in May."

"Then technically if your parents wanted you out they could just say the word. At eighteen it's your decision. You don't want to leave do you?"

"I just wonder if it's for me. I mean I've done all this but now what? Back to sweeping up the leaves on NAAFI Road? Silver service waiter in the Officers Mess? I suppose its changed me Sir."

"You're good at your job, and there is plenty of opportunities in the Army with your skills on the radio," said Captain Lacey.

"And you've got to travel halfway round the world to kill people and your only seventeen!" interrupted one of the Sergeants laughing.

"It's your choice. When we get back there will be some leave, think about it then and if you still want to go, and until you sign the forms, you can go. We can't stop you," said Captain Lacey.

"Thanks Sir, but I don't think I'll change my mind," I said happy in he knowledge that in a few months I would be away from the bullshit.

"Your one of us now," said the Sergeant looking at me seriously. "You said yourself that you've changed, and trust me, from now on civvies will never understand."

I didn't understand what he meant until much later.

The sunbathing under oily skies continued for what seemed like weeks until we were given the order to move. Tracked vehicles were rounded up and driven onto low-loader transport vehicles, the massive flatbed lorries that used to take us on exercise in Germany without wrecking the Autobahns. These were driven to the Saudi port of Al Jubayl, where the armour would be shipped off back home. Wheeled vehicles could make their own way down to Al Jubayl, before they too would be shipped off. The personnel themselves would be going home in waves, the main parties being the guys with young families first, which included "Bugsy" as his wife was almost due to give birth, then other married personnel, and lastly, and depressingly, the single soldiers.

It was two men to a vehicle, and I was with Dave in a Bedford lorry full of tents and cooking equipment belonging to the sloppos from the Catering Corps. Dave had mellowed slightly, as I must have earned his respect and he, in turn, had been less of a knob to me. Although as I couldn't drive, he had to drive all the way from just south of Kuwait City, on the infamous road to Basra, down the coast to the Saudi port of Al Jubayl. The convoy of Bedford lorries and Land Rovers stretched as far as we could see through the desert, and it was a couple of hours before coming to a Military Police checkpoint that waved us onto the motorway itself.

"Fucking hell," I said as we passed hundreds of vehicles shattered and burnt, bulldozed to the side of the road.

"Looks like they had a bit of a nightmare," said Dave, "and this is just the road south of Kuwait City, it's the northern one that's worse."

The ground was scorched black around the road, and every few miles required driving through a chicane of bomb craters, some of which were terrifyingly wide and deep. The depressing scenery of burnt out transport was never ending, debris littered the area for miles around. Everything from buses and tractors to tanks were broken black shells lining the road, the ones that weren't up-ended still pointed northwards hopefully. We drove for hours, Dave pleading with me to take over the driving. He even tried to explain a double clutch, or something like that, but I was having none of it and was happy to make sure he didn't fall asleep, even though I was having trouble keeping my eyes open myself.

We reached the town of Al Khafji, scene of the first ground battle almost two months previously, marked the Kuwait/Saudi border. I couldn't tell if this place was just a run down dump of a border town or had been hammered by the fighting until I saw the tower-like building in the middle of town, battered and scarred by incoming bullets and artillery. Local children, dirty and sand covered from the dust cloud of our passing convoy ran up to our vehicles waving and shouting, we threw them the boiled sweets from our rations, but threw them as far as we could to get the children away from the road. Every few hundred yards an open patch of land had been taped off. At one of these places I saw a bird fly down to land before trying to pull something with its beak, in a split second there was a puff of smoke and feathers, the bird had disappeared.

"Fuck me! Did you see that?" I said looking at Dave with a confused expression.

"No, what?"

"I think I've just seen a pigeon land on a mine," I said wondering if that sounded odd.

"How do you know? What happened?" Dave said, looking at me like I was insane.

"It...er...got blown up," I said.

We eventually left the battered town of Al Khafji and the motorway south through Saudi Arabia was big and craterless, thankfully with no scenery of burnt out steel and debris, the war was getting further away. We finally reached the holding area outside the port after about eight hours of driving. At the holding area there were vehicles and men from almost every nation involved in the ground war; a huge six - wheeled APC from the Czech Republic, jeeps from Norway and Canada, some painted in various shades of beige colour, some left green, with flags and regimental insignia hanging from antennas.

"Shed, check them out," Dave said as we pulled up next to a long line of scruffy, roofless lorries.

"That's the fucking Mujahedeen," I said looking at the tall bearded Arab men in the back of the lorry.

The rows of men sat with Kalashnikovs between their knees, long dusty brown shirts and trousers led to black sandals, turbans were wrapped around their heads, some had their faces covered, protection from the dust. These were part of the Arab forces involved in the ground war and had retaken Kuwait City, entering Kuwait from its southern border.

"Salaam Aleiekum!" I shouted out of the window to them.

The men all turned and looked towards me smiling and repeating the phrase, their thin, handsome faces beaming. I raised my fingers to my lips in the eating gesture before showing them what the boiled sweets looked like, then threw an open tin into their lorry, some that were not watching our mimed conversation visibly flinched on seeing a metal tin thrown into the lorry, the others laughed at them as they shared out the sweets. I wanted to stay with them and learn about them, they were so fascinating and beyond any kind of people I had ever met before. With their hands on their hearts they bowed in thanks for my gift of Army issue boiled sweets.

"Allahu Akhber!" I shouted, knowing they would love that one.

"Allahu Akhber! Allahu Akhber!" They all shouted in unison as they raised their Kalashnikovs to the sky.

Our trucks started moving and we parted, the Mujahedeen waving with their "Allahu Akhbers". I waved back hoping I would meet them again.

We were stationed in military accommodation on the outskirts of Al Jubayl. It was a gigantic Barracks, but Saudi Arabian style, with nice bunkbeds, carpets and air conditioning, it even had a laundry and ironing room. The base was home to hundreds of soldiers, most of which were British, but there were also a lot of Canadians who we got on with quite well as they didn't particularly like the Americans either. Needless to say the laundry and ironing room was always full of British soldiers pressing their kit, and I felt sorry for some of the Guardsmen I saw polishing their boots until they shone, we did the military routine of minor bullshit, but we were just waiting to get home. Our vehicles had gone along with our rifles, which were no longer necessary, and guard duty on the base was done by the Military Police. We bought phone cards to enable us to phone home from the banks of payphones nearby.

"Hello Mum," I said nervously.

"Stephen is that you?" said my Mother, as the voices of my brother and I sound the same.

"No, it's Simon."

"But you're in the Gulf," said my confused Mum, "oooh! Bill, it's Simon phoning!" she shouted to my Dad who was in the garage with his TVs.

"I'm still in the Gulf, I was just phoning to say I'm OK and I'll be back soon."

"When are you back? Are you OK? Have you got a suntan? You weren't near those boys that got blown up were you? They were all from Coventry you know."

"Yes, I know Mum…"

"Your Dad hasn't stopped watching the news, are you brushing your teeth? We were ever so worried when you wrote to us when it was raining," my Mum went on. "Here's you're Dad."

"Hello Simon," said my Dad, I could tell by his voice he was smiling.

"Hi Dad, I'm OK and everything's fine, we'll be flying back in a week or two, then I'll be home on leave," I said trying to get as much information across before I was cut off.

"That's great. It's really good to hear from you," said my Dad, who was always less worried about my teeth than my Mum.

The conversation went on, my Dad just glad that he could hear my voice, my mum complaining that I was too young. I didn't quite know what to say, and the conversation wasn't easy and I was selfishly relieved when I finally ran out of credit.

We killed time until it was our turn to get on the plane home by going into the town of Al Jubayl. The streets we full of people no matter what time of night, local Arabs and their families and immigrant Thai and Indian workers mingled alongside soldiers from hundreds of nations, including pretty female Norwegian nurses which everybody noticed; not just because they were female but also because they had blonde hair and blue eyes, anybody with blonde or ginger hair and blue eyes was immediately stared at by the locals. Children wanted to hold everyones hand and stroke their hair, we noticed Arab men walking around holding each others hands. Traders would call us into their shops urging us to buy something, it took us British a while to learn to haggle, prices had already been inflated by the locals and watching a British soldier come into your shop and pay full price without haggling must have made their dreams come true. Some of us were naturals at it but for most, like myself, it felt a bit rude. Most of us bought gold to take back, somebody bought a Hookah Pipe much to everyones amusement. I loved the hustle and bustle of the town, the mixture of languages, the smiles and friendly manner of the local Arabs, the smells of mint tea and spices and the general organised chaos. I heard the call to prayer again, beautiful even though from a knackered P.A system, it echoed down the streets of the town calling to them from the Mosque, drawing people in like a magnet.

The soldier population of the base dwindled to a few hundred single men from various Regiments, as the married soldiers and those with families boarded the planes home to parties and warm welcomes. Eventually it was our turn and after almost four months here it was with some sadness that I said goodbye to the Middle East, and although I was leaving, I knew the place and the things I had done here, would never leave me.

It turned out that there was almost nine thousand Iraqis that surrendered to the Allies, approximately a hundred thousand Iraqis were wounded and around fifty thousand dead. Six hundred oil wells were ignited, the last of which was extinguished only in November of that year. Of the British casualties there was just over twenty dead, including the nine soldiers from 3 RRF who were a result of "friendly" fire; the oldest of the Fusiliers was 21, the youngest 17.

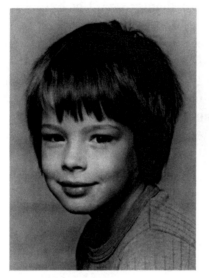 

Aged 3 or 4.   With my brother's air rifle.

With my brother and sister,   With my sister at the Junior Leaders
aged 3.   passing out parade, June 1990.

Standing guard after our Land Rover broke down.

Pete and I at the vehicle holding area.

In the back of the cramped FDC, I'm on the right.

Sequence of three launchers firing…

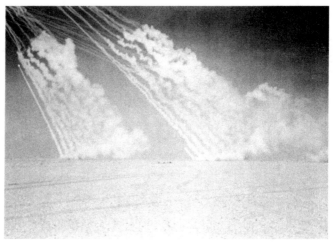

Trying to dig a trench in full NBC kit during a brief stop in the charge forward.

Left: Standing guard at the Quarry.

Below: When the war ends, the FDC takes "root".

Attempting to get a post-war suntan.

HQ Battery relax as an oilwell burns in the distance.

Clean at last.

Welcome home, as Bill and Emily Hutt greet their Gulf soldier son Simon.

ET9749TCTC

From classroom to the war zone

Within the space of a few months Nuneaton teenager Simon Hutt went from sitting in a classroom to fighting in the war torn Gulf.

But now the 17-year-old soldier is back with a very relieved family at his St Nicolas Park Drive home.

Serving

Simon went straight from Higham Lane School to Bramcote Barracks, where he trained, before joining the 39th Heavy Regiment of the Royal Artillery.

He was then sent out to the Gulf in October, where he was one of the youngest serving soldiers

Simon, a gunner, said: "It

By ANDREW PUNSHON

was boring waiting for the war to break out, and then it was frighening because you did not know what was going to happen next.

"But thankfully it is all over now and I am looking forward to a good leave."

His parents, Emily and Bill, have decorated the outside of the house with Union Jacks and bunting greeting his safe return.

Mr Hutt said: "We are delighted that Simon is safe and back home with us.

"We have already held a party for him, and it was terrible for us during the war, since we were not sure if he was safe and what was happening to him."

An article in the local paper with me looking slightly uncomfortable. Needless to say, I didn't have a particularly "good" leave.

5. Cold Turkey

The best thing about leaving somewhere is the feeling of coming home, the excitement and anticipation making time seem to speed up or slow down to a frustrating crawl. It was a more subdued return flight, soldiers lost in their own thoughts of an impending return. Germany had never looked so welcoming as we flew high over the dark grey clouds covering the country, one step closer to home. The married soldiers had already been here a few weeks, the debris of parties and celebrations long since tidied away. Now it was our turn to have the flags flown for us and the champagne sprayed around; the newspaper headlines all screamed "Welcome Home Boys", and we were determined to milk it for all it was worth.

After flying for several hours, watching the sights of industrial Germany flash by through the window of the coach was surreal. The last three months of desert and its beige and grey landscape, seeing the curvature of the Earth in the 360 degree horizon and the giant blazing disc of the sun, now Germany felt claustrophobic. Houses were packed close together and on top of one another, street signs and billboards on every flat vertical surface, little gardens with a handful of flowers attempting to inject colour into the uniform drabness. The black clouds here held rain instead of the residue of burning oil wells, people walked around with umbrellas and collars up and faces looking miserably downwards to the shiny wet pavements. Occasionally someone outside would see us in our desert uniforms in the coach and attempt a smile or a wave, it was hardly a ticker-tape parade but I suppose Germany, due to its history, has an uneasy relationship with anything military. The noise in our coach gradually increased as we drove through Paderborn and Sennelager until finally we reached the gates of Dempsey Barracks, home of 39 Regiment Royal Artillery, by now we were shouting, singing and cheering. Some of the soldiers on guard duty, men from 56 Battery who stayed behind, stood in line at the guardroom, turned around, and dropped their trousers, their "Moony Salute" was greeted with more cheering. It was party time and the coach was rocking with cries of "'ere we go, 'ere we go, 'ere we go." As we pulled up outside the Regimental Gymnasium next to the other coaches, where a large banner, wet with rain, predictably read: "Welcome Home Boys".

I don't know what we should of expected really, after all our families were in the UK. The large space of the Gym was almost empty, long tables had crates of beer and a cake stood alone on one of the large tables. A handful of the married men and officers along with their wives had come to make a bit of an effort in welcoming us back, it was to their credit, or more likely their wives credit, that they had turned up at all. Cans of lager were thrust into our hands along with a slice of the cake, we looked at each other bewildered and deflated.

"It's fucking wank isn't it?" said Bugsy, who was one of the first back and his wife still hadn't given birth.

"I feel like shit now," said Pete, visibly angry.

"You've just got to remember your families are in England, ours are here. We had a fucking great reception if that's any consolation."

"Fuck off," I said, laughing.

Men started to drift off, all we wanted to do now was to get into town and get pissed together, this was too depressing.

"Hold on lads," said the Quarter Master Sergeant, who was responsible for all the tables and chairs that had been laid out. "Can a couple of you just unload that wagon over there, won't take five minutes."

Pete and I looked at each other; everyone else did the same, not quite believing that our homecoming parade was turning into more of a funeral cortege.

"Fucking hell, I'll do it!" said Tim, who worked in the stores anyway.

"Thanks Tim," said the QMS as everyone else avoided eye contact and moved away.

"Fuck it! Hold on Tim!" Pete said.

I looked at Pete and sighed before the two of us went over to the Bedford Lorry and helped Tim unload it.

"Cheers boys, I'll buy you a beer," the QMS said.

"It's OK Sarge, we've been given free ones," I said sarcastically.

"Tosser," said Pete under his breath.

We spent the night getting drunk and after over three months of imposed abstinence it was a cheap night, most of us didn't even make it out of the Barracks. We needed to get home and let off steam, thankfully it would be only a few days before we went home on three weeks leave. The thought was that there was no point keeping us here longer than necessary, and besides the vehicles hadn't all arrived back yet and when they did the married personnel could deal with them.

With heads pounding and hands shaking through the mother of all hangovers, we were given back our boxed up possessions that had been packed away in December. Men silently grabbed their last letters home that sat on top of their kit in the box, ripping up the emotional words without hesitation or comment. I thought of the Fusiliers again, I'm sure most of us did. The next few days were spent lounging around in tracksuits and getting drunk, the anticipation of our return home felt like we were children waiting for Christmas morning.

It wasn't long that in a mad blur of yet more alcohol and excitement we arrived at Birmingham Airport; a hundred soldiers with skinhead haircuts and faint tans. People smiled knowingly, allowing us to be noisy and boisterous as we raced from the airport to the train terminal. Finally at New Street Station in Birmingham, we all said our goodbyes as we boarded different trains to various parts of the West Midlands or further afield. Pete and I sat on the train to Nuneaton; I had been on this train many times in my youth, the short twenty-minute dash to the big city of Birmingham where we would enjoy its hustle and bustle, laughing at their strange accents before coming home in the afternoon. Today it felt special. Other passengers also gave us that knowing glance as we watched the City give way to fields and farmland, we sat in silence occasionally smiling at each other as home came ever closer. I felt more and more nervous as we went past the playing fields that I recognised, all too quickly we had stopped at Nuneaton and my legs felt like jelly.

"What the fuck do we say to people?" I said to Pete as we walked from the train to the Bus Station, where he was getting the Bus home and my parents would be meeting me.

"Dunno mate, it's weird, it's like we're just home on normal leave when I want to shout to these fuckers that I've just been in a war."

People rushed around in their daily routine. There was no ticker tape parade again, not that we wanted that, but no acknowledgement either.

"Shit…I'm dreading this," I said as I saw my parents car come into view.

"Look, you know where I am," said Pete.

The car slowed and pulled up next to us.

"You sure you don't want a lift mate?" I said, as my brother got out of the passenger side holding a camcorder, filming us.

"Oh fucking hell," I said quietly.

"Good luck mate," Pete said before we put our arms around each other and hugged.

"Good luck."

I made polite uncomfortable smalltalk with my Dad and brother before pulling up outside our house.

"Welcome home," said my Dad, turning the car onto the driveway.

Yellow ribbons had been tied on the trees up and down the street, suspended between the upstairs windows a huge Union Jack had been hung and words had been sewn across the centre which read:

WELCOME HOME SIMON

I was quite moved, this was my ticker tape parade. Neighbours and other residents poked their heads out of their front doors to watch, then from out of my front door came all my friends. My parents had organised them all to come round and welcome me home, the house was full of my family and about fifteen of my civvy mates. I still didn't know what to say, and every one seemed strangely tense, maybe it was me giving off an I-don't-want-to-be-here feeling. I was still being filmed and everyone was smiling and laughing, patting me on the back or shaking me by the hand and saying it's good to have you back, welcome home, where's your tan? There was some cake and a bottle of champagne to be opened, there were cards for me, not only from friends and family but also from others in the street that I had never met but who had seen the flag and yellow ribbons, most said welcome home, one was a thank you card. I was humbled and appreciated everything they had done, after all it's not every day a family member returns from a war. I was uncomfortable though, I didn't want to be the centre of attention and certainly didn't want to be filmed feeling uncomfortable. I wanted to hear everything my friends had been up to; the problem was everyone wanted to hear what I had been up to. I noticed that when I spoke the room fell silent, everyone stopped to listen to what I had to say which made me feel even more awkward. I wished I was down the pub with Pete.

I soon settled into my routine on leave that consisted of sleeping, watching TV, but mostly getting drunk. Nobody at home asked me about the war, they were just glad to have me back; the things I did tell them were covered in a gloss of niceness; the truth but with all the bad stuff left out. Yes, I knew about the Fusiliers but they were miles away, and yes, we went down the Basra road but it had all been cleared away by then. It was all the things they wanted to hear and nothing more. Only once in a pub did a particularly stupid girl ask me if I had killed anyone, much to everyone elses disbelief. The worst thing was that when I answered "not directly," she looked almost disappointed. My friends were their usual selves, determined to treat me as they always had done, to them I was still just "Shed" the same kid that they had got drunk down the park with. They didn't ask awkward questions or want to know any details.

The problem was that I could feel that I wasn't the same. My discomfort and embarrassment soon gave way to impatience and irritation. I was unnecessarily snappy and would provoke strangers into fights when out on the town at the weekends, my friends would bail me out, telling the Police or strangers on the receiving end of my anger "Sorry, he's just back from the Gulf," where there then would be a nod and a sad acceptance of my behaviour.

                              * * * *

     I'm sitting in "Madison's", Nuneaton's number one, (and only) nightclub. It is the early hours of the morning and I am drunk as usual, I don't know where all my friends are or even if I have had a good night so far. I sit on my own on a sofa facing the dancefloor. Beautiful women in short skirts dance with men in matching shoes and trousers, dance music hammers repetitively, strobes and coloured lights flash in time to the beat like a migraine. Everyone is smiling, happy, kissing, drinking and dancing. I look at them all and try not to hate, it's not their fault, they don't know what I know, I'm jealous of their ignorance and angry at them for having a good time. In my mind I all I can see is the burnt Iraqi, with his frozen scream and fingers pointlessly trying to shield his face. I realise that I don't belong here, I'm a soldier who belongs with his brothers, they understand without having to explain. Something has changed and I know that from now on I will forever be an outsider and the thought of leaving the Army to be a civvy is soon gone. I now understand what the Sergeant meant when he said after the Gulf that people would never understand.

                              * * * *

     Leave soon comes to an end, and my goodbyes aren't filled with tears and sadness from my parents this time. Its been good to see my family but I'm eager to get back to being a soldier, I've had enough.

     "How was your leave?" I ask Pete as we wait for our train out of Nuneaton.

     "Absolutely fucking shit mate!" Pete says shaking his head, "yours?"

     "The same, I'm so glad to be getting back, seriously- I hated it."

     "I didn't get in touch because I thought you'd be having a great time," said Pete.

     "That's what I thought, I didn't want to drag you down," I replied laughing.

     "I take it you won't be leaving the Army any time soon then?"

"No chance!"

Back in Germany everyone seemed to have had the same experiences when they were on leave. The feeling of being the outsider and generally not enjoying it, except Tommo the notorious porn lover, he had kept in contact with one of the women who had sent a naked photo of herself to "A Soldier in the Gulf". Tommo had met up with her and the dirty deed was done after a few drinks and very little in the way of romance, I suspect the event itself didn't quite match up the fantasy the woman had.

The wagons had arrived back in camp when we were away on leave, most of the stuff had been sorted out and packed away into the garages. Now the FDC where I had lived for three months was just another APC, stripped of its communications equipment and its rooftop cage now empty of rations and water and tents. We now had to get it back to its normal state of green and black paint, taking the welded on Jerry can holders off and generally make it look like it was new and shiny. The bullshit had started and everything that had been taken to the Gulf had to be cleaned, polished, blasted with water, repainted, oiled, taken apart and reassembled, items such as the rubber pads on the tracks had to be changed as they had been worn down by the desert sand. The mechanics of the REME serviced the engines; the oil, water and coolant was drained and replaced. Whilst all this was going on the routine of camp life kicked back in, the Regimental guard duties consisting of marching onto the parade square looking as smart and polished as possible before spending the next twelve hours overnight either sleeping, patrolling the camp or standing in the concrete box at the gate which looked out onto the street, often seeing the other squaddies coming home after a night on the piss.

On my eighteenth birthday in May I was called to the Battery Admin building. Everyone knew what for, and cries of "don't do it!" rang out as I headed to the building to sign my full time adult Army contract, no longer would my parents be responsible for me, I was now, officially an adult.

"You've definitely changed your mind then Gunner Hutt?" said Major Lacey, who had been promoted from Captain.

"I don't think I'm cut out to be a civvy Sir."

The Battery clerk handed over the sheets of paper, smiling and shaking his head.

"It's not too late you know," he said.

"Shut it!" the Battery Sergeant Major said, "It's funny how when it comes down to it, and after all the complaining about how crap the Army is, people still sign."

"Absolutely," said Major Lacey smiling, "you're part of a bigger family now Gunner Hutt."

I could sign up for three, six, or nine years service. I signed without hesitation for six years, the Battery clerk shook his head.

"Your ours now," the Sergeant Major said laughing. "And just think, now you're eighteen you can go in pubs and buy alcohol, get married, vote and buy a porno mag."

Even Major Lacey laughed at that.

It was good to get back into uniform and into the Army structure of discipline and order, and it didn't take long for everything to be back to normal, such is the way of the Army. The beige had been resprayed in the usual colours of drab green and black, and the broken and worn bits of equipment that used to hang off had now been replaced. When we were off duty we would all go into town and into the soldiers bars getting hammered on strong, cheap lager, taking the piss out of the Light Infantrymen who didn't go to the Gulf and hoping to pull one of the local women that one of your mates had had the previous week or, even better but slightly more risky, the wife of a soldier that was away on exercise. We may have played hard but we didn't work hard, if the job needed doing then it would get done, the problem with the Army is that a job could always be found that didn't really need doing, a pointless task could be found just to keep you occupied.

We had a competition; who could get away with doing nothing for the longest. The favourite was to get a dirty boilersuit on, pick up the largest spanner you could find then walk around camp and people would assume you were doing some kind of task. Pete held the record of four hours, constantly bullshitting anyone who questioned him that he was going somewhere to do something of vital importance.

A few months after our return from desert we were presented with our Gulf War Medals, marching onto the parade ground in dress uniform, the whole Regiment stood to attention. Our Commanding Officer gave a speech; the usual bullshit about how proud he was to get us ready in time when nobody thought he could, the fantastic job we did in the war and that he was getting an MBE, or some other gong, for being such a great guy. All I could think of was "I spat in your tea - you tosser," and tried not to laugh. The medal was silver and had 24866218 Gnr Hutt S.E. R.A stamped around the edge, the clasp said 5 Jan to 28 Feb 1991 and there was a rosette to signify we were involved in the ground war itself. I felt immensely proud, it may have only been a bit of metal on a strip of coloured material but it was something that I would one day show my grandchildren and say "I earned that, look, its got my name on it." Medals weren't handed out like confetti; some soldiers spent their whole careers without ever receiving one. Some soldiers in our Regiment had the General Service Medal for serving in Northern Ireland, but not many. The Governments of Kuwait and Saudi Arabia also gave us all medals, the Saudi one particularly ornate, along with a certificate stating I had helped in the liberation of Kuwait written in beautiful Arabic calligraphy that reminded me of my time in Al Jubayl.

There was a remembrance service and dinner for soldiers of the Gulf War; a handful of soldiers from each Regiment or Battalion that served would be attending. Often soldiers are "dicked" to do some kind of task, usually a man is chosen at random for a particularly thankless or pointless job like weeding or emptying toilets, but for some reason my face always seemed to fit. Certain men would invariably have the shit jobs whereas I always fell on my feet, just as on this occasion. I was one of the guys that would be buggering off to somewhere in Germany for a day to be waited on and fed, before a church service that would be broadcast on the Forces TV channel. It felt strange to be wearing our Desert uniforms again, but this time they were clean and immaculately pressed with the badges of the Rams Head of 1st Artillery Brigade and the red and blue artillery flash sewn onto our sleeves.

Somewhere in Germany a huge marquee had been erected with rows and rows of tables laid with silver cutlery and china plates, and covered in white sheeting. We had been informed at the last minute, for security reasons, that Prince Charles and Lady Diana would be present. A hundred soldiers turned to look at them as they came in and sat down. At the top table along with the Generals and other dignitaries sat our future King and Queen. The food and non-alcoholic wine was served, all cold meats and salads. It was rushed, with miserable looking waiters and waitresses dishing out shit food and water to squaddies who thought they would be getting a Sunday Dinner.

"Call yourselves Silver Service? I've done better myself in the Officers Mess," said Dave, the other HQ Battery representative.

"I bet they aren't eating this shit," I said turning to look at Charles and Diana.

"I see he's in his civvies today, not wearing the medals his Mum gave him," said Dave.

"Look darling, this one Mummy gave me for having the biggest ears," I said doing the quietest prince Charles impression I could. A Sergeant from another Regiment looked over sternly as the rest of the table around us tried not to laugh.

Prince Charles chatted away politely to the big cheeses next to him whilst his wife stared at her plate looking miserable and probably wishing she was somewhere else.

"She could at least pretend to look interested," said a Corporal from one of the tank regiments.

"Jesus, I know the foods shit love, but cheer up for fucks sake," Dave said, making sure the angry looking Sergeant couldn't hear.

The food, what little of it there was, was soon finished and we stood as our VIP guests left for the church service.

"They're probably off to the chippy now," said Dave.

"God save the Queen and a battered sausage for the wife please," I said.

For some strange reason Coca-Cola sponsored the whole event, and we received a souvenir of a little metal badge of a map of

Germany with the Coca-Cola logo which went into the bin immediately. The Gulf War - even better than the real thing. The church service was just like all Army church services; lots of loud passionate singing and guys trying not to fall asleep, I did manage to get my left arm on telly though.

Another month and another civic reception, and another chance for me to be picked for a "jolly", this time with Rob Capewell and four other men from the two Gun Batteries. Birmingham City Council was holding a reception for the city's two local Regiments; ourselves and 3rd Battalion the Royal Regiment of Fusiliers, who lost nine of their men in the "friendly fire" incident. We were flown back to the UK, staying at the nearest Army barracks, which happened to be Bramcote, Nuneaton. Then to Birmingham town hall to be greeted by the Mayor and filmed for local TV. Before we lined up in front of the town hall we walked through Birmingham City centre in full uniform, which we had never been allowed to do previously due to the IRA threat.

"So where are you from?" the Mayor asked Rob who was standing next to me.

"Stoke-on-Trent, Sir."

"And where are you from?" the Mayor asked turning to look at me.

"Er...Nuneaton, Sir."

"Mmmm, closer than Stoke I suppose. Are any of you actually from Birmingham?" said the Mayor frowning after meeting a few of the others who were from Wolverhampton and Stafford.

"There are plenty of guys from Birmingham in the Regiment, they're just a bit of a liability Sir," Rob said trying not to laugh; luckily the Mayor saw the funny side.

"They're not allowed out to meet the public Sir," I said smiling.

The Mayor chuckled.

In the Town Hall itself it was a more relaxed affair, walking around eating cakes and drinking tea, local councillors spoke to us like we were human beings rather than a piece of public relations to get through as soon as possible.

"They're a bunch of two faced bastards," one of the councillors said quietly as we sat with a couple of them on the sofas. "The people in charge refused to fly the Union Jack."

"What? So much for the public support," Rob said.

"The majority were right behind you, even if some don't agree with the War, at the end of the day you're British Soldiers."

"Bunch of wankers!" I said.

"The worst thing was," the other councillor went on, "when those Fusiliers died they refused to fly the flag at half mast. It's fucking disgusting."

"The idiots in charge are in the minority, I hope you don't think we're all the same but it's a big city and the people at the top are powerful."

"It's a good job politicians don't fight wars then isn't it," said Rob.

Back in Germany and with the medals and civic receptions out of the way it was back to normal, the war was history, a distant memory to the public. It was time for 39 Regiment to test its capabilities again, this time in Western Europe where there was no expanse of desert or burning oil wells. The exercise was, rather predictably, called "Exercise Black Rain." Two weeks spent in the forests and fields of a wet and miserable Germany, everybody went through the motions of doing their jobs, which by now they knew inside out anyway, although this time the voices over the radio were flat and disinterested. Pretend Fire Missions were sent without the ground shaking and dust churning roar of the launchers actually firing, now there was thirty seconds of silence before a voice would come back over the radio with a pathetic "Rounds Complete." It was, literally, a pointless exercise. After two weeks of mud and pretending to the local population that we weren't there, we returned to camp, and the clean up began all over again. Vehicles spray washed and boots polished and cleaned of mud until the next exercise.

Now that the vehicles were back to normal and the receptions and presentations out of the way, I didn't understand what were doing here in Germany anymore. I missed the real war of the Gulf, the memories of it invaded every thought and its horrors invaded my dreams. I tried my best to justify everything we had done in the Gulf but there was no point to it, as Major Lacey said, "good men die for no good reason." I had thought we had a new role as global policeman and if half the western world could mobilise to liberate Kuwait, think what else it could do. The UN now had some teeth, even if it didn't finish the job in the Gulf and get rid of Saddam Hussein.

"It's the oil mate," said Pete matter of factly. "Kuwait is a shitty piece of desert, we liberated it and the oil flows again."

"It's bullshit though, it can't just be about the money can it?" I said.

"Well it ain't about getting the bad guys is it? If it was we'd be sitting in Baghdad right now."

While most of the former communist states of Eastern Europe underwent peaceful political transitions, transforming into democracies overnight, one country's revolution wasn't so gentle. We watched TV pictures of Yugoslavia falling apart; first Slovenia then Croatia and Bosnia, different states of Yugoslavia, breaking away from the dominant state of Serbia. Slovenia, because of its geographical location, gained independence after a week or so, war raged everywhere else. The Serbs, who had control of Yugoslavia's infrastructure, weapons and the bulk of the Army attempted to crush the Croatian fight for independence. The Croats had no access to weapons and had to build an Army from scratch. The UN considered it a civil war and imposed an arms embargo so no weapons could get in and Croatia struggled to defend itself as the UN sent envoys to urge sides to "talk". On TV I watched Serb artillery shells hammered at the ancient port city of Dubrovnik, in Eastern Croatia scruffy, bearded Serb men in long greatcoats marched slowly through the Croatian town of Vukovar which, after being under siege for several months, finally fell. The bearded men were a far cry from the pathetic Iraqi conscripts I had seen before, these men seemed evil, even carrying a skull and crossbones flag into the town.

"This is bullshit, why aren't we doing any thing to help them?" I said to Pete.

"It's fucking politics mate, they haven't got any oil have they?"

"They don't look like they signed up to the Geneva Convention," I said sarcastically.

Later, reports appeared of two hundred people being murdered after seeking sanctuary in Vukovar Hospital. The term "ethnic cleansing" was used, referring to the Serb method of dividing the previously ethnically mixed towns of Serb, Croat and Muslim and "getting rid" of the non-Serb population, usually innocent civilians. At around the same time the civil war in Rwanda was in full swing and reports of boy soldiers, high on drugs, were using machetes to maim and murder their neighbours.

The more I heard the more disgusted I became, not at what they were doing, but at what we were not doing. I felt used by my country in that we could slaughter thousands of Iraqi conscripts in the name of oil but not stop a civil war and its ethnic cleansing by either arming the good guys or physically stopping the bad guys. Maybe my notion of bad guys and good guys was naïve, but either way I had begun to lose my love for the British Army and my Country and its system. The big killing machine that had rolled through the desert was a politicians tool, brought into life only when we had something to gain, human life it seemed, had no worth. So we sat, impotent and confused watching men in suits talk on TV about "resolutions" and "embargoes" while villages were "cleansed" by bearded Serbs or Rwandan boys with machetes.

I was now becoming disillusioned and angry, many of the others felt the same way. It was probably the post-war comedown, after the highs of war comes the lows of peace, the cold turkey of withdrawal. It was all I had known; straight from training aged seventeen into a war, maybe my expectations of Army life were based on that and to cope with the anger and impotence I felt as I watched the News, I began to drink heavily. A soldier drinking heavily is not unusual, a teetotal soldier is very unusual. As soon as work was finished and we were off duty we would hit the bars or sit in our rooms drinking until we passed out, sometimes lunch breaks consisted of a few bottles of strong, cheap German lager. Every off duty moment was spent drinking or trying to get drunk, then work as usual the following day with hangovers or often still drunk from the night before. We would have parties at weekends that would make rugby players blush, I once challenged Pete to drink a bottle of Crème de Menthe, he in turn challenged me to drink a bottle of Blue Curacao; that night ended in rivers of multicoloured vomit and my eyes, ears, nose and mouth were stained blue for days. The moment I knew I had a problem came when I woke up one morning and immediately wanted a drink, and opening a can of lager had a liquid breakfast, I was a borderline alcoholic at eighteen. And the start of 1992 was a drink-fuelled blur.

I wanted to slow down but at the same time wanted to blot everything out, I had lost any focus I had. Needing a new challenge Pete and I applied for the Special OP's course, these guys were the eyes of the artillery, they were super fit and lived in holes in the ground for weeks at a time observing the enemy. I didn't last long, I just wasn't fit enough, Pete was naturally fit and was cruising the course but decided to leave along with me. I felt like shit, for coming back to the Regiment and for bringing Pete down with me. The drinking started again and it wasn't long before I progressed to drugs.

In the early nineties drugs weren't so much of a problem in the Army, and a few of the soldiers in the Gun Batteries were known smokers of drugs but the Army turned a blind eye. It wasn't long before we found ourselves in the middle of the woods with these guys getting stoned, the guys we were now mixing with were total losers and I often wondered what the fuck I was doing there in the middle of a forest in Germany getting caned. It did block out any of the thoughts I didn't want, the drink at weekdays then the drugs at weekends. It was an unpleasant spiral downwards and the more I did it the shittier I felt, and the shittier I felt the more drink and drugs I needed. It didn't affect my work, what little work I did anyway, and nobody noticed I had a problem.

Having another moment of clarity and realising I needed to be away from the losers I was mixing with, I volunteered for a tour of Northern Ireland, which I thought would clear my head and get me fitter so I could try for the Special OP's again. A week after my Northern Ireland request I was informed I had been put forward for an advanced radio operators course. This meant more money and more prospects and as the courses didn't come around too often anyway Northern Ireland would wait. I stupidly continued to drink and use drugs and, inevitably, a week before I was due to go on my signals course I was caught smoking drugs along with the others and, unfortunately, Pete.

I was charged and dealt with within the Regiment and "awarded" thirty days detention in the Regimental Prison. I knew as soon as I was caught that any career in the British Army that I may have had was now gone even though I had just turned 19, and whether it was a feeling of wanting to give up or the drugs still in my system, I refused to soldier.

"Stand still!" the Regimental policeman shouted at me outside the Adjutants office after my sentencing.

"YOUDONOTLOOKATANOFFICERLIKETHATYOUDO NOTANSWERBACK..." he was red faced and ranting at me, "ABOUT TURN!"

"No," I said quietly.

"What? You've got one more chance," he said knowing I meant it.

"Sorry...no."

"Are you refusing to soldier Gunner Hutt?" he said menacingly.

"Dunno....suppose so."

Refusing to soldier means that you are refusing to obey orders or do anything you are told, if you last for thirty days you're a free man. It does mean however, that you never leave your cell, only have a single blanket and are fed bread and water. I was walked to the cells, and everything belonging to the Army was taken from me, I sat on a bare mattress in a freezing cell in my underpants. The Battery Sergeant Major came to speak to me, a motivational pep talk, but my anger had got the better of me and I couldn't take any more and didn't want to listen. It was only when Pete, who had also been given thirty days detention, spoke to me that I listened. Here was my closest friend that I had been through everything with and who I considered to be like a brother; and I had dragged him down with me, and rather than call me a selfish wanker he was telling me just to keep my head together. I refused to soldier for almost an hour, quite pathetic really.

It turned out that Army prison was good for me. There were no drugs or alcohol, and no distractions. Instead there was an intense fitness regime, bed blocks and kit layout inspections, it was like basic training and I loved it. The slightest misdemeanour meant severe punishment.

"NBC kits...GO!" the Sergeant in charge of the Guardroom screamed.

We would all sprint inside get our NBC kits and gas masks on before running back outside and standing in a line to attention.

"Long johns and best boots...GO!"

Running inside and stripping off before donning green long johns and shiniest boots. We looked ridiculous.

"PT kit....GO!"

Other soldiers would watch out of the windows of their accommodation blocks cheering us on as we got sweatier and our smartly pressed kit got slowly ruined.

"Helmets and webbing...GO!"

"Right....kit inspection 6PM...GO!"

By the end of it our stuff would be all over the place and our highly polished boots cracked. Everything had to be redone. There was about eight of us in the guardhouse, mostly for drugs but a couple of guys who didn't go to the Gulf were in for stealing stuff from soldiers rooms while they were away. There was a camaraderie that made it bearable, we were all in the same ball-breaking boat so we might as well make the best of it.

Eventually we served our time and I was determined not to surround myself with idiots like these again or get involved with drugs. Pete and I did celebrate our release to excess and get paralytic on vodka, the last thing I remember was someone hosing me down in the shower as I wondered where all the shit I was covered in, came from. Me, as it turned out.

After my release Pete and I were separated for the first time. We were fantastic friends but together were a bit explosive, and I was definitely holding him back. I was sent to 176 Battery and my new job was as a signaller on the Battery Ammunition Control Point; in other words the Land Rover in charge of organising the resupply of ammunition to the launchers. It was a five-man crew in a crappy little Land Rover, and a big step down from the FDC and its role as the heart of the Regiment. The Gun Battery wasn't as closely knit as the guys in HQ Battery, I even had a room to myself and I missed sitting around watching TV with my roommates Pete, Tommo and Jeff, although Jeff was always out with his Polish girlfriend anyway. I didn't know any of the guys in my accommodation and although most of them had also been through the war it wasn't the same, I hadn't stayed up all night painting vehicles beige or drank Blue Curacao with them.

It was lonely and depressing, and on my first exercise with the gun battery in the BACP, I threatened to kick the shit out of one of the other crew members as he wouldn't wake up for his shift on the radio in the middle of the night, the officer in charge of the wagon heard this and gave us both a bollocking and my reputation became instantly worse. As soon as I got back to camp I put my name forward to do some adventure training, sailing from Southampton to the Canary Islands, if nothing else it would at least get me out of this place. It was now the middle of 1992, and I was now depressed, angry, and isolated without the support of my other Army friends from HQ Battery. It was just over a year since the war and yet so much had happened. The war undoubtedly effected me, although I didn't realise quite how much; its intensity and power began to feel normal when the war suddenly stopped, maybe part of me didn't realise the war had ended. I felt guilty that I was the small cog in the big machine and when I said "Fire Mission" people died horrific deaths, they weren't the bearded evil men slaughtering civilians in Eastern Europe, they were old men and boys who died so we can have cheap petrol in our cars. I thought I had made a difference in helping liberate Kuwait, I hadn't, I had followed orders that the men in suits had made.

Alone in my room with the summer sun shining through the window I watched the TV reports of the war in what was Yugoslavia; a Serb-run concentration camp had been found and filmed in Omarska, Bosnia. The skinny Bosnian men reminded me of the prisoners of Auschwitz or Belsen as they peered helplessly from behind fences and barbed wire, their ribcages and cheekbones jutting out against a thin film of skin. This was the twentieth century and it shouldn't be happening.

As I opened another beer I wondered if the world was mad, or was it just me?

6. Point of No Return

There were around five of us from 176 Battery making our way in a cramped minibus from Germany to the UK, where we would spend a few days on leave before meeting in Southampton and sailing as part of the crew of a yacht around the Canary Islands and back. It beats sweeping roads or guard duty in camp, although I didn't know these guys at all and the thought of spending the next two weeks in their faces wasn't something I was looking forward to. It took most of the day to get from Sennelager to Antwerp where we boarded a huge Royal Navy landing craft that would take us across the channel. The landing craft was noisy, claustrophobic and dirty but its Navy crew seemed to like being so close, we on the other hand couldn't wait to get off the stinking heap and its weird, touchy-feely sailors, but an engine breakdown meant another ten hours in the sea. We eventually got ashore and the sailor jokes started as we rushed to the nearest Train Station to ensure we wouldn't be stranded overnight.

It was late and three of us headed for the midlands but only got as far as Reading before a helpful guard informed us that we would now have to wait until morning for the next train, so we went to the nearest night-club. We were initially refused entry; first because I had a visible tattoo, and then refused because we were clearly soldiers. I was all for telling them to stick it and sleeping at the Station as it wasn't worth the hassle, but eventually the Lance Bombardier in charge persuaded the bouncers to let us in. I drank over-priced and watered down lager with two other guys I hardly knew, whilst Readings glitterati looked at us as if we were something they had trod on. Sleeping on a bench in the Train Station would have been more enjoyable. The following day I was back home in Nuneaton, and nothing had changed apart from my own attitude. I only had two days before I had to be in Southampton so I attempted to make the most of it. It was the first time home on leave since I had been in trouble with drugs.

"How many times have we warned you about drugs," my Mum went on.

"I know Mum, I really regret it." I said honestly, but I didn't really want to be having this conversation with my parents, I didn't need reminding that I had screwed my Army career up.

"It's the Armys fault. You should never have been in the Gulf," my Mum said.

"No it's not," I said half-heartedly. Mum was probably right, the drink and drugs were used to block out either the memories of the war, or the monotony of peace.

"What are you going to do now?" said my Dad trying to hide his disappointment at me.

"After this, I'll get back and try and start again, maybe try and change Regiments," I said making it up on the spot. In reality I was lost. I couldn't change the past and didn't know what to do next.

Most of my friends were at University now, spread out across the Country from Sunderland to High Wycombe, the few that weren't at University had jobs to go to, but I still managed to have a beer with Matthew who I used to play "Army" with when we were boys. People could tell I wasn't the same, I was disillusioned and unhappy, and I would tell everyone who would listen that the Gulf War was pointless. Usually when I had been home on leave I was the party animal, I had money to spend, unlike my student friends, and usually had a couple of weeks to spend it all on having a good time. This time it was different, although I was home for only a couple of days people wondered why the party animal had been replaced by someone so bitter. It felt like the time I was on leave after the Gulf, when I had become angry at people because they could go out and have a good time without a care. Then I had the Army to go back to, the big family that understood, this time I had to share a boat with a group of strangers before returning to Germany and a career in tatters.

Saying goodbye to my parents, I boarded the train from Nuneaton to Southampton, glad to be leaving but in reality dreading where I was going. I listened to Pink Floyd on my faithful Walkman as the train moved off and the landscape passed by. I hadn't been travelling long when I had one of my moments of clarity again which made my stomach churn.

Pete and I had often read of soldiers going AWOL and joining the Croatian Army, who having had to build their army from scratch, had no well trained or experienced soldiers in the initial stages of the war and desperately needed volunteers. Men from all over Western Europe answered the call; many going AWOL from the British Army or the Foreign Legion to fight the Serbs. People with connections to Croatia came from as far away as Australia, and North and South America. Some came because they thought the war was wrong and wanted to defend Croatia, others came for the adventure. I thought of the Bosnian prisoners in the Omarska concentration camp, the evil bearded men strolling through the beaten city of Vukovar, whose defenders fought to the death. This was it, this was the answer and it was so obvious all along. I could make a difference and for once in my life I would be standing up and doing the right thing. AWOL soldiers usually came back and had nothing but a slap on the wrist from the Army, I could volunteer to fight for Croatia then hand myself in to the Army and start again, maybe reapply for the Special OP's. The more I thought the more sure I was, no more monotony of Regimental life, it would be back into the intensity of a war. It would also ease the guilt of fighting in the Gulf, this time I was definitely going to be one of the good guys, defending a Country from the threat of an ultra-nationalist "Greater Serbia".

I wished to myself that I had had this idea sooner then I could have brought all my best Army gear with me, all soldiers buy their own kit; usually the most comfortable and hard wearing. My boots and combat jackets that I had bought cost me fortune because they were the best, but they were sitting in my locker. As it was I had my olive green Bergen, my sleeping bag and bivvy bag, the rest was just tracksuits and shorts, the kind of stuff you take when sailing around the Canary Islands rather than going to a war in Eastern Europe. My mind was racing, I had until I got to Southampton to make sure this was what I wanted to do as we were meant to meet up at the docks in the afternoon. I had to buy some kit for a start; boots would be essential, batteries for my Walkman and some more tapes, splashing out on a load of Army surplus clothing would look suspicious as I went through customs on my way to Croatia. I had to sort out travel and withdraw as much money as I could, who should I contact? Someone will have to know just in case, I stopped myself from thinking the worst, no, a few months then I'll be home.

I arrived in Southampton with the adrenaline pumping and any doubts I had were now gone, only a stomach churning fear and anticipation remained. I knew all the others on the sailing trip would be in the city so I had to be careful, if I was spotted that would be it and tomorrow I would be sailing off into the Atlantic. I headed into the city centre and withdrew as much money as I could before going to a travel agent. I had worked out that to avoid any suspicion, and not even knowing if anyone flew direct to Zagreb, Croatia's capital. I would go to Vienna, the nearest big city, then take the train to Zagreb and hope they would have some kind of Army recruitment office.

"OK. The Dan Air flight to Vienna goes from Gatwick tomorrow morning. Is it a return ticket?" the female travel agent asked.

"No, just one way," I replied without hesitation.

I bought a pair of Doc Marten boots as they are comfy and reliable, and immediately put them on to break them in. I also bought a load of AA batteries and some cassette tapes to go with my now overplayed Pink Floyd - The Wall; I bought U2 - The Joshua Tree and Depeche Mode - Violator, ones I already had but had left in Germany. Another war another soundtrack. As I was so focused on getting tickets and boots and getting to my destination I had forgot about the seriousness of what I was doing and was only reminded when I almost bumped into the officer from 176 Battery who was in charge of the sailing trip, just as he was going into the camping shop that I had just come out of, luckily he didn't notice me. It wasn't too late to change my mind, I still had another couple of hours before the deadline of meeting at the Docks and as I slowly walked back to the Train Station I thought long and hard about what I was about to do. I then realised I had to do it, to change my mind now would mean a future of "what ifs?" Then I remembered a quote- "I'd rather die on my feet than keep living on my knees", and as I boarded the train from Southampton to London I couldn't remember if it was James Brown or Martin Luther King who said it, either way I wasn't going to be living on my knees any more.

I arrived at Gatwick airport late in the evening, I had stared at my watch throughout the train journey as the deadline to meet the rest of the crew approached then passed while I was traveling. I would now have just been officially reported Absent Without Leave. Phone calls would have been made to my parents to make sure I had left and that I knew where I was supposed to be, they in turn would explain that I had got on the train early this morning and start asking where I was, the Army Officer on the other end of the phone would hear the panic in my parents voice and say not to worry he'll turn up soon but we have to report him AWOL. My parents would put the phone down and then spend the night awake, worrying. I started to get angry with myself for putting my parents through this again and I remembered my Fathers face when he heard that I had used drugs. My flight wasn't until ten o'clock the following morning so I tried to sleep, and then I had a few beers to relax me. I thought about phoning someone, but I thought it better to wait until I was out of the country. Instead I wrote a postcard to Pete as by the time it got to him I should, in theory, be in Croatia. I was glad Pete wasn't with me, this was my sole decision and for once I couldn't drag him into it, although if he was here he would take absolutely no persuading to join me and would do it out of a loyalty and friendship that I didn't deserve. I was on my own this time and the postcard I wrote was full of apologies, I told him where I was going and what I was going to do and that I would be back in a few months. I also knew that the Army would eventually see the postcard and my whereabouts would be established, and my parents would be informed and their fears would then be multiplied. I had another drink, posted the card, and wandered around they grey, functional and over-lit airport lounge trying not to think too much as I listened to U2.

The morning came quickly and I spent half an hour in the toilets washing away the grubby feeling that I always get when I've had to sleep in a public place, I also had a shave and brushed my teeth which made me feel that much more awake despite only having a few hours of alcohol assisted sleep. I checked in at the earliest opportunity, feeling the desperate need now to get away, the guilt of worrying my parents and the paranoia of being AWOL still wouldn't go away. Thankfully, soon enough I had boarded the Dan Air flight to Vienna with the handful of other passengers, most of which were suit-wearing and briefcase-carrying businessmen on their way to vaguely unimportant meetings. As I sat in the aircraft's seat in a scruffy fleece and Doc Marten boots, I could now smile to myself, I felt relieved as this was the point of no return. I couldn't turn around now, and as the plane took off and England got further and further away, the fear and guilt went with it. Now I just wanted to get into a uniform and carry a rifle, to defend peoples homes instead of oil wells. I felt positive about what I was doing now and any regrets I may have had were drowned out by my reasons for joining the fight. I felt alive.

We flew over the Alps and although it was only a two and a half hour journey we had some food served which was possibly scrambled eggs which had somehow been turned into a rubbery cube. The airport in Vienna was uncannily similar to Gatwick in that it was all grey and functional, and after collecting my bag without a hitch I was happy that it was "stage one" over with. I wanted to be heading to my destination as soon as possible and I hate hanging around unless I have something to wait for. I was glad the Junior Leaders had taught me some German although the only time I used it when stationed in Germany was to ask for a beer or chips or to drunkenly tell a girl I had a big cock. I asked at the information desk for the "Bahnhof" or Train Station, but as is always the case the attendants English was better than my German. There was a free bus to the two stations; North and South. I assumed that due to its geographical location, Croatia was reached via the South terminal and jumped on the bus that took us on a short journey through Vienna and its beautiful architecture before reaching Vienna's "Sudbahnhof". I could feel the cold through my fleece and see my breath as I left the bus in bright winter sunshine, and I hoped to God I was in the right place. It was another industrial open plan building though this time a lot older, draughtier and with more character than the airport. A huge display of arrivals and departures hung from the high glass ceiling clicking and flicking as the times and locations came and went. I saw on the board exactly what I was looking for - Zagreb.

Without consulting any of the information desks I purchased a one-way ticket to Zagreb, which left in a couple of hours. It would be my third Capital city in one day which wasn't bad going. After at first getting the German words for arrivals and departures mixed up and sitting on an empty train that had arrived ten minutes before, I finally found myself on the right platform with an hour to go. Now, I thought, was the time to phone someone. I was far enough away so nothing can be done but at least my friends and families worry of not knowing might dissipate slightly. I couldn't phone my parents, I realised selfishly, as they would beg for me to come home and I would have to give in, whoever I did phone I knew would be lumbered with the bad news. I phoned one of my best civilian friends; Adam.

"Where the fuck have you been? Everyone's looking for you," he said angrily.

"I know, I know mate, I'm in Vienna."

"What?"

"I'm off to Croatia to fight," I said, needing to get the information across.

"Fight? In the war? You're fucking joking mate."

"No, it's something I've got to do, look I'm sorry."

"Your Mum and Dad are going mental with worry, what if you get yourself killed?" he said giving me a reality check.

There were long pauses interspersed with sighs as Adam tried to find the right words. "Why do you want to go a fucking warzone when you're meant to be sailing around the Canary Islands?" his voice sounded exasperated.

"I'll be back in a few months, don't worry."

"Just be careful for fucks sake." Adam knew I wasn't going to be talked out of it.

The conversation came to a close with the pips going and we said rushed goodbyes. The guilt came again, I had just placed a massive weight on his shoulders and I wondered if everyone was better off not knowing where I was, I could imagine my Father being glued to the twenty four hour news channels again as he was during the Gulf War. My mind raced away with itself again as I walked to the train that would take me further away from home, England and the relative safety of Western Europe and into the heat of a civil war. It was another round of convincing myself that I was doing the right thing for the greater good- I'd rather die on my feet than keep living on my knees.

The train had old-fashioned compartments with sliding doors and the dark wood was worn smooth as glass, I made myself as comfortable as possible and hid my green rucksack so I didn't look in any way military. Just as the train moved away from the platform I was joined by an old woman with multiple bags of shopping, she staggered as the train moved off and my attempts to help her with her bags were met with waves of her hand as if she was swatting a fly, eventually all her shopping was stowed away precariously in the overhead racks and she sat down, mumbling to herself.

"OH SHIT!" I said as I checked my pockets.

The old lady was too busy trying to keep her top set of teeth in her mouth to notice my sudden panic. To my horror I realised my wallet was gone, I had took it out in the phone box and had laid it out next to the phone book but had forgot to pick it up when my conscience went into overdrive. What a fucking idiot! I was furious with myself for not concentrating. Luckily I had my passport and train ticket in a separate pocket in my fleece, and a spare stash of money, about £50 in another compartment in my Bergen and the change from the train ticket in the back pocket of my jeans. I didn't have any credit cards and the only thing they could use would be the £150 in cash, my Army ID card however, was meant to be my ticket into the Croatian Army. I knew they wanted experienced soldiers at the start of the war, but they wouldn't just take any idiot, and at the moment I looked like just any idiot. "Fuck it," I thought, I've come this far so something will turn up, and the lack of money meant I couldn't simply buy another plane ticket back to England, I would be stuck in Croatia whether I liked it or not.

The landscape was incredible, and the train wound its way around the sides of huge snow-capped mountains and wild untouched forests as we sped south through towns with German names. The old woman's mouth continued to battle with her top set, her jaw and lips going round and round like a chewing camel. I listened to Pink Floyd as the mountains gradually got smaller though no less impressive as it got dark and we arrived, with the old woman now snoring, at Maribor, on the border of Austria and Slovenia. I had my tickets and passport ready, I had also picked up a flyer for a Croatian jazz festival in Zagreb, I don't know whether I looked like some kind of funky beatnik but I was trying my hardest not to look like a soldier. The black-clad border guard had her bright blonde hair scraped back into a pony tail and she knocked on the doors of each compartment, I felt like I was in a black and white war film and half expected her to ask sternly "papers please." I smiled politely as she prodded the old lady awake and we both tried not to laugh as her teeth rattled her awake, a shared joke between a pretty Slovenian border guard and me, a cursory glance at my passport and the flyer in my hand and I'm on my way to the jazz festival - groovy.

Before I know it the train is slowing again and yellow lights could be seen illuminating buildings outside. The platform at Zagreb station seemed rammed with people despite it being late at night, a couple of men in Army uniform could be seen waiting, the rest looked like students, young couples kissed their goodbyes and a man with a guitar tried not to knock anyone with it, all of them are wrapped up against the cold, it all seemed so normal for a country that is at war but then again what did I expect? Stage two of my journey is over, but now what? I hadn't really thought about what to do when I got to Zagreb, should I find some kind of Army recruitment place if there is one or just keep heading east until I hit a front line? A vague panic sets in, I've got to my destination but can't cross the last hurdle, suddenly I'm exhausted, hungry and pissed off that I haven't got my wallet with me. I step onto the platform and the only thing I can think of is to ask someone in uniform, at the minute it seems as good an idea as any.

The cold air hits me as I step onto the platform and into its yellow glow and I wished I had more than this fleece I'm wearing. I looked around for the exit so I could find some food and information but Junior Leaders didn't teach me any Croatian, I tried to walk through he crowd of people looking for a way out. I started to think what a stupid idea this was; travelling all the way to Zagreb to fight against the Serbs only to turn back, penniless, because I don't know how, or where…

"Hey, you English?" A man in uniform stands by himself. I noticed him from the train because he looked scruffier than the others, now I also notice he has blond curly hair.

"Er…yes mate…how did you…"

"You come to fight?" he says in a Dutch accent.

"Yes mate, I'm Simon," I say smiling and relieved that I have a contact.

"I'm Peter from Holland," he says as we shake hands. "You English, you always have the green rucksacks and boots," he laughs, so much for my undercover jazz aficionado then.

"I am on my way to the front with HOS, if you want I can take you to HOS headquarters, they will sign you up and pay for your ticket."

"Fantastic mate, I didn't quite know what to do after getting to Zagreb."

I had read about HOS, they were the armed wing of one of Croatia's far-right political parties and separate from the Croatian Army but they were, however, always at the front. These were the men that had bravely stayed and fought to the death at Vukovar; ignoring their own commanders order to surrender. Most foreigners initially joined HOS as they accepted anyone and they were also purely front line infantry troops, the foreigners had volunteered to be there to fight so their casualty rate was high. Peter bought me a coffee at the station served in a small cup which was black and strong, I explained why I had come and that I was AWOL British Army but I had lost my ID card in Vienna.

"Fucking Zagreb commandos," said Peter looking at some young lads in combat gear smoking and drinking.

"Who?"

"Guys hang about here in uniform but never go to the front and fight, they try and impress the women and whatever TV crews come past wanting an interview, it's bullshit."

"But they're Croats aren't they?" I said.

"Most of them. Just because it's their country doesn't mean they want to die for it. And they say any kind of shit to the TV crews, they give us a bad reputation."

"Bad reputation?" I ask.

"Going on about Mercenaries and killing Serbs, everything the TV crews want to hear but it's all bullshit. We aren't here for the money, if you are you'll be disappointed and should turn back now."

"No, I'm not here for money."

After the coffee Peter took me into the city to the HOS headquarters. We sat in the foyer of a drab building, posters of men in dark glasses trying to look menacing covered peeling paint and cracked plaster and on every poster were the words "ZA DOM SPREMNI". At a small desk sat a man in a black shirt and trousers with dark glasses also trying to look menacing. Eventually the man in charge, complete with what must have been the HOS uniform of dark glasses, came down and greeted us without a smile. After a conversation in Croatian that started to get heated, Peter shrugged his shoulders and we turned and left.

"More fucking Zagreb commandos," he said.

"Didn't they believe I was a soldier?" I said.

"They said if you can lose your ID card in a Train Station, what else could you lose," Peter laughed and lit up another cigarette.

"Fuck. What now?"

"We'll go to the front, that's what most people do anyway, and register your name there, they can hardly turn you away can they?"

"What does Za Dom Spremni mean by the way?"

"It means Ready for the Homeland."

Peter organised everything with some of my remaining money at the Train Station using his fluent Croatian and I had to buy my ticket to somewhere in Slavonia, as the area of the East of Croatia was called, I was glad I had him to tag along with as he was an experienced foreign volunteer. I liked the guy and trusted him, but then again there wasn't anyone else. Peter Van Ekeren's hair was in short, tight blond curls, which made him stand out amongst the mainly dark haired locals. His hair, along with his blond moustache and Dutch accent made him look and sound like a 1970s porn star, however his teeth were chipped and his face lined, his fingers a nicotine stained orange. It was hard to tell how old he was, in his thirties at least but his lined and worn face masked any youthfulness, his blue eyes were tired and yellowing from the chain smoking and sleepless nights. The train was packed with people, most of which seemed to be the young student types that I had seen at the platform. The guy with the guitar was there and soon after the train was moving off he started playing folk songs, everyone was laughing and joking and it reminded me of my friends at University back home.

Peter opened his battered brown suitcase that was filled with photos and souvenirs; pictures of a group of men in white uniforms standing in a snowy forest, a shattered church, a tank destroyed. Peter talked me through each and every photo; the foreign volunteers in the town of Novska, the church that housed a Serb sniper, and the tank he took out with the RPG. I was exhausted trying to keep up with all the information he was giving me, and realised this time yesterday I was in Gatwick airports departure lounge, now here I was after passing through Austria and Slovenia, in Northern Croatia on my way to a front line.

Peter explained that there was no longer a war in Croatia, the Serbs had been beaten back and shaky peace deals had been negotiated, though they were still enemies. The Serbs consisted of local militias who defended their own towns and villages, Paramilitary groups of volunteers such as the nationalist Četniks and some regular Serb Federal Army units, the JNA. The Serbs had turned their attentions to Bosnia Herzegovina, a mixed state of Muslim, Croat and Serb, which like Croatia had declared its independence in 1991 but soon disintegrated when the minority Bosnian Serb population took up arms. The Croatian government quietly sent several regular Croatian Army brigades, the Hrvatska Vojna or HV, into Bosnia to protect the Croats living there and renamed them the Croatian Defence Council, Hrvatsko Vijece Obrane or HVO. The HVO and HOS units where we were going were in Northern Bosnia, an area called Posavina. The Posavina corridor had been one of the most heavily fought over places in the war as it was the only uninterrupted supply route from Serbia in the east to its territories in Western Bosnia of Krajina and Banja Luka. To the south of the corridor was the ABiH, the Army of Bosnia Herzegovina, to the north, Posavina, was the pocket of Bosnian Croat forces; the HVO and HOS.

"They are sick, crazy men," said Peter.

"The Serbs?" I said.

"All of them, the Četniks, the paramilitaries, are the worst, don't ever get captured," he laughed.

"Well I'll try not to obviously."

"There was one guy," he started, and after a few hours on this train, I knew a lot of his stories started "there was this one guy…"

"…a foreign volunteer, got lost on a patrol. The next day the patrol found him stripped and nailed to a tree, his passport and ID pinned to his head."

"Was he dead?" I asked stupidly.

"Of course he was fucking dead! Usually if you get captured you would get executed, it was only because this guy was a foreigner that he was nailed to a tree."

"No rules then?"

"No, our side sometimes has to do the same, not the nailing to a tree thing, but it's the unwritten rule. None of the foreigners do it, I suppose executing people isn't what were trained to do, but hand the prisoner over to a Croat whose had his farm burnt down or his parents murdered and buried in a ditch and what do you think will happen. War's a dirty business."

The train rattled on slowly into the darkness, stopping at every small town whose names had too few vowels and too many V's and Z's. The student population on the train gradually thinned out at every stop, all would smile and nod at Peter and the other uniformed men on the train as they left and the train became quieter, the guitar and singing now gone. It was well into the night and I could now feel the cold in the draughty train. Peter continued with his stories and I got the impression that they were all true, although slightly embellished with bullshit, but I didn't care as at the moment I was still going in the right direction. Eventually we had to stop and change trains. A handful of people now remained on the train, most of them in uniform returning to the front after being on leave. The Station was a small, badly-lit grey building in he middle of nowhere, and as we had several hours to wait until the next train in the morning, I got out my sleeping bag and had a few hours of restless sleep.

When I woke, a layer of freezing fog hovered above the ground and the few people waiting hopped from foot to foot in a vain effort to keep warm. In daylight this place was even more depressing with its frozen fields and leafless brown hedges and trees. We got on the new train the second it stopped at the platform in the hope it may have been warmer, predictably it wasn't. We were happy to be moving on though and I was glad that out of all the Army kit I had, I had brought my sleeping bag. The train trundled on slowly eastwards through the clearing mist, Peter continued with his stories and his chain smoking although I could tell he was slowly running out of steam. The towns and villages of V's and Z's continued and we stopped at every one, though most of the time nobody got on or off. The landscape became increasingly bare and flat, winter forests and brown fields surrounded us, and there were fewer and fewer signs of civilian life. We eventually reached the last large town we would see - Osijek. It was the first time I had seen war damage since I had been here. I had seen the sandbagged buildings and windows criss-crossed with tape in Zagreb but the buildings we saw as we approached the outskirts of town were riddled with bullet scars, there were also large holes punched in walls from anti-tank weapons, the place looked untidy and the grass was long.

"This is as far as the Serbs got," said Peter also looking at the damage.

"Did they take over the town?" I said.

"No they got to the outskirts, almost surrounding the town, they shelled it and almost had it under siege."

"Why didn't they get in?"

"At Vukovar, which is only twenty minutes away, they had to take every house, every room and cellar, and they took heavy casualties. They didn't want to do that again, their next objective of Osijek was well supplied and had plenty of very motivated soldiers, lots of them foreign as well," he said as we stopped briefly at the platform. "This was a town too far for the Serbs, the turning point where we pushed them back."

A few more soldiers boarded the train from the almost deserted platform to continue the journey that took us south, towards Bosnia. I now felt out of place in my civilian clothes and as I was only nineteen but looked younger, people didn't look at me as if I was here to fight. The train continued on southwards through identical deserted villages and the war damage was more evident the further we went, a burnt out vehicle could be seen, black and rusted, houses damaged by explosive shells were left crumbling and abandoned, fields were unharvested and corn rotted and turned brown on the stalks. Only a few civilians could be seen, usually old men on cold-war era tractors, too stubborn to become refugees.

It wasn't long before the train made its final stop and we stepped out again in to the cold air and a run down Croatian village.

"We're about fifteen miles from the front lines, we have to cross the border between Bosnia and Croatia first though. Unfortunately the border is the River Sava, and it's a big fucking river," said Peter.

"I'm sensing there won't be a bridge," I said.

"Nope, the place where were going is a pocket inside Bosnia about fifteen miles across with the Serbs east and west and defending the Posavina Corridor to the south, to the north is Croatia and safety."

"But to get to safety you better be able to swim?"

"Yep, and wait till you see the fucking river!"

Peter spoke to one of the military policeman who seemed to be everywhere now, and flashed his HOS ID card. I sat down on a bench next to the road as Peter attempted to find a lift to the crossing point with the aid of the MP. There was no way I would have been able to get here on my own and now that I was here there was no way back, I had come a long way and made a big decision, and my thoughts of home were further from my mind the closer I got to the front. The village was almost deserted; most of the civilian population had become refugees and had gone to safer parts of Croatia, those who stayed had too much to lose if they left. The grass was long and vegetation left to rot, this was a once loved village abandoned in the threat of war. Soldiers now stood around the streets, their "HV" insignia visible on their arms, and for the first time I noticed they were carrying weapons. Heavy trucks rumbled through the cold, grey, dusty streets heading in every direction, in the back of the trucks men sat holding rifles, some trucks towed large calibre recoilless guns or heavy mortars. Everything was grey and dust covered, the trees and bushes were bare and colourless, and everything was left, decaying.

It was mid afternoon and by the end of the day Peter assured me, we would be at our base in Bosnia, country number five in two days. Looking around at the battered village and the overgrown vegetation I reminded myself why I was here. This was somebody's home.

"We have a lift to Babina Greda, the town closest to the river, in an hour," said Peter interrupting my thoughts.

"Nice one, is that a bar over there?" I said pointing to a place on a corner that soldiers kept coming in and out of.

"Yeah, lets have a coffee. The guys are HV - Croatian Army, most of them are conscripts and for most of them the war is over. Some don't like HVO, and many certainly don't like foreigners coming here."

"Understood."

We drank our coffees quickly, the suspicious stares becoming intimidating. With Dutchman Peter's blond curly hair and me, a teenager in civilian clothes, we must have looked very suspect anyway. We found our lift and eagerly jumped in the cab of the truck that took us to Babina Greda, the driver was full of thanks as we were foreigners coming to fight, unlike the reception we had in the coffee house, and offered us some Rakija, the locally made plum brandy.

"Ah Simon, your first taste of Rakija! Welcome to Croatia!" Peter said taking a deep gulp.

"Cheers!" I said, I wasn't really a spirits man ever since I had drank the whole bottle of Blue Curacao in the competition with Pete back at 39 Regiment. I drank the firewater anyway.

"JEEEEZUS!" I managed to say through a burning throat. Peter and the Driver laughed hysterically.

Babina Greda was a larger version of the grey and dusty village we had just come from, only this time there were more soldiers as it was the last town before the border and the crossing point. Keen to get out of there, we walked the rest of the way to the river not wishing to wait for a lift, and found the small ferry that crossed at the narrowest part of the river. To say it was the narrowest part doesn't do it justice, it was the biggest river I had ever seen, this "narrowest point" seemed longer than a football pitch and the water looked ice cold.

"Fuck swimming this!" I said to Peter as we stood on the ferry, being pulled across by a cable on the other side.

It took over half an hour as the current was so strong to cross the gigantic freezing river before we eventually set foot on Bosnian soil, more military police checked ID cards and pointed us in the right direction. I looked back at the ferry loading up with soldiers and vehicles for its return trip and realised that stage three of my journey was now over; I would be walking into the fire from now on. The landscape got progressively worse as we walked down potholed roads and past fields that were churned into deep brown mud by tank and armoured vehicle tracks and past isolated buildings, almost all of which were bomb damaged. We headed for the HOS base on the outskirts of Domaljevac just a few miles away, as it was starting to get dark.

In the growing gloom I started to feel the rush of adrenaline and fear, as I heard the recognisable crack and snap of rifle rounds far off in the distance.

7. Black Legion

The HOS unit was based in what looked like an old farmhouse at a dead end road on the edge of the village. Word soon spread of the new arrivals and some of the Croats came out and had a quick look in my direction as I hung around in the yellow gloom of the small grubby courtyard. Peter was greeting everybody already. There seemed to be a party going on and a guy in a black boiler suit was drinking and singing along with a few others in various types of makeshift camouflage uniform, all held Kalashnikovs.

"I can tell you're English," the boiler-suited man said with a German accent.

"Yes mate," I said. I was the new boy and knew I should be cautious.

"Welcome to HOS," he said laughing drunkenly.

I saw that Peter was introducing himself to what must have been the commander of the unit and they seemed to know each other as they shook each others hands, smiled and started speaking Dutch. He beckoned me over to a covered cookhouse and meeting area complete with exposed beams, long tables and benches.

"Hi I'm Nico, I'm one of the guys in charge of this lot," said the commander.

He was also Dutch but looked younger than Peter, he was tall, with short, jet-black hair and a thin moustache.

"We served together in Novska, the place I told you about," said Peter, turning to me. We helped ourselves to a bowl of some kind of stew that bubbled away in a huge metal tub in the corner.

"I'm Simon, British Army," I said trying to look like I did this thing all the time.

"Peter told me. Most Brits who come here are ex-army and I've never met a bad one yet," he said reassuringly. "It's good to have well trained people."

It was getting late and I had been travelling for the last few days non-stop. Nico showed us where we were sleeping, I was on the floor of a small downstairs room in another farmhouse along with three others whose bedding was strewn across one side of the wall. Again I was glad I had my sleeping bag.

"Tomislav and some others sleep here, they're at the front at the minute, in fact another English guy used to sleep here until last month, his name was Davy," said Nico. On the dressing table I saw a T-shirt with the Scottish saltire on.

"So what happened to him? Or shouldn't I ask?" I said.

"Shot in the stomach, he survived," Nico laughed. "We'll get your uniform and stuff tomorrow. Peter will tell you everything you need to know." And off he went.

I unfurled my sleeping bag and bivvy bag. This was going to be home for a while. Just as I was unpacking and admiring the 1970s style wallpaper a man walked in.

"'Ello, how you doin'," he said with a strong Northern accent.

"Sound mate. I'm Simon, nice to meet you," I replied, glad to have another Englishman around.

He looked and sounded exactly like Bernard Manning, only his camouflage uniform and Kalashnikov made him look more menacing. He was in his forties, short and round with a ginger moustache that spread across his face, joined onto his sideburns and exploded into a mass of deep red hair that was almost an afro.

"They call me Smiley, I think it's a piss take," he lit up a cigarette.

"The foreigners tend to stick together round here, there's a couple of Brits, an American and a few Germans. Make sure you watch your back, a few of these HOS blokes are fucking nutters," he said casually.

We chatted away for a while explaining that I was an AWOL soldier and found out he was from Rochdale, when I asked why he was here he got a bit defensive, and thought best not to push it, after all we all have our different reasons. After a few minutes another guy came into the room. This time I could tell he was English; he was in his early thirties with blond hair and moustache. He wore a British Army issue forage cap and combat trousers.

"Alright Terry?" said Smiley.

"Not too bad mate," he said in a West-Country accent, "I'm Terry." We shook hands.

"I explained that the foreigners stick together," Smiley said.

"The English always stay together because were all usually ex-forces, some of the Germans are OK, and you'll probably meet Farmer Joe tomorrow," Terry said with a laugh. "He's the American Vietnam vet."

Smiley said he had to go and left us, saying he'd see us tomorrow. I got the feeling that they were checking me out to see how long I would last before going home or if I could be relied upon when the time came, and I was doing exactly the same to them.

"Don't take too much notice of Smiley. He's only here because he didn't pay his Poll Tax," Terry laughed conspiratorially.

Terry explained how the system worked; there were three separate teams of eight to ten men that protected our section of the front lines which consisted of only a couple of houses. Twelve hours on, then twenty four hours off, one of the teams was made up of all the foreigners lead by Miran the Slovenian, whose English was "shite" according to Terry.

"Want to meet the Mujahedeen?" he said.

"What?"

"I stay with them just up the road, they're sound blokes, mostly Turkish and Saudi Arabian. Sometimes they come on our shift but they only come with the foreigners, they hate the HOS guys." We walked together up the road to the other farmhouse and I remembered the Mujahedeen I had seen in the Gulf.

"I get the impression the HOS boys aren't popular," I said fishing for information.

"Most are OK and are just here to fight, there's plenty of good blokes here but there's some that are total arseholes, always on drugs. The gangsters and criminals are the minority but they're dangerous, it's only in the last month that things have gone downhill.

Have you seen them doing the 'Heil Hitler' shit yet?" By now I was wondering what I'd got myself into, two days ago I was meant to be going sailing.

"They're a nationalist paramilitary group with the backing of one of the right-wing political parties here. This party sided with the Nazis in World War Two. Back then they were called the Ustaše, or Black Legion, because they wore all black, which is why some of these idiots wear black and give it all the neo-nazi bollocks."

"I'm not here for that kind of shit," I said seriously.

"That's why the foreigners stick together and distance themselves from it, none of us are here for that kind of shit. We're here because we heard the stories of HOS being brave soldiers, nothing to do with their politics but some of these guys are a disgrace to the blokes who died at places like Vukovar," Terry said. "Up until a few weeks ago our job was to harass the Četnik defences by firepower and forward assault, I took part in three of the raids."

"So whats gone wrong?"

"We took casualties, some good men from HVO and HOS died. Then HVO pulled out and HOS had no effective leadership, the young guys took over and we went into a defensive role. I don't know really, in the last couple of weeks it seems the unit has been left high and dry."

"Looks like I joined at the wrong time."

"It's another reason for us to stick together and besides, could you imagine Smiley in a black boiler suit? Doesn't bear thinking about!" We both laughed, I decided that whatever happened I would stick with Terry, we were on the same wavelength.

The Mujahedeen house was spotless. No litter or drunken partying or waving rifles around. In the front room a dozen patterned rugs were rolled out, all equally spaced and all pointing to what I assumed, was east. Most of the men were out.

"Terry, Terry, Terry, who is friend?" a young looking Asian man said.

"This is Simon from England. Simon, this is Murat from Turkey," Terry introduced us politely.

"Murat great Mujahedeen," said Murat striking a pose.

"Murat great taxi driver!" said another, older looking Asian man.

Murat stomped off in a huff. The other Asian man was called Mahmood. Mahmood made coffee for all of us as Terry explained that both men were from Turkey and had come, with the others, to help Bosnian Muslims and that Murat had indeed been a taxi driver prior to becoming a volunteer. These men looked so different from my experience of the Mujahedeen in the Gulf, those men were tall willowy Afghans covered in the dust of the desert. These two in their green camouflage uniforms just looked like Turkish soldiers rather than holy warriors.

"The Serbs are scared shitless of them, they don't have any fear because they're all going to paradise when they die."

"Nice," I said.

"They're here for the right reasons, and I'd rather be fighting alongside them than some of the HOS psychopaths," Terry said as he poured coffee from the samovar. I noticed they all wore green berets with a Bosnian flag badge, Terry also had one and must have been some kind of honorary member.

We chatted away for ages and told him about the journey and Peter and his stories, "the truth wrapped in bullshit," as I described them. I discovered he was here for the same reasons as me; to do what he thought was the right thing, although his experience of HOS in the last few weeks seemed to have soured his view which was why he was so close to the Mujahedeen. The coffee was beautiful but by now I was exhausted. I eventually returned to the warmth of my sleeping bag hearing the occasional burst of gunfire in the distance and U2 on my Walkman who still hadn't found what they were looking for.

I was woken the following day by Tomislav and his men. They had finished their shift at six and now they were getting their heads down. I said some brief hellos and left them to it. I wanted to get kitted out as soon as possible, at the moment I felt like a spare prick at a wedding, walking around in a fleece and Doc Marten boots.

The base looked dirtier in daylight. It consisted of several farmhouses on one side of a strip of road, at the top was the Mujahedeen, our farmhouse, then at the end of the road was the headquarters and administration building where we had met Nico the previous day. Set in-between was a civilian farmhouse complete with an elderly couple that were making the most of their situation. In daylight I could see the graffiti scratched into walls, from the basic "HOS" to a huge swastika that covered the whole of one of the farmhouse walls. Our building was fairly tidy as it was just used for sleeping, with the kitchen being the busiest area with various faces coming and going. The room was constantly filled with the smoke of strong Croatian-made cigarettes.

I found Peter in the kitchen, smoking as usual and boiling water for coffee, he looked slightly hung over.

"You've met some of the other guys then?" he said through squinted eyes.

"Yeah, they filled me in on how they operate, I just want to get my shit together and get to the front. I feel pretty fucking useless at the minute," I said.

"Plenty of time for the front. We'll see a guy in a minute that'll issue you with kit and a weapon. At least we'll stay together on the same team."

"You know Nico then?"

"Yeah, he's a fucking asshole though so take no notice of him."

Smiley came in with a tall, scruffy, leather faced man who must have been in his fifties. Peter, Smiley and the tall guy said their hellos, they must have met last night, the tall guy also looked hung over, although I thought it may have been his natural appearance.

"Hi, I'm Joe from Arizona. They call me Farmer Joe," said the tall man shaking my hand. I noticed one of his fingers was missing.

"Got it in 'Nam," he said, noticing I was looking at his hand.

"Fucking hell, 'ere we go again," Smiley butted in.

We all talked away for a while, carefully getting to know each other but at the same time not giving too much away. I could tell we would all get on as there was lots of piss-taking which was always a good sign. I'd never met such an odd bunch of guys in my life but I'd followed Peter so far and felt at ease being with these strangers who I would be trusting my life with.

A blond, acne-scarred Croat man issued us with the uniform which consisted of two shirts, trousers and jackets, I didn't need boots, but picked up an olive green woolly ski mask that I could fold up to make a hat. There was no webbing or pouches to carry the magazines, nor was there any field dressings in case of an injury.

"This used to be Branko's gun," he said laying a Russian made, folding stock AK-47 on the table in front of me along with five empty magazines.

"He kill many men with this," Acne Man smiled.

I didn't bother to ask what happened to Branko.

He brought in a ledger and I filled out my name alongside the serial number of the weapon and signed for all my kit. He also gave me a patch to be sewn onto my jacket; a black and white picture of the Grim Reaper with the words "SINOVI SMRTI" - Sons of Death, written above, and "CRNA LEGIJA" - Black Legion, written below.

My first shift would be that night from six o'clock. I got changed straight away, getting comfortable with my new gear. In the kitchen Peter showed me how to strip and reassemble the Kalashnikov that I then did over and over until it took seconds.

"You'll never need to clean it anyway," he said as we filled the magazines with bullets. "You could bury these for a year and they would still fire."

I was now all geared up and ready to go.

"What the fuck is that?" I said looking at the kitchen wall. There were thin red lines of liquid sprayed across the wall.

"Yeah, I noticed that as well and asked one of the Croatian boys," Peter said. "One of the blokes used a syringe to spray his own blood."

"What the fuck for?" asked Smiley.

"He'd been using the syringe to shoot up with and was off his head."

We all looked at the pattern on the wall with disgust.

"You might have seen him, dirty bloke with along red beard."

"That's you isn't it Smiley?" Terry said making everyone laugh.

"This is the funniest thing. Guess what his name is?" said Peter trying to hold it together.

"Sili!" he said. And by now everyone was pissing themselves with laughter.

"Very fucking silly!" said Terry.

The front line was a village called Lijeskovac, a derelict place bisected by a canal. This position was several hundred metres into no-mans land, as the actual front line belonging to 104 Brigade HVO was well behind us. The canal separated the enemy and us; there was a road that ran over a bridge linking the two sides, though the bridge was covered in huge anti-tank mines. Our side consisted of half a dozen buildings, either half built or half destroyed. On the left hand side of the road facing the canal were only two houses, one of which was used as our forward position. The right hand side was slightly more built up and therefore had more houses to use as cover, although there was one main building that was always used. On the other side of the canal was the main part of the village itself, also almost half destroyed although the buildings were closely packed together providing plenty of cover for the enemy.

Our enemy in this stretch of the line were the Četniks, a Serb ultra nationalist paramilitary group made up of Bosnian Serbs and Serb irregulars with the occasional Russian volunteer, they often sported long beards, and their uniforms were mainly similar to ours. There was no Geneva Convention here, stories of captured Croats and Bosnian being found dead having been tortured were commonplace and the treatment to foreign volunteers even worse, confirming the story Peter told me on the train. I was pretty sure both sides were as bad as each other, though the foreign volunteers were in agreement that we wouldn't have any part in the mistreatment of prisoners should the situation arise.

Along with myself, Peter, Smiley, Farmer Joe and Terry were three young German lads who could only have been seventeen or eighteen, if they were English they would have been hanging around street corners asking people to buy them cans of lager from the off-license.   Gustav was tall skinny and blond with a deep voice. Rommel, was the "leader" of the three Germans, having Croatian parents he could speak the language and was the only one of the three that could speak any English, he wore a German World War Two era peaked cap - hence the nickname Rommel. The last of the trio was called Norbert, much to the amusement of us English who called him "Nobby", short and slightly fat with a black crew cut, he really did look out of place. Also on this trip to the front was the two Turks, Murat the taxi-driver, and Mahmood. The rest of the group consisted of two Slovenians, Miran our leader, and Sasha. Sasha was around my age and had started to train as an officer in the Yugoslav Army before the outbreak of war. Miran was tall, in his fifties, scruffy and had a few teeth missing, nobody quite knew why he was in charge.

A couple of vans took the twelve of us to the front, listening to the beautiful violins and high-pitched guitars of Croatian folk music on the way. It was only a fifteen-minute drive in the now smoke-filled van, but nobody looked nervous and nobody spoke, Maybe we were all in a trance listening to the music. We got out of the vans and did a final check to make sure we hadn't forgotten anything. I began to feel nervous and focused, the adrenaline flowing. To me we seemed to be making too much noise and there were eleven others and most of them hadn't "switched on" yet. There was a quick dash along the sides of fields and hedgerows. I kept on stopping to make sure there was enough distance between me and the man in front in case he trod on a mine, that way I'd be OK. It was basic military training.

"Hurry up Simon," it was Rommel, directly behind me.

"Fucking hell!" I said quietly.

I thought this wasn't the time to teach him basic infantry fieldcraft, so I carried on running up to the road, hoping there was nothing hidden for me to tread on, where we then split into two sections, one to each of the houses. Now I followed Peter, Miran, Smiley, Farmer Joe and Sasha into the house on the left, my fear of the unknown outweighed by my trust in the people that had done it a hundred times before.

The house was a brick shell. It was massively exposed and the firing positions consisted of a single brick removed from a front wall. Downstairs were two rooms knocked into one, although one of the rooms was probably a garage as it opened out completely to face the road to our right and the other house containing Terry, the two Turks and the three Germans. Lined up leaning against one of the walls was a selection of anti-tank weapons. Upstairs consisted of a corridor with a large hole in the wall facing out to the front with an old washing machine which was used as a makeshift barricade, only one front-facing bedroom was safe as the area above where the "garage" was, had collapsed and was held together by the remaining roof timbers. The safe bedroom was on the left hand side of the house and also had a single brick removed in the wall, and through the side window the front line and the canal stretched to the horizon. Another set of stairs lead to the roof area, which was simply a low wall with roof timbers across it. Around the house long grass and vegetation had overtaken the bricks and rubble that were strewn across the whole area.

Miran and Peter got a fire going, all we had to do was keep a look out to see if anything was happening. Since the HOS unit had become defensive, as Terry said, it rarely did. The canal and bridge would be too difficult to attack across and the only thing we had to be on our guard against were the snipers. Coffee was made and we drank it relaxing around the fire as Smiley took watch from the upstairs bedroom. It was almost last light.

"What do you think of it so far?" asked Peter.

"Not much of a defensive position," I said stating the obvious.

"Nice and easy, they no attack, we no attack," said Miran.

"It's bullshit, if I wanted to stand guard I'd be at Buckingham Palace," Farmer Joe said through a cloud of cigarette smoke. Miran held out his hands and shrugged his shoulders.

"Ninety-five percent of this war is waiting and watching, it's the other five percent you've got to be ready for," said Peter.

The three of them nodded in agreement, Sasha drank coffee as he looked out from the downstairs hole in the wall. The conversation continued between the three of them comparing war stories.

"And some of these HOS guys couldn't organise jack shit!" Farmer Joe said.

Miran did his usual shrug of the shoulders with his palms raised as if to say, "I agree but I'm just doing my bit." The fire was put out, it was now dark and suddenly I was freezing.

I was glad there were so many of us in that house, in the darkness every shadow seemed to move and my mind imagined there was danger around every corner. I stayed awake all that night, constantly moving to keep warm. Some of them slept, they had done this hundreds of times before and as Miran said "they no attack, we no attack." From the upstairs bedroom window I could see tracer rounds being fired into the sky on the horizon by bored soldiers with the now familiar crack and rattle of gunfire, these red and green phosphorous tipped bullets looked like fireworks, the only light apart from the moon. The hours ticked by slowly in silence until eventually it was almost sunrise. In the morning the village was covered in a mist that hovered just above the ground like dry ice, there's always a smell at dawn of freshly cut grass and moisture, it was the same in the Gulf, it's a clean, new smell. The sun rose slowly under a cover of cloud and the mist gradually disappeared. Downstairs the fire was going already and the first cigarettes of the day were being smoked.

"No problem?" Miran said to me.

"No problem mate," I replied.

Sasha smiled and gave a thumbs up as Smiley's smokers cough went into overdrive.

"Smoking's dangerous for your health you know," I said.

"I could get hit by a bus tomorrow!" laughed Smiley in between coughs, his bright orange nicotine-stained fingers still holding the cigarette.

"I've been waiting here ages and I still ain't seen no bus," said Farmer Joe.

The other shift turned up on time and there were a few brief conversations before we were off and running back down the fields and hedgerows to the waiting van and more Croatian folk music.

The shifts were always the same, only at night we would talk in whispers or try to sleep through the freezing cold. The personnel would often vary but it was Peter, Smiley, Farmer Joe, Terry and myself that were the constant presence. Over the next few days new faces would arrive, a couple of Romanians and a Hungarian called Elias Laszlo. They didn't have much to do with us and were in different teams. We noticed that some people that we'd seen around the farmhouses had now gone, we were told they'd either had enough or they were on leave. About a week after I had been there I met some other British volunteers, word would soon get around that a group of foreign volunteers were operating together and guys from other units would come round to meet us. John was also an AWOL British soldier who had been here a couple of months, he had a bandage around his head as a result of being hit by shrapnel from a Serb mortar. Ivan was from the Republic of Ireland, he was tall, skinny, and softly spoken and wore a wide brimmed "digger" hat pinned up at one side which covered his pony-tailed hair. We asked if they wanted to join us but said they would never work with HOS, and so would we like to join them in their HVO unit, we said that at the minute it was a case of "better the devil you know." Although we were sure we'd see them sooner rather than later. I also put other names to faces around the HOS camp. I only saw Sili the junkie once, he wore a long dark green trench coat and a peaked cap that covered his ears, the only exposed skin was his grey face half hidden by his Z Z Top beard. The man I saw on my first night in the boiler suit was Andreas, a young German with spiky black hair and an earring with a cross hanging from it. The Croatians Željko Čelik and Marco Tigrić would often stop to talk with us and especially Terry, we considered Marco one of the nicest blokes we'd met so far in HOS, he was thickset and had homemade tattoos and it seemed he had a lot of respect from the rest of HOS.

I settled into my own routine, on returning from the shift I would sleep, always with the unloaded rifle next to me alongside my boots. On waking up I would strip and clean my Kalashnikov, wash and shave, then polish my boots. Then I'd meet the others to drink coffee and talk.

"Who's the geezer on the badge," I said pointing to the patch on Peter's arm that had a picture of a man with a large black moustache and the words "Srbin".

"It's the previous commander, apparently killed in action, they had this patch made in commemoration. He was a Serbian guy."

"Bullshit. He was killed by Jelko," Farmer Joe said referring to the second in command of the unit, the acne-scarred man who had issued my kit.

"Yeah, it's true, the liaison officer of the Mujahedeen told me the same thing," said Terry.

"Look, we all know some of these guys are crazy fuckers but as long as we stick together they won't touch us," Peter went on, "they fucking need us more than we need them."

He was right, we had been here just over a week and already we were becoming powerful. Peter had somehow become our unelected leader, though nobody minded, he had the confident attitude of someone who knows what he's doing. And we could sense a power struggle between Peter and Miran.

Sometimes a sniper rifle or a heavy machine gun would be brought with us to the front. Miran would always use the sniper rifle, which was a World War Two era bolt-action rifle with a scope, but you could always tell if he had hit one of them, as they would then start firing anti-tank grenades in our direction, which weren't particularly accurate.

"Are you OK? Are you OK?" It was Smiley screaming from the house opposite.

"Fine thanks, what's the panic?" I replied.

"A fucking RPG round just exploded in your doorway!"

"Yeah? Didn't hear a thing mate!"

The heavy machine gun was a belt fed World War Two copy of a German weapon called the MG-42, Peter often used it as a pretence to hose down known Četnik positions, not that in the whole time I had been there I had actually seen the enemy and as they changed their positions regularly we could never tell if we had inflicted any casualties anyway. In fact we thought he only used it to do his "Rambo" impression that seemed to be the preferred method of training among many of the soldiers we saw.

It was at night in the freezing cold and unable to sleep that I often wondered what my friends and family were doing. These were the times when our whispered conversations were no longer piss takes, I could talk to Terry and Sasha for hours; getting to know them but at the same time never really talking about our pasts, we were talking but we were all strangers to each other as much as we were strangers to the local population. Smiley never gave anything away, if he didn't like where the conversation was going he'd say "Nema, nema," in his best Bernard Manning voice which was Croatian for stop or no. Peter's conversations always had a hint of bullshit, and I discovered why Farmer Joe was called Farmer Joe. He was obsessed with pig farming and his plan was to make pigs eat more greens to make them healthier, and therefore the meat would taste better. I didn't know if pig farming was a major industry in Arizona, I somehow doubted it. I never found out exactly what he did in Vietnam, he could have been a cook for all anyone knew, but we discovered that if you let him start talking about pig farming he would be quite happy and wouldn't stop until you told him to. He was a great guy, but completely bonkers.

"Tank! Tank!" Murat came screaming into the room.

We were in the house on the right hand side of the road this time, which was fine as the main room was enclosed and couldn't be seen, it even had two sofas. Terry, Smiley, Sasha, Mahmood, two Croats and myself were sitting on the sofas. An hour or so earlier two men with huge beards came to our position with a heavy calibre sniper rifle, this was a professional sniper team that went to various positions all along the front line, he would fire a couple of shots, then bugger off. Inevitably he would kill some Četniks and inevitably they would retaliate with tank rounds or RPGs, by the time they had retaliated our bearded sniper had long gone. Nice work if you can get it. We heard the tank rumble around the corner then stop, we didn't even have to look, it was always the same routine after a sniper had done his thing. A bit of tit-for-tat.

-BOOM-

Everyone sat on the sofas trying to get as small as possible, feeling the ground jump as the tank fired.

The sound of a tank round going past is a bit like a high speed racing car going past at top speed. The tank was firing down the main road. Murat was pacing, then sitting, then standing. The round hit a building behind us with a *-crump-*.

-BOOM-

The round screamed past the outside wall. Everybody looked at each other; Murat was shaking and started stuttering to Mahmood in Turkish.

"We go! We go!" he shouted flinging his hands in the air.

Everyone looked at him as Mahmood told him to calm down. Although if one round were to hit the room we'd all be in the shit.

-BOOM-

Smiley lit another cigarette, we were packed into the room and we could hardly breathe for the smoke and fear.

"I'm not coming on holiday here again," I said.

Smiley and Terry's faces broke out into a huge nervous grin, Murat looked at me like I was mad.

"I shall be writing a strongly worded letter to my MP," Terry said.

"They told me club 18-30 was a bit rowdy but this is ridiculous," I said as I noticed my hands shaking.

Murat started pointing and jabbering in Turkish, Sasha was smiling nervously.

-BOOM-

"I've just fucking decorated in here as well," said Smiley.

"The estate's gone downhill since the new neighbours moved in."

"TURN THE FUCKING MUSIC DOWN!"

The round screamed past, it felt like it was millimetres away from the outer wall.

"To think I could be sailing around the fucking Canary Islands."

"I'm glad I didn't bother with that extension now."

The banter continued, Terry, Smiley and myself giggling like maniacs until the tank stopped firing. The others were sniggering nervously, not quite understanding the joke, but laughter is contagious and the tension disappeared like the screaming explosive tank rounds flying down the street.

"This is the famous British sense of humour Murat," Terry said.

"Četniks must have caught us in happy hour!" said Smiley.

It was one of the most bizarre experiences I'd ever been through.

The days and nights at the front continued to follow the same pattern of "we no attack, they no attack." The only difference was that Peter and Miran had started to hate each other and something had to give. I liked Miran, he was in his fifties and was too old to be one of the HOS "gang" and he went about his shift at the front like a man doing a shift at a factory, he had no family or children back in Slovenia, in fact, I probably felt sorry for him. He was in charge of us so that HOS had one of their men in command, an outsider in charge would be bad news for them as it would mean we had too much power and authority. We were also starting to get disillusioned with what we were doing, it was just guard duty and the atmosphere between us and the rest of HOS deteriorated to the point where Peter would not share the same house with Miran when we were at the front. Peter even considered the idea of shooting Miran and blaming the Četniks, but we were having none of that and told him as much and he soon forgot that plan. Miran was getting pissed off with all of us, he knew he had lost his authority.

"I've spoken to the commander of 106 Brigade HVO, he said he'd love to have us as an intervention group," Peter said.

We were in the kitchen, Terry, Peter, Smiley, Farmer Joe and myself and as usual all of us were bitching about the state of affairs. The Mujahedeen had moved out a few days previously to a round of handshakes and "Allahu Akhbers," we all missed our strange allies.

"Intervention?" I said.

"Kind of Special Forces, it's all observation, recce, and a bit of behind the lines aggro," said Smiley through his usual cloud of smoke.

"The commander said we'd be our own unit, we'd work alongside their other local intervention group," Peter said.

"HVO don't treat you like shit," Farmer Joe had spent time in 104 Brigade.

"Proper soldiers, not these gangsters," said Peter.

"We're wasted here, we should be fighting, and that's what we all came here to do," said Farmer Joe.

We all new the risks in leaving HOS, they would want us dead, we'd pissed the leaders and their gangster henchmen off enough so far so to leave them seven or eight men short would be the final straw. Nobody would send a search party if we went missing. Who else would be with us? The three Germans? Sasha? It was unlikely, they would know the risks too, and besides most of them were in the comfort zone of just guarding the front for twelve hours then coming back and sleeping or drinking. We discussed the idea in whispers, if they found out our plan they would simply take us by surprise and we'd disappear.

"Tonight, at the front we'll discuss it more, in the meantime don't mention it or speak about it to anyone," said Peter.

Terry and me looked at each other and started to giggle.

"This message will self-destruct in fifteen seconds," said Terry. The discussion deteriorated into a round of James Bond impressions.

That night it was the five of us along with the three Germans and Sasha, now that Miran no longer went on shift with us. Although everyone except Peter was on friendly terms with him, he had reached the point of no return with Peter, and at the very mention of Peter's name Miran would draw his thumb across his throat. The Germans and Sasha knew our feelings toward the rest of HOS, it was difficult to hide. They were glad the Miran and Peter issue had been temporarily sorted, but the tension between HOS and ourselves was still there. Sasha just wanted to get on with what he was doing, being Slovenian meant he didn't fit into the "foreigner" category and had family only a days train ride away, he had too much to lose by joining us. The Germans on the other hand were bored stupid, being so young and with no military background meant that they acted like children who had already grown tired of their Christmas presents. They got on our nerves if they were left to their own devices but when we were around they tended to switch on a little more. We assumed they would want to go where we went but they mixed more with the HOS soldiers than they did with us and it was obvious that their first loyalty was to each other. There was plenty of running back and forward across the road that night. There were even more whispered conversations in the darkness.

"Who made him leader anyway?" whispered Terry when we were on our own.

"I know he's full of shit most of the time, but he's got the balls to stand up to them," I said.

"Yeah, I suppose so and I wouldn't want to do it," Terry went on. "What do you reckon then?"

"I don't know. We've got a good team with Sasha and the three stooges over there," I said.

"I reckon HOS want rid of us now anyway, were becoming a pain in the arse."

"Yeah, it's only a matter of time I suppose."

"At the minute we've got the men to say "right, that's it were fucking off", a few days down the line, maybe one of us goes home, or they kill Peter, we'd be fucked," Terry said.

"Better to jump now than be pushed later I suppose," I said.

"They won't be pushing that's for sure!" said Terry.

"I'm more scared of them than the fucking Serbs," I said honestly.

"And we thought we were the good guys," said Terry looking out over the village.

The night passed in a flurry of whispered plots and a growing feeling of dread for what was to come. This wasn't what I came here for; I was one of the good guys. I watched the sun rise and burn away the mist, inhaling the smell of the dawn.

Back at our farmhouse I had a restless sleep, we had no definite decision as to when, how and what if? We met in the kitchen again and had further whispered conversations. We were sure nothing was going to happen anytime soon.

"Could 106 guard us on the way out?"

"No, the commander doesn't want to fuck with HOS either, he'll send a van and driver that's it," explained Peter.

"So we tell them were off, hand in our weapons, and say don't go changing? Yeah, that's gonna happen!" said Joe.

"We've no chance trying to shoot our way out," said Smiley.

Ideas and suggestions flew round until we were repeating ourselves, Peter would go to 106 again and see what more they could do. In the meantime we'd carry on as normal.

"Lets get some food," said Smiley.

"That's the best suggestion I've heard all day," said Terry sarcastically.

"I hear the goulash is the chefs speciality."

"I thought that was Stew."

"It was soup with lumps in."

"Just like Momma used to make. Mmm."

As the five of us walked up the road we could hear a radio blaring and the HOS boys shouting and cheering, another drunken party followed by a morphine chaser, something we were getting used to. It wasn't music on the radio though, it was a man shouting. Looking quizzically at each other we walked into the courtyard.

We recognised the voice. It was a speech, the speaker was shouting, angrier and angrier as the as he whipped the crowd into a frenzy. The HOS boys were loving it, boiler suited Andreas and the others were shouting the words along with the man before the final climax of the speech, deafening, my stomach was churning, they were laughing, shouting, angry and with hate filled faces. The man stopped speaking but the crowd were roaring, I knew what was coming.

Through gritted teeth they screamed it, their right arms thrusting up and forwards in the Nazi salute, bottles or Kalashnikovs in their left hand.

"SEIG HEIL!"

"SEIG HEIL!"

"SEIG HEIL!"

8. End of a German

We all looked at each other in a stunned silence as the tape was rewound and played again, then walked quickly, avoiding eye contact, to the eating area where we scooped up the meatballs onto plates and sat down. I noticed I no longer felt hungry and stared into my plate.

"We've gotta eat," said Farmer Joe quietly.

"Wankers," said Terry.

We ate in silence, trying to shovel the tasteless stew into our mouths as quickly as we could. We all wanted to be a million miles away from these people but tried to act as normally as we could, as if listening to the rantings of Hitler was like eating a bag of chips.

"SEIG HEIL!"

It went on and on. I felt physically sick. People just don't do this. This was a bad place, it felt evil, I didn't belong to it and I wanted no part of it. We were supposed to be the good guys and I was here to do the right thing, to stand up for people, risking my life to stop people being driven from their homes and ending up in mass graves, not risking my life for these idiots. This was all wrong. Maybe I was being naïve, was I doing the wrong thing but for the right reasons? What the fuck am I doing here? We dumped our plates and walked out, again trying not to make eye contact with any of the crowd. They were too busy drinking and singing. I tried to make a mental note of the faces, and with sadness I noticed the three young Germans were joining in. Back in our kitchen we sat down and cigarettes were lit, Smiley's hand shook.

"I've never seen anything like that before in my life," he said exhaling smoke.

"Is that what we're dealing with? We're screwed," said Farmer Joe.

"It's just the drink," said Peter. "It's only the minority of them."

"I'd hate to see that when they're sober," said Terry.

"I can't believe the German guys were there," I said.

"They're only kids. They just want to look like part of the gang," said Terry.

"This is fucking bollocks. Fucking bollocks," Smiley said, getting redder in the face.

We were all at a loss for words, we thought we knew some of the HOS boys were psychopaths, but not this bad. If we wanted to change units and go to 106 Brigade we would need a damn good plan and we would have to be very careful.

The following morning I noticed used morphine syrettes littering the ground. The syrettes were mini syringes full of morphine that came with the field dressings and were meant to be administered upon injury, I realised now why we weren't issued any, and they must be worth a fortune on the black market. Empty bottles of the locally home brewed Rakija were also strewn around. Hitler would have been proud.

The shifts at the front continued, days on, days off, nights on, nights off, in the monotonous regularity of it all we kept a low profile, waiting for the right moment, and building friendships with people we thought we could trust.

The location of our HOS unit and that of several HVO brigades was in Northern Bosnia, an area called Posavina. The main town in the Posavina pocket was Orašje on the southern bank of the River Sava. We had been to Orašje with Murat and Mahmood not long after arriving in Domaljevac. It was a depressing place, every wall was sandbagged five feet high and masking tape held shattered windows together. It was a typical Soviet style grey urban landscape. We didn't see any civilians in the street, only off duty soldiers. Croats were allowed to carry weapons into the town; the foreigners weren't due to an "incident" some time ago. The few bars and cafes that were open were full of off duty soldiers, it was an uncomfortable place where we were met with suspicious glances and whispered mutterings. We had a free haircut though; a zero blade all over was the order of the day before we wandered around to the river Sava. It was massive, even compared to the point at which Peter and I crossed it the week or so before, it was a stunning sight amongst all the grey drabness and bomb damage. In the distance we could see a huge bridge, the centre of which had been damaged and tilted into the river at a forty-five degree angle, the bridge once linked Orašje with the larger town of Županja on the Northern, Croatian side of the Sava. Now the only means of crossing was the ferry that we had used.

Another night shift and the moon illuminated the front line like silver floodlights, making the village look like more of a ghost town than it already was. It was the coldest I'd known it, my breath forming a silvery cloud as I hopped from foot to foot to stop my toes going numb, rubbing my hands together before shoving them deep into my armpits, wishing I'd brought some gloves. My face felt like it was burning, I rolled my ski mask down to cover my face but realised it covered my ears and all sound was muffled. I'd spent the first few hours of the shift carving "Nuneaton Borough F.C. on tour" into the plastered wall with all the skill and patience of a professional stonemason, I was going to add "'92" but my fingers started to go numb. Everyone was the same, hands shoved deep into pockets, pacing or rocking to keep the circulation going. The moonlit silence occasionally broken by a wet sniff from a dripping-tap nose. Nobody talked, we were trying to make ourselves comfortable, some tried to sleep but found if they stopped moving they started shivering. The front may as well have been daylight because of the full moon, and coupled with the cold we were confident nobody would try anything in this. Sitting on the sofa I took my arms out of my sleeves and wrapped them around myself inside my jacket and bent forward trying to reduce the surface area of my skin and keep my body heat in. I slept on and off, waking every ten minutes to find myself shivering before warming up enough to fall asleep again. Eventually the dawn mist invaded every room bringing its fresh smell with it, the sun seemed to rise in seconds giving every surface a pale yellow warmth.

"Fuck me, I'm glad that's over," said Smiley.

Terry, Sasha, Smiley and myself were sitting on the sofas warming our hands on the fire that now burned slowly in the room. A couple of cups of coffee and the next shift would be here, I was already fantasising about the cosy warmth of my sleeping bag.

We heard running and the telltale rattle of magazines in pockets, the next shift was here. A head appeared in the doorway.

"WHAT THE FUCK ARE YOU DOING?" It was the Hungarian Elias Laszlo. He was shouting and agitated, I saw Smiley slowly and unnoticeably point his rifle at Elias with one hand.

Elias was raging in Hungarian now, his eyes wide and darting everywhere. There was more talk behind him before he was patted in the back and lead away. These guys weren't the shift that usually replaced us.

"What the fuck was that all about?" I said quietly.

"He looks like he's off his head," said Smiley who had both hands on his Kalashnikov now. We all did the same.

"I don't like it whatever it is," said Terry.

We sat nervously looking at each other, we didn't know what was going on or what was going to happen next.

"Maybe they're going to get rid of us here?" I said.

"Wait here," said Sasha moving to the doorway. Sasha spoke to some of the other Croats, and the voices got louder and angrier. Before it turned into a full-scale row there was a shout, the argument stopped. It was Terry's friend Marco Tigrić.

"Didn't you hear it?" asked Marco standing in the doorway. We looked at each other with blank faces.

"Someone's been killed by one of the mines on the bridge an hour or two ago," said Sasha.

"No. Didn't hear a thing," said Terry.

"OK, wait here, we have to get the bodies," said Marco who then moved off with the rest of the small group.

"I didn't hear any mine go off," said Sasha.

"None of us did. They should tell us if they're sending a patrol out on our shift anyway," said Terry. "But at least they're not here to kill us!"

Sasha explained what he knew from his brief conversation; Andreas the German, Elias and two others went out on a patrol behind enemy lines, on their way back someone triggered one of the anti-tank mines on the bridge, killing all of them except Elias, who ran for help. The argument was because they couldn't understand why we hadn't heard the explosion. It would be pointless trying to explain to them that had we known there was a patrol out we would be alert to them coming back, we could have shot them thinking they were Četniks, and what were they doing out on a night like that? It raised more questions the more we thought about it.

"Lets just keep quiet and go with the flow here," said Terry, "they're obviously on edge and want to blame someone."

We were nervous because we were dealing with people who weren't thinking straight, anything could happen. It went quiet for a while, we were all looking at each other and I could tell we were thinking the same thing, until eventually I couldn't take any more and said in a whisper,

"I hope they brought plenty of bin bags!"

"They'll need rubber gloves and wellies on," Smiley said with a giggle.

"Couldn't have happened to a nicer guy," said Terry sarcastically.

An hour passed before they were ready to relieve us, nothing much was said to the incoming shift, only the usual cursory nods before we were off down the fields and into the clearing where the van usually waited. One of the vans was already leaving, the rear suspension taking the strain of all the men inside. There was also an old black Mercedes car there, belonging to one of the local 104 Brigade commanders, along with our usual van and a light blue VW camper van that I had never seen before. Several men milled about waiting for us as the rest of the body recovery party must already have gone or were in the vans ready to go.

"OK, OK, you three in there, you two in there, the rest over there." It was the local commander ushering us all into the three remaining vehicles. We made sure we said nothing and went along with his orders, after all he sounded like he knew what he was doing and even better, he wasn't HOS. Terry gave me a huge grin as he was pointed towards the Merc, I headed to the light blue camper van.

The side door was already open and the van looked to be full of men already, one of them Elias. They all stared at me with grim expressions as I stepped into the van, which had been stripped bare and a plywood floor put down. I hesitated for a split second, then crouched down and slid the door across behind me. I saw why they had left a space in the middle of the floor. Stretched out in front of me with feet pointing to the front of the van was what was left of Andreas. The body was face down. His trousers had been blown off and inches away from where I sat were two long, pale legs laying in front of me with the boots on intact, he was still wearing his black bomber jacket although it looked strangely flat, almost empty. One arm of the jacket curled behind him and lay in an unnatural position in the middle of his back, poking out of the cuff was a pale hand, the fingers curled. There was no head. Every part of the body had a thin film of moisture on and I noticed that he was wearing light blue underpants. The explosion must have tore through his chest and took his head off, his hips and legs were intact, and probably his spine held a few bits together. I sat wondering how strange it was that the explosion took his trousers off, trying my hardest not to stare at those cold dead legs that were right in front of me. Everybody was trying not to look, and nobody spoke. I caught Elias staring at me and looked away wondering where Andreas' head was. I didn't feel any pity or sadness for him, only that it was a shitty way to end up, headless and trouserless in a camper van full of soldiers who knew what colour your pants were. My enduring memory of him was of an angry drunken face shouting "Seig Heil". I guess maybe he got what he deserved, unlike the Iraqi I had seen burnt into his jeep. My first experience of death in Bosnia and like Terry said - it couldn't have happened to a nicer guy.

We pulled up at what looked like a Hospital, the other vehicles were already there. I couldn't get out of the van quickly enough, and took deep breaths of fresh air, it seemed everyone else in the van had the same idea. Catching sight of Terry, I headed straight towards him.

"Fucking typical mate, you get the Merc and I get the van carrying a headless German. Wanker!" I whispered.

"They obviously saw I was a man of class," replied Terry with a smile.

"Lets get the fuck out of here, I don't fancy unloading the body," I said.

Back at the kitchen of our farmhouse the five of us drank coffee, and smoke clouded the small room.

"One of the dead blokes lived in this other farmhouse," said Farmer Joe.

"He was local?"

"Yep, the place where the well is, they're his parents."

"They had to go back for someone's foot, it was hidden in the long grass."

"The other guy was Sili!" laughed Peter. Which then resulted in a round of "Silly" jokes.

"They couldn't find any of his body, he must have caught the mine and been vapourised," said Peter.

"He must have stamped on the fucking thing to set it off," said Smiley.

"How can you miss them anyway, they're not hidden and have a four foot pole sticking out the top!" said Terry.

"They must have been high," said Farmer Joe.

"They wanted to try the night vision goggles Elias brought with him," said Peter. "That's why Elias went with them."

"Well they worked a fucking treat didn't they? It was nearly a full moon, they had to be off their heads to go out on a night like that," I said.

"We can't tell them were leaving now, they really would go apeshit," Peter said.

The general consensus was that four idiots had gone out on patrol, three of them were stoned, and those three had died for no reason and now we would all have to pay our respects as if they were heroes. Would they do the same for us? That was highly unlikely. As far as we were concerned it was all bullshit and in my opinion Andreas was scum and embodied everything I had come out here to destroy, yet he was on our side. It was a pointless waste of life that could have been avoided, and now we would have to go through the pretence of giving a shit about these junkies and Nazis.

The atmosphere in the camp had become darker than usual after the three deaths, people spoke in whispers and for some; such as the three Germans, it was the first time they had seen a corpse. For these people, the reality of being so close to death had sunk in. Elias still walked the camp wide-eyed and twitchy, his first brush with death leaving very vivid memories and we all avoided him. For us a shift at the front was now relief from the camp atmosphere. On one of our stints at the front someone in another shift had scratched in huge letters "Make love not war!" on one of the walls, which then had been crossed out and redone to read, "Make war not love!"

"We'll get the funerals out of the way, then we go," Peter said, "do we all agree?"

"We've got to get away from this lot," I said.

"We know the risks, but its got to be done," said Terry.

"We'll do it in the middle of the day, have the 106 van waiting," said Peter.

Everyone was in agreement that enough was enough. We would tell them we were going, then just leave, and hope for the best. Peter was on good terms with his fellow Dutchman Nico, even though he thought he was an idiot, but he was leader of HOS in name only, the problem was with the real man in charge, Jelko, the man with the acne scars. He was the real man in charge of all the black market activities and the supplies of morphine and alcohol. He wasn't a soldier, he was a criminal with a gun and the hardcore of gangsters and junkies would be loyal to him.

"We'll cross that bridge when we come to it, lets get the funerals out of the way first," said Peter.

The sun shone into our faces as around twenty of us stood to attention in ranks at the edge of the grassy graveyard. There were only about eight or nine other graves there. All side by side with a few metres separating them, all were basic wooden crosses with single lettering screwed on spelling out names and years. It must have been HOS' only graveyard, a small patch of fenced in field in-between houses with long grasses and weeds that were gradually overtaking the fence. In front of us was the rectangular hole in the ground, a pile of fresh earth piled high next to it with an assortment of flowers spread on top. A newly made wooden cross as yet unweathered by the elements stood at the head of the hole. Bright white plastic letters spelled out:

ANDREAS BÜHNER 1971-1992

A Priest with a slightly bored expression stood next to the cross ready to do his business for the day. I wondered how many times he's had to do this and if he even cared, if he had met Andreas he might have felt differently. All he ever saw was wooden crosses with names on them and some of the names were foreign. Andreas was going to be a long way from home, if he had a home. Nobody would be tending his grave. The more I thought about it the more depressed I felt about the whole thing. A nasty piece of work buried in a place thousands of miles from home surrounded by blokes that pretended to care, give it a year and maybe a lot will have forgotten, I knew I never would and it made me angry that I was starting to feel sorry for him.

A small procession appeared behind us down the road, a dozen men in uniform, their faces blank and expressionless, amongst them were Nico and Jelko. Squinting in the sunlight I saw that a large rectangular wooden box was carried shoulder high by six men. These men stood out from the rest and a wave of disgust hit me. My sympathy for the man evaporated when I noticed they were wearing the fascist uniform of all black and jackboots. I was starting to sweat in the sun as I thought of these people dressing his headless corpse in his favourite black gear or maybe they had they just tipped his trouserless remains into the box, either way I didn't suppose dignity mattered when you're only a pair of legs and a bit of spine.

Attempting to keep in step they marched to the grave. A firing party of half a dozen men stood to our right, bringing up their rifles into the "present arms" position as they drove their feet into the ground with a thump, they had obviously been practising. The men in black stumbled over the freshly dug earth around the hole in the ground, three of the men manoeuvred around to the other side of the grave and the box was laid on the ground. The HOS main men stood around the grave and with heads bowed the Priest began.

The Priest swung an incense burner from a long chain as he spoke in Croatian, probably saying that Andreas was a great bloke and a brave soldier and that he's now in Heaven because he was such a nice guy. Or at least words to that effect, even the Priest looked like he didn't believe it, maybe he'd said it a thousand times to a thousand boxes of remains so that eventually the words became meaningless. It went on and on, everyone was fidgeting, trying to ignore the mosquitoes that had seen we were sitting ducks and the sweat that was dripping down my sides from my armpits was making me feel sticky and dirty. Eventually the Priest finished with a particularly lazy flourish of the incense burner. There was a pause for a few minutes, heads bowed even further as men remembered their own mortality rather than the death of Andreas. There was a shouted command and everyone looked up straight into the sun, the firing party raised their weapons into their shoulders and pointed them skywards, another shouted command.

-BANG! -

The silence was broken as six men fired a single shot into the sky. It sounded like a machine gun as birds took flight from nearby trees.

-BANG! -

There was another pause.

-BANG! -

There was then a shouted command, upon which the firing party lowered their weapons.

The men in black slowly and carefully lowered the coffin into the ground until it came to rest at the bottom of the hole. There was no fidgeting now, every man stood transfixed by the sight of the soldiers last journey. There was no outpouring of grief, only a stony-faced sadness, hard men watched squinting in the sun as the box disappeared into the earth. I felt the sadness, not for Andreas, but for all the others, the strangers who had been buried here thousands of miles from home.

The Priest walked away, onto his next appointment. The main men around the grave laid a wreath, some threw flowers onto the coffin below. One by one we filed past the grave picking up a handful of earth then dropping it onto the coffin and some waited with heads bowed above the hole in the ground, silent in thought. I noticed Elias, who stood above the grave but stared into the distance for some time before turning away, the tears in his eyes from reliving every moment of the explosion over and over again. My turn came and I felt uncomfortable, it was all too staged, the collective sadness was real, the mourning of this man wasn't. By the time it was my turn the plain wooden lid was covered in a film of earth and petals, underneath the dirt and cheap wooden lid was the headless remains of a man that I wished I could have liked. I gently poured the soil onto the lid as if not to wake him, then walked quickly away, not looking back. Peter, Terry, Smiley, Joe and myself made sure we hung around the graveyard for a while as a sign of respect, they didn't like us already so we didn't want to make our situation any worse by buggering off sharpish. We made quiet smalltalk as the sun started to set, before we saw the first people go then left shortly afterwards, unnoticed as the men in black got to work with their shovels.

Tonight the HOS gang would remember their fallen hero with Morphine and Rakija, with maybe a few "Seig Heils" in Andreas' honour. Tomorrow he'd be history.

"What a pile of shit," I said. The five of us were sitting in the kitchen, talking about the days events in whispers.

"It could have been any of us," said Peter, HOS' nazi leanings didn't bother him as much as the rest of us.

"We don't go out stoned," said Farmer Joe.

"Buried in a bit of Northern Bosnia that the rest of the world doesn't care about, dying for fuck all," said Smiley.

"There's a full wake for the family of the other guy tomorrow," said Peter.

"I've never even seen the guy," said Farmer Joe.

"They want guards of honour standing at the doors of the house."

"Fuck that!" said Smiley.

"Still, they're dead soldiers, they deserve some respect," said Peter. "It's different for this guy, he was local, this was his home."

I had glimpsed what must have been the mans family while getting water from the well. The elderly woman was wailing, rocking back and forth, using her black headscarf to mop her tears as her husband sat on the step with his face in his hands. The open display of utter grief shocked me and reminded me of my parents.

They wanted a guard of honour, someone standing to attention in the doorway during the wake which was to last all night until he was buried the following day. We had just finished our day shift at the front and were sitting down in the cookhouse eating red-hot freshly made goulash when Nico asked us if anyone would do it tonight. I agreed, much to the derision of the others. What was one hour of my time? Seeing the mans parents made my decision for me, I didn't know the guy himself but his Mother and Father weren't to blame for the company he kept. It also kept the HOS people off our backs.

"I'm taking one for the boys!" I said.

"I'll do an hour too," said Terry.

"Bet you won't see any of the other motherfuckers doing it," said Farmer Joe. Maybe so, I thought, but this was his home. Besides, Terry was in too.

I could hear the low wailing of a woman's voice as I approached the house at about eleven o'clock at night. The doorway illuminated by the glow of candlelight and a group of soldiers stood by it smoking and quietly talking.

"Honour guard," I said on seeing Nico.

"Thanks, we really appreciate this," he said. "Come this way." He ushered me into the house where I could feel the warmth from the blazing open fire. Cigarette smoke hung in the air and several men in uniform milled around quietly. The mans Father came to greet me in the hallway with a bottle and a couple of small glasses. His face looked crumpled and his eyes red and sore from two days worth of grief, he smiled a toothless grin at me and swayed, the hand with the glasses in supporting him against the wall.

"Hvala, hvala Ingliiski," Thank you English, he said. His breath was pure alcohol.

I nodded my thanks to him as he handed me a glass, Nico gently took the bottle of Rakija from him and poured us both a drink. The old man knocked it back in one gulp, as I did the same I noticed his smile disappear and his eyes fill with tears, without a word he turned and went into the front room where his dead son lay. The Rakija tasted as it always did, burning its way down my throat and into my stomach.

I turned and looked into the room, in the far corner the Mother with her black headscarf sat on a wooden chair, still rocking backwards and forwards, wailing and sobbing uncontrollably, another headscarf wearing female relative was attempting to console, or control her. The room was the same as any other family home with photos and ornaments on walls and mantelpiece. Above the blazing fire was a huge picture of the Virgin Mary staring down on the scene below, surrounded by gold leaf with a Rosary hanging from it. The coffin lay in the middle of the room supported by a long table, the top half of the coffin lid was open and their dead son lay there as if asleep in his black suit and tie. I didn't recognise him. He looked as if he was in his early twenties and sported a wispy moustache and mullet style haircut. His face was a greyish-yellow and a dozen dark spots, each an inch wide were spread around his face, I assumed these must have been puncture wounds caused by the explosion. I couldn't help but wonder how much of him was left beneath the lid of the coffin, maybe it was the opposite of Andreas and his chest and head were the only parts left, or the puncture wounds to his head were the only damage. The undertakers looked like they had done a good job anyway.

I felt that sudden wave of sadness and anger again on seeing this family fall apart, the family were here before the war began and before HOS arrived bringing their darkness with them. The parents must have seen so many funerals of other soldiers, always praying their son wasn't the next one. Now they'll grow old never knowing what their son could have been, only their memories of him left. They only had their religion and each other to give them comfort, but as the Virgin Mary looked on expressionless and the mans Father sat drunkenly sobbing with the glass of Rakija in his hand, I could only turn away and leave them to their tears.

I took my position in the doorway and stood to attention, the anger growing in me as I stood motionless as people came in to show their respect, then went out a few minutes later with faces drained. Now and again someone would hand me a glass of Rakija, which I would throw down my neck. I chatted quietly to Marco Tigrić, Sasha and Željko Čelik, showing them how to "present arms" and various other drill movements from the British Army. After a couple of hours someone else took over. I was glad to get away, trying to understand it drained me, there was no reason for the death of this man whose name I didn't even know. One idiot stands on a mine which eventually means a whole family is ripped apart, or in Andreas' case will probably never know that their son's remains are in an overgrown graveyard somewhere in Northern Bosnia. My thoughts went back to the Gulf and the charred statue of the man melted into his seat of the Jeep, an unnecessary waste, somewhere a family is destroyed.

I walked slowly to my room breathing in the cold air to help clear my head, the others had gone to bed and I felt alone. I was a long way from home surrounded by madmen where a life could disappear in an instant. I thought that maybe I wasn't cut out for this soldier business, the British Army had turned me into a robot but I still had my humanity. I really wished that I didn't care about the families or the pointless deaths, but on the other hand that would make me just another Andreas, killing for killings sake. I could hear drunken singing from the cookhouse and thought that maybe that passes for their expression of grief, or maybe it's just any excuse to get drunk and stoned. The mans family had God, Jelko and the gangsters of HOS had morphine. Mentally drained, I got into my sleeping bag where I soon sank into a Rakija induced sleep. I must have been asleep just a few hours when I was shaken awake.

"Wake up, wake up," said a Croat voice in the darkness.

"What? What's up?" I said sitting up, thinking it was some kind of emergency.

"Your turn. Guard of honour."

"I've done my turn mate," I said laying back down again.

"Yes, you have another turn," said the voice almost pleading.

"Fuck off! There's another forty other men here, ask them," I said surprised by my own reaction.

"But it's your turn." The voice knew he was losing this particular battle.

"F U C K O F F !" I said the words slowly and menacingly. End of conversation.

The voice stomped out of the room muttering Croatian obscenities under his breath.

"I've had enough of this shit," I said.

In the morning the five of us were in the kitchen again, talking about the mans wake and its aftermath over black coffee and bread and jam. I had told them about being woken up to do another turn as honour guard.

"So much for any of those fuckers doing it, could you imagine trying to wake them last night? Not a chance." I was really going for it now and I was no longer whispering.

"Lets get to 106 ASAP," said Farmer Joe, who got absolutely hammered on Rakija whenever possible but didn't like the drugs or Mafia-style operation that this HOS unit had become.

"We've done the funerals, the gangsters here have shown their true colours, it's time to go," said Terry.

"We can't just go now, they'd love any chance to shoot us in the back," said Smiley.

"I know. From talking to most of them they're more interested in the drugs and making money on the black market than fighting the Četniks, it's not the HOS I knew from last year," said Peter.

"We aren't making a difference here, I know we all have our reasons for being here but this isn't what I'm here for. In the last couple of months it's all gone to shit," said Terry.

"These aren't the good guys," I said.

"We have to make the arrangements to be picked up and stuff. If we get tonight's shift out of the way, the following morning we'll have to sleep, that doesn't leave us enough time," Peter said.

"We have to leave in the daylight," said Terry.

"What if you do the day shift as normal the following day without me so I can arrange everything, then when you come back we sleep. The following morning we'll have a van waiting and we tell them the good news," said Peter.

"I can come with you in case anything happens to you, two of us will know the details. If that's OK with everyone else," said Terry.

"Fine with me," said Smiley. Everyone agreed. Much as we liked Peter we knew he could be full of shit sometimes, Terry was the perfect second in command and even if we were two men short at the front, nothing ever happened anyway.

That last night shift seemed to go on forever, we were cold and apprehensive about leaving, but we had reached the point of no return. Sasha and the Germans knew something was up and eventually we told them. Although Sasha was a "local" we trusted him. And, just as we thought, he wouldn't go with us.

"They would find me, but good luck to you."

"We would look after you, you're part of the team," I said.

"But I live here, it's not the same. This will be our last time at the front together, I will miss you and I will say nothing to anyone else about this."

"You're a good man Sasha."

"It will be strange without you, but good luck."

He was right, we didn't live here. When we had had enough we could get ourselves home to Rotterdam, Arizona, Rochdale,

Bristol or Nuneaton, far enough away from the reach of HOS. The Germans were a different proposition, every decision they made was by their own three-man committee, and after seeing them join in with the mini-Hitler rally I had my doubts about their loyalties.

"When you get there, then we will come," said Rommel, their semi-official spokesman, after some debate.

"We like being with you at the front, but we don't want to get killed by Jelko and his boys."

"So if we get out of HOS alive then you'll come to us," said Terry.

Rommel smiled. "Yes, it's a big risk. Like you say - if you get out alive."

"OK, just remember to say nothing, when we get there we'll arrange to get you out," said Peter.

"I don't know who is crazier, those HOS people or you for trying to leave!" said Rommel. "I really hope you make it."

9. Out With a Bang

It was a 6AM to 6PM shift and we were like school kids on their last day of term, the sun was bright and warm and tomorrow we would be joining a proper unit rather than the right wing psychopaths we were with.

The team that day consisted of Smiley, Farmer Joe, the three Germans and myself. Not exactly the SAS by any stretch of the imagination, as Peter and Terry were at the Headquarters of 106 to organise our arrival the following day. We decided that myself, Norbert and Rommel would take the house on the left with Smiley, Farmer Joe and Gustav taking the house on the right. The Germans bitched about it non stop, they didn't like being split up but we had no choice as they had no basic army training and were a serious liability if left on their own. The day started just like any other day at the front. I always went in to get my bearings, making sure I knew where everything was in case the previous shift had moved anything or a wall had fallen down. This made me familiarise myself with everything again, I did this at every shift. Only then could I relax, get a brew on or eat. At least that was what I always did, rather than some of the guys method of going in and going to sleep, which they did all too often.

The house looked like it always did; at least nobody had taken a shit in one of the fire positions anyway, which had happened the previous week in the house on the other side of the road. I made sure Nobby and Rommel knew I was the boss today, and tried to keep everything as simple as possible.

"Fire position?" said Nobby.

"It's where you stand and shoot from when the shit hits the fan."

"Ze fan?"

"Rommel, can you explain to him what I've just said?" I said trying to keep calm.

A lot of German waffling ensued, at the end of which Norbert smiled and said, "Ah... Ja, is OK." And pointed to where he was meant to be in the event of shit hitting the fan.

"And no fucking about or running off, just stay here!" I nodded at Rommel who, though younger, was the cleverer of the two. Rommel translated for me and after another conversation with Norbert,

"No problem, Simon," they both said.

Not that a fire position was much good in that house, with its roofless attic, one room upstairs, and downstairs being a bit too "open plan" to be used as a very good defensive position. And besides, a few good hits and it would have collapsed on top of whoever was in it saving the Četniks a lot of ammunition. I got the feeling that the Germans had never been told any of this stuff before and yet we'd done it continuously for the past month. These young lads had volunteered to fight, for whatever the reasons, and needed looking out for or they would be dead all too soon. They got the water boiling and the mint tea was made and if there was one thing they did well, it was make a nice brew. There was our usual breakfast of fresh bread with jam and each man took turns to keep watch from the upstairs room while the others ate. The winter sun was shining weakly and there wasn't a cloud in the sky.

A few hours in and I ran across the road to Smiley's position, sending Gustav back across to the other Germans. Smiley and Farmer Joe were sitting in the front room doing their normal comedy double act routine of having a heated debate about total crap. We had coffee courtesy of Farmer Joe, who chain-smoked along with Smiley as we discussed how we could go out with a bang. After twenty minutes of coffee drinking, piss-taking and me complaining about their smoke we decided to make our last shift at the front a memorable one by firing some of the Rocket Propelled Grenades which were kept at the two forward positions. Mainly because none of us had ever fired them, but also to give the Četniks something to remember us by, it would be a long, dull day otherwise and we could rub Peter and Terrys nose in it. At a set time each position would fire an RPG round over the canal into a Četnik target where they were known to occupy.

"You should use the Ossa," said Farmer Joe referring to the huge anti-tank bazooka, his eyes lighting up at the thought.

"The backblast would make the fucking house fall down, stick to the RPG, you can't go wrong," replied Smiley.

"I wouldn't know how to use the fucking Ossa. I'd be up on the roof pressing every button on the bastard and get shot before it fired," I said to Farmer Joe.

Smiley laughed as he blew out smoke.

"And I'd end up with a fucking broken shoulder. No chance mate."

"It would cause the bastards the most damage though, I'll fire it," said Farmer Joe, who was by now getting quite excited.

"I'm not carrying that thing across the road."

"We'll stick to the RPGs, keep it simple. We just want to fire it. That's all," said the typically sensible Smiley. Sensible was a word lost on Farmer Joe.

I could hear the three Germans shouting and laughing from across the road, then their weapons being fired on full automatic.

"Fucking hell, you leave the kids alone for five minutes," I said.

Swapping places with Gustav again I ran to the house and glared at Nobby and Rommel.

"What the fuck are you doing?"

"Target practise," answered Rommel, looking as if I'd asked the stupidest question in the world.

"Shooting at a pile of bricks from twenty feet away isn't target practise you twat, we're at a front line!" I was almost screaming in his face as the red cloud of brick dust settled. I took a deep breath.

"You've wasted ammunition you might need."

I filled them in on the plan to fire the RPGs and told them to stay downstairs, the Germans seemed to read between the lines and understand that I wanted them nowhere near me upstairs when I fired the RPG. There was some more German conversation punctuated by Norbert nodding and giving a thumbs up.

"We'll be in our fire positions," Rommel said. At least some of the things I had told them had sunk in.

The RPG is a shoulder launched anti-tank weapon and, like the Kalashnikov, one of the most widely used weapons in the world. There were several anti-tank weapons leant against the wall, including the huge "Ossa" that Farmer Joe almost wet himself over. I picked up the unloaded RPG and tried it on for size, it was light and I could have easily ran with it resting on my shoulder. I tried the firing mechanism which was a matter of cocking it with the thumb then pulling the trigger, easy, or so I thought. The grenades were all ready to go, each one looking like a pineapple on a large stick, the "stick" being the rocket part and the "pineapple" being the grenade. It was no wonder it was the weapon of choice for just about every terrorist in the world, although it was idiot-proof I wouldn't want Norbert carrying one around anywhere near me.

By now there was only about forty-five minutes until we were to fire, and giving the other two the thumbs up I made my way to the upstairs room carrying the grenade, RPG and my own rifle. I had already picked my target earlier on, amongst all the derelict red brick houses and jutting timber of Četnik occupied Lijeskovac was the side of one house painted white that looked relatively unmarked. We knew that this was one of their forward positions as on a previous shift Peter had seen three or four armed men scurrying into it, though not quick enough to react and open fire at them. I however, had still not seen the enemy in the entire month I had been here. They also varied which forward positions they used unlike ourselves who only had the two houses to choose from, so there was no guarantee they would be occupied. Nevertheless, it was big and white and if I missed it with the RPG I would never hear the end of it.

For the next few minutes I took my time to look though the small hole in the bedroom wall that served as the upstairs fire position and observed the other half of the village. It could have been a ghost town, it looked as if it had been abandoned fifty years ago and left to the rats and long grass while the houses crumbled, it was only if you looked closely you could see the countless bullet holes caused by bored soldiers firing at nothing in particular. What if the building was occupied? My mind started to race and my heartbeat quickened as I took some deep breaths to keep calm. Don't think, just fire at the wall. It was time to check myself and get it together. Mostly for a sense of psychological comfort but also if I had to run I wouldn't have stuff spilling out of my pockets or trip over my shoelaces. I took off my woolly hat, rolled it up and put it through my shoulder boards, then checked my rifle. The safety was on with a round chambered ready to fire, I folded the butt down, put the sling over my shoulder and across my body so the rifle was flat against the middle of my back. My four other magazines were full and secure, with all pockets done up, I was ready.

I grabbed the RPG in one hand and the grenade in the other and went up the next flight of stairs to the open air attic room on the third floor. This room had a low wall and a few roof timbers opening out into the sky, the ceiling was long gone and it was ideal for firing the RPG as the blast from the rear of it would destroy anything close behind. Crouching on the floor I lay the RPG down, looking carefully to see where the grenade fitted into the launcher, then slid the long cylindrical part of the grenade down the tube until it locked. Needing one last look at the house, I shuffled to the outer wall and raised my head slightly over the edge of the brickwork, it was a long way up and I could see the whole layout of the Četnik side of the village like a 3D map, with the dirty wall of the white house right in the middle of my view on the left hand side of the main road. There was a light breeze waving the long grass but other than that nothing moved. I ducked back down out of view and checked my watch, it was exactly midday.

Still crouching, I nervously lifted the RPG onto my shoulder and flicked up the sights. My palms were sweaty and my stomach felt tight, my whole body telling me to sit down and forget it. This was what I'm here for, I volunteered to do this and I'm supposed to be on the side of the good guys. In a split second I thought, "Fuck it" and stood up sharply, RPG ready and looked down the sights towards the white wall a hundred metres away.

"SHIT!"

As quickly as I was up I was crouching down again behind the wall. Christ, I hoped no one saw me. Looking through the sights down the length of the RPG I saw that I hadn't pulled the pin out of the grenade and as pulling the pin out makes the grenade armed, I would have just fired what would have been a lump of pointy metal into the enemy village which was not much use unless it hit someone directly on the head. I took a few deep breaths and pulled the pin. Here I go again, I thought, and jumped up cocking the lever of the RPG with my thumb.

I stood for what seemed like an age getting my aim on the house and tensing my whole body, pulled the trigger.

-click-

The hammer fell but there was nothing. My stomach turned to ice as I ducked behind the wall again.

"Fuck it! Fuck it!" I said out loud.

At that moment I heard a huge bang then a whoosh of Farmer Joe letting rip with his RPG. Now they will have woken up and I had been up and down like a jack-in-the-box swearing loudly, if anybody had seen or heard me they would be ready this time. Looking at the RPG the only thing I could think of was that the safety catch must have been in the "on", rather than the "off" position. What a fucking Muppet. This was my last chance and I was panting hard now with the adrenaline. Shouldering the RPG, I cocked it ready and I wasn't messing about with getting my aim right this time. Up I jumped. In one moment I had pointed it in the general direction, pushed the safety catch in with my forefinger, and pulled the trigger. The hammer fell again with a snap.

It was as if all the oxygen around me had been sucked out, changing the air pressure and taking my breath as a yellow flash enveloped everything for a split second, there was an ear splitting crack, then silence. I watched the smoke trail of my RPG rocket speed toward the house in the distance before exploding a second later into a red flash and a cloud of dust, right in the lower middle part of the white wall.

"Fucking hell!"

I couldn't hear my own voice, only a high-pitched ringing that drowned everything out. A thin mist of brick dust and plaster caused by the backblast swirled around me. Realising that I was still standing and staring at my handiwork, I ducked down with the now dust-covered RPG. I was shaking and my heart felt like it was going to explode it was beating so hard. If they hadn't noticed me before, they have now. With my ears still ringing I ran down to the second floor bedroom.

I felt strangely safer now that I had a roof above me and couldn't be seen and leaning the empty RPG against the wall I peered through the small hole in the wall which overlooked the enemy positions. I could see that everything was still, the light breeze blew a small cloud of dust and smoke across the front of the buildings from the white wall before it thinned out and disappeared altogether above the main road. The wall looked the same as before apart from a crater with a hole about a foot wide in the centre, it looked as if I had hit the building downstairs. The hole had a hazy appearance, the dust and debris had not fully settled inside the room I had hit and it was the perfect, albeit lucky, shot. Smiling to myself I walked downstairs to Nobby and Rommel, if there was anyone in that room they would now have a serious headache at least.

"What?" My left ear still sounded as if it was tuned to the test card. Rommel still jabbered away excitedly as I turned my head so he could speak into the other ear.

"Didn't you put anything in your ears?" Rommel had a grin that spread across his face and was talking at a hundred miles an hour. Of all the stupid questions.

"I got the house, perfect shot, forgot about the ears though," I said.

"I know, we saw the rocket hit from down here. It was excellent," he said, not pausing for breath.

Norbert could no longer contain himself either and described what he saw in German coupled with plenty of hand gestures and rocket noises just so I understood, and ended it with a hearty chuckle. Rommel patted me on the back, "Fantastic."

"Ja, ist gut, gut. Četnik-boom!" Nobby laughed.

"Keep your eyes open just in case they want to fire one back," I said loudly, trying to get the Germans to concentrate.

I lay the RPG back against the wall downstairs where I found it and put my woolly hat back on before walking to the back door, I needed to calm down. The Germans continued their own action replays, trying to outdo each other with their sound effects. Still everyone was smiling. Out in the fresh air again I felt the adrenaline drain away, my heartbeat returned to normal and I was no longer breathing hard. Looking over to Smiley's house I saw Farmer Joe.

"Did ya get 'em?" shouted Farmer Joe.

"Right in the middle mate!" I replied as Smiley appeared. "How about you?"

"The fucking idiot missed by a country mile!" shouted Smiley creasing up with laughter.

Farmer Joe laughed and gave Smiley the finger. It had been around twenty minutes since we had fired on the houses and we were chatting casually across the main road, secretly I was glad to be relieving the tension. I told them I could hardly hear a thing because I hadn't put anything in my ears at which they started pissing themselves with laughter at my expense. I gave them the finger.

Back in the house and it was business as usual and back to what remained of a long day. The Germans still seemed to be on the RPG high, they even asked if they could have a go at which point I explained about how exposed the roof was and that I stood up half a dozen times, so if they wanted to they were more than likely to get their heads shot off before they got chance to aim the thing. They changed their minds. More mint tea was made and canned meatballs heated on the fire, we now relaxed just sitting and talking in pidgin English and broken German, eating deliciously fatty meatballs with one of us occasionally checking the enemy lines for activity. Back to the nice, quiet and dull final day that we expected. At least an hour had passed without any movement or incident and we assumed that the white walled house must have been empty.

I went upstairs to get a view of the enemy positions, it felt safer up here as I could almost see the whole of the village past the canal that separated both sides. The hole the RPG made looked like it had been there forever, just another piece of war damage. I stood with my back to the far wall and looked through the gaping hole in the corridor wall above the washing machine that served as a barricade, it gave a better view of the main road that ran over the canal.

Then I saw them.

Around a hundred and fifty metres away two men on the Četnik side of the village walked casually towards us down the right hand verge of the main road towards the bridge, side by side. The one on the left walked with confidence, looking straight ahead all the time. He wore an olive green bomber jacket with the white Serb two-headed eagle on a red background clearly visible in his upper arm and a woolly hat similar to mine, the butt of his Kalashnikov in the crook of his elbow and his hand on the grip pointing the rifle skywards Rambo-style, he was clean shaven and must have been in his late twenties. The one on the right looked more nervous, constantly looking around, his shoulders slightly hunched, coiled like a spring as if expecting something to happen. He held his rifle with both hands in the ready position and was dressed in dark green camouflage, he had the trademark heavy black beard favoured by the Četniks but short hair, he must have been in his thirties. This was the enemy I had never seen, the evil men that marched through Vukovar or ran the concentration camp at Omarska. The reason I was here, these were the real bad guys.

The soldiers were walking down the street in order to make me open fire on them and give my position away, and that took some balls. I must have really pissed someone off for them to want me that badly. I couldn't warn the other two downstairs in case the two Četniks heard me and knew I was onto them.

* * * *

I fumble with my rifle, locking the butt open, clicking the safety catch off, I put the rifle into my shoulder and I aim. I'm about to kill a man and I feel no fear. My heart pounds, not in the panicked adrenaline rush of firing the RPG, this is a stranger, calmer feeling. I have never felt so focused, nothing else matters but them and me. Everything feels like it's in slow motion even though I'm going a million miles an hour, my actions are instantaneous. I lean into my Kalashnikov to take the recoil and keep balance. I'm still back from the open window itself so they can't see the muzzle flash of my rifle when I fire. A couple of well aimed shots is all that is needed, I was an excellent shot with the British Armys Self Loading Rifle that I had used before. I am confident, focused.

They are still sauntering along the road and seem to be becoming tenser, they know what is going to happen and are waiting for the shots to be fired before diving into the nearest cover. With my sights set to a hundred metres I aim for Bomber Jacket - unlucky mate, you shouldn't have looked so cocky.

I slow my breathing down, taking the tension in the trigger. I am about to kill a man. I have never felt so alive.

-BANG, BANG, BANG-

My three single shots echo loudly in the enclosed corridor and spent cartridge casings bounce of the wall and onto the floor. I hear the Germans shouting something to me. The men are still walking, I had missed.

They speed up, a slight jog now, Beardy looks terrified, Bomber Jacket looks up and I think he's smiling. I can't tell where my shots had landed. Why hadn't he dropped? Were my sights set wrong? Ready again, I open fire.

-BANG, BANG, BANG-

Nothing.

They break into a run. Still towards me. I can hear the hissing of the blood pumping in my ears as I shout something to the Germans.

They are almost at the last building before the bridge. Clicking the safety catch to automatic I have to let rip and hope I can see where my rounds are landing. I snatch at the trigger. The sound of machine gun fire in that enclosed space is deafening, empty cartridge cases clatter off walls and fall to the floor all around me as my rifle hammers away into my shoulder, I grit my teeth.

DIE YOU BASTARD, DIE YOU BASTARD.

Rapid puffs of white brick dust. I see their expressions change - I can see their fear. I adjust my fire towards Bomber Jacket.

DIE YOU BASTARD, DIE YOU BASTARD.

Beardy Man flinching, head down, Bomber Jacket's mouth opens, he spins sideways, loses his grip and his rifle drops to the floor.

DIE YOU BASTARD, DIE YOU BASTARD.

Beardy ducks into a doorway. I see brick dust and splinters of wood.

DIE YOU BASTARD, DIE YOU BASTARD.

Bomber Jacket falls face down to the floor.

DIE YOU BASTARD, DIE YOU BASTARD.

A doorway, a hedge, a lifeless body.

A heavy machine gun jumps into life somewhere to my left, its incoming bullets batter the bedroom wall next to me. I stop firing. Bomber Jacket lies face down in a crumpled unnatural heap, his olive green coat is slowly turning a darker shade.

I hesitate. Beardy runs from the doorway and in a single movement grabs Bomber Jacket's collar and drags his limp body into the building. I open fire again and rounds shatter the doorframe, missing Beardy but thumping into the already dead Bomber Jacket. My Kalashnikov clicks, I have emptied my magazine.

There is a pause and a silent calm - I am God.

The heavy machine gun has found my position and bullets thud in short bursts into the outside wall of the bedroom. I load a fresh magazine. The machine gun is in the Četnik position a hundred metres away that Peter had hosed down a few days previously, It was one of their closest to us. Everything had suddenly become instinctive and clear, there were no grey areas here, just life and death, black and white. I am on a survival autopilot. I have just killed a man and feel nothing and now a machine gun is pounding into the wall next to me. This is good, I'm fucking enjoying this.

The machine gun is firing five round bursts as he was still waiting for me to show myself. I edge my way into the bedroom. After he fires his five rounds I spin round with my rifle in the fire position and fire a short burst through the missing brickwork in the wall on full automatic at the area where I think the enemy gun is. He immediately returns with a more concentrated ten round burst punching into the wall and then stops, at which point I return fire, sending splintered wood from his bunker into the air. I jump into the corridor and check the main road and Beardy's position, there is no movement but I fire several rounds into the doorway to make sure he knows I have him covered.

Why aren't the Germans firing at anything? Are they just sitting in a corner and shitting themselves or can't they see? What about Smiley and Farmer Joe? I suddenly feel very isolated. The private tit-for-tat firefight between me and the machine gun seems to go on forever, on every few bursts I check the other fire position and let off a few rounds towards Beardy's building, although there is no return of fire.

It seems machine gun man has the same idea as me, fire then get your head down. However, his more powerful rounds are taking its toll on the wall and I can only see the area of his bunker, not the gunner himself.

"Fuck it!"

As soon as he opens up I stand up, and jump towards the fire position and fire. I can hear the machine guns bullets buzz and hum as they fly towards the outer wall, each one landing with a powerful thump as they hammer on the outside, taking my breath away with the pressure change. Neither of us back down, two men trying to kill each other a hundred metres apart, both firing weapons on full automatic. The noise is immense; rounds ricochet off the wall or embed with the force of a pneumatic drill into the brick, spent cases spray into the air and land with a high pitched rattle, littering the floor. The roar of machine gun fire, brick and plaster dust, the smell of cordite and sweat.

-click-

I duck down and roll away into the corridor behind the washing machine and change the empty magazine in one movement. The machine gun stops, there is a seconds pause before hammering away again, this time his fire totally concentrated on the hole in the wall where he was expecting me to appear. I crouch in the corridor facing into the room.

I watch as the bedroom wall on my right where the fire position is starts to weaken and begins to bow inwards, the plaster starts to crack, it feels like a sledgehammer is hitting the wall as bullets start to find their way through, buzzing and zipping past me and hitting the wall on my left with a dull slap and a puff of plaster dust.

I think I am laughing.

"YEEEEEEEEEEEEEEHAAAAAAAAAAAAAAAAA!!!!" I scream as I jump up into the bedroom and towards the ever-widening hole.

I'm firing at the bunker with single shots, trying to aim every one of them as the machine gun rounds continue to batter away against the wall, the occasional large calibre bullet finds a gap and zips past me like a fat bee, hitting the wall behind me with a thump. I'm firing directly at his bunker and I can see the muzzle-flash of his machine gun as he fires back in one continuous burst, the dust from the bricks obscures my view but I can see my rounds hitting his bunker.

I'm not backing down this time - you can blink first you bastard.

As if on cue he stops, his barrel has probably overheated and I switch to automatic and empty what's left in my magazine into the Četnik bunker, laughing through gritted teeth as my Kalashnikov clatters. As soon as I hear the click of the empty chamber I duck down and scuttle to the corridor again.

"ARE YOU OK SIMON?" Rommel shouts.

"FUCKING TOP OF THE WORLD!!" I shout back, changing my magazine again.

Machine gun man starts up again with shorter, more accurate bursts. Now the bricks start to cave in, throwing red dust into the air, huge scabs of plaster and chunks of brick fall to the floor, bullets zip past, feet from my face and smack against the wall next to me with more regularity, still the sledgehammer machine gun continues. Out in the corridor I check the view down the road and fire a couple of rounds into the doorway of Beardy's building. Looking back into the bedroom I realise there is no safe place to fire from, the once single missing brick is now a gaping hole. Decision time. Then I hear a loud rumble drowning out the sound of the heavy machine gun.

* * * *

It was coming from the furthest part of the village where the road turned to the right behind some buildings and out of view. An unmistakable revving of a massive diesel engine, it was their tank. In a split second I had to weigh up my options, I could try to take it out with an RPG but didn't fancy going up on the roof again, one hit on this wall from a tank shell would bring the house falling down. Suddenly I could feel my invincibility evaporate, I was scared and with each rev of the tanks engine the fear multiplied. I could see the exhaust smoke rise from behind the far building. The machine gunner kept up the steady clatter of bullets into the bedroom wall. I froze, they want to kill me and they know where I am, I could hide behind a wall from the bullets but a tank shell was a different matter. My body screamed at me to curl up in a ball, close my eyes and maybe it would all go away. I'm not laughing anymore. I don't wait for the tank to appear, I run downstairs. My clarity replace by confusion and panic.

"Did you hear the tank?" I said breathlessly to Rommel.

They had stayed in their fire positions but had not fired a round.

"Yes, but we can't see any targets," he said.

"Did you see the two guys walking down the road?"

"No."

"How could you not see them?" I said gasping for breath.

They looked at me and I saw the fear.

"OK, we've got a little war going on, they're a bit pissed of with me shooting some of their men and want some revenge, now they're using their tank. So any minute now we can expect a high explosive tank round to be fired at this building," I said it calmly and slowly so Rommel could translate, even though I wanted to be as far away as possible. At the last sentence their eyes widened. Norbert looked like he was on the verge of tears.

"Lets get out the back," I said ushering them through the doorway.

Rommel had the hand held radio, as he was the only one who spoke Croatian. "Can you call for some support?" I said pointing to the radio. He gave it a go. Obviously they had handed him the radio and that was it, no instructions on callsigns or procedures. The response was some major swearing in Croatian, the wankers. Even I gave it a go in English.

"Fuck you Čedo!" came their reply. They must have thought the enemy was talking on their frequency, though the amount of Englishmen on the Serb side must have been pretty minimal. We were on our own until 6PM, without support or means of escape. We were stuck, trapped here whether we liked it or not. Checking my watch I saw it was about two o'clock, we had four hours left.

"Check your ammunition, how many rounds have you got left? No dickhead, a rough guess will do!" Norbert had started to get each bullet out of his magazine. Going across the road to Smiley for more ammunition would be too dangerous.

"Is this your own private war or are we all invited?"

It was Smiley and his face told me he was worried. They hadn't seen the two men either, only heard the incessant close range gunfire and now the tank starting up. I gave Smiley a quick update on the events so far.

"We've got about half a magazine each," said Rommel.

The tone of his voice told it all, like a naughty schoolboy caught red-handed. I rolled my eyes. Now the responsibility hit me, I had to look out for these two, they were kids.

"YOU PAIR OF CUNTS! THATS WHAT HAPPENS WHEN YOU WASTE YOUR AMMO!" I shouted.

I had to calm down; they were looking to me for some kind of leadership, someone to hold their hand. Shouting was no good; they were more scared than I was.

"OK, I've got one spare mag left, take this one and split it between you so you've got a full magazine each. If you see a target - AIM YOUR RIFLE, fire single rounds, they all have to count," I felt like I was in the Junior Leaders again. "We'll fall back to that house." I pointed to the next house fifty yards behind our position. "Then wait until they fire their tank rounds or get bored with us not firing back, then go back in," I said, then looked over to Smiley where Farmer Joe was now also in attendance.

"We're falling back to this house until the tanks fucked off, I reckon my RPG must have done some damage!" I tried to laugh.

"We'll keep our eyes open and keep you covered, shout us when you're going back in. And I thought this would be a nice easy day!" said Smiley.

"I ain't goin' anywhere." Farmer Joe shouted. "Motherfuckers gonna have to kill me."

Smiley and I looked at each other in silence, Farmer Joe had a way with words and we knew he meant it.

"Go, go, c'mon," I said to the Germans urging them on to the house.

They couldn't run quick enough and I followed, giving Smiley a mock salute. Rommel and Norbert were on the ground floor and started emptying the magazine I gave them of all its rounds and reloading them into their own as quickly as they could.

"You, bottom left window, you bottom right, I'll take upstairs. We'll give it an hour or two and see how it is, OK?"

The house was a carbon copy of the forward position but was almost completely intact, only the scars on the outside showed it was in a warzone. It looked like it had been newly built then abandoned as there was no evidence of it ever having been lived in, there was usually an old washing machine that seemed to be in every house at the front. I went to the upstairs corridor and saw that the window was made of dozens of different glass panels about six inches square, this was the position in the other house that I had fired down the road from and some of the panels had gone. I stood back from the window and watched the scene through chipped and shattered thick panes of glass. There was no movement now and the only sounds were the occasional gunshot from the other side of the canal from men on high alert thinking they saw something. The tank had turned its engine off. The Germans whispered a conversation downstairs. The sudden realisation hit me that I had left all the loaded anti-tank weapons in the house - fuck it! I wasn't going back in there to get them. I watched intensely for any movement or tell tale sounds, though every sound made me feel like someone was sneaking around ahead of me. My panic had worn off and the nervous focus was back, I felt in control again as my mind started to wander.

They must have wanted me badly enough to risk their men down that road, they wanted revenge for the RPG in which case they must have had men in the building, three? Four? Were they dead? Bomber Jacket certainly was, I saw the moment on his face. I had just taken the lives of four or five men and didn't feel anything. Should I feel anything? They were trying to kill me after all. I noticed my left ear was still ringing.

I convinced myself that the possibility of them attacking was slim, the bridge was full of huge anti-tank mines and the canal was too exposed to risk any more lives. I made myself smile with the thought that they probably don't want to risk the tank because they think I'm a brilliant shot with the RPG.

An hour or two passed with my mind babbling away, going through every event and the ringing in my ear had now turned into a high pitched squeal, I watched our original position through the cracked glass which made it look even more nightmarish. I checked

156

on the other two every so often, they stayed in their fire positions - there's nothing like fear to focus the mind. Maybe this had taught them a lesson, a very steep learning curve, although we weren't out of the woods just yet. There was no tank round and eventually I knew the Četniks had lost the initiative as the moment had passed. Maybe their shift had changed, or maybe they just thought, "fuck it" it's not worth the risk. They only needed one tank round into that house and it would have come tumbling down, thank God it was my last day here, tomorrow they might regroup and attack, they still wanted revenge after all.

It was now four thirty and starting to get dark, I wanted to be back in that house before it was pitch black or our minds would see the enemy in every shadow. The adrenaline was still pumping, though not on turbo as it had been and my mind was screaming at me not to go back in. Creeping out the back door I called to others across the road. Farmer Joe appeared.

"Five minutes and we're going back," I said quietly, holding my hand up to signify five minutes.

"Četnik chicken shits!" he said. "Looks like they've all gone back to sleep."

He had an air of disappointment about him, Joe lived for moments like this.

"See anything?" I asked.

"Not a goddam thing, bunch of pussies."

"Right boys, time to go back in," I said to the Germans whilst trying to look confident. "They haven't used the tank so we'll assume they've knocked it on the head for the day." Rommel translated after finding out what "knocked it on the head" meant. "We'll go careful into the house because we don't know what's in there and sit tight until six, just over an hour away."

The Germans nodded and looked slightly relieved. I had never done any Northern Ireland training and didn't know the finer points of house clearance but whatever I did know was more than Rommel and Norbert.

"I'll go in first, then you Rommel, then Norbert. Check every room is clear, then assume our original fire positions," I explained.

After translation Norbert looked even more relieved that he was last in. Now the adrenaline kicked in again, once we were in the house we'd be fine.

"Lets do it."

Putting the Kalashnikov into my shoulder in the ready position I ran to the other doorway, then signalled the other two to follow who then stood against the wall. I was fairly sure the house was still empty but in the growing gloom my fear amplified all paranoia. Breathing hard I went in as fast as I could, my eyes and rifle quickly scanning the room before running to the stairwell. Rommel followed as Norbert ran to his original fire position. I ran upstairs, ready but relieved, if they were here they would have been downstairs, or at least booby-trapped something. All clear. Giving Rommel the thumbs up I ran back outside and shouted over to the other house.

"No problems, see you in a bit."

"Coming round for dinner?" laughed Smiley who also looked relieved not to be involved in a firefight alongside two men, one of which had a death wish, the other couldn't speak a word of English.

I stood in the corridor in the same position as before when I saw the two Četniks walking down the road, well back from the hole in the wall and surveyed the damage to the wall of the bedroom. There was now a gaping hole and the floor was littered with bricks, plaster and empty cartridge cases, the whole scene carpeted in a layer of dust. The time dragged as it became darker and I felt gradually safer, the enemy couldn't see me in the shadows either.

Eventually I heard voices behind our position, the next shift had arrived and thankfully it was time to go. Tomislav was downstairs and Rommel was trying to fill him in on the details. The rest of his men started to get themselves comfortable and listened to the conversation.

"Right, the upstairs is fucked because of the machine gunning and show him the building where our RPG hit," I said to Rommel who quickly translated into Croat. Tomislav looked serious as he chatted away to Rommel, I wanted him to have as much information as possible.

"He said did you get any?" said Rommel.

"Yes, one of the guys walking down the road and maybe some in the building."

Tomislav patted me on the back and smiled. I wished them good luck and we were off running down the field like men possessed, the fear now evaporated.

Smiley and Farmer Joe were already at the VW van smoking cigarettes next to Gustav as the three of us got there slightly out of breath. Gustav ran to the other two like they were long lost lovers and a loud three way conversation in German started with plenty of sound effects thrown in. I looked at Smiley and Farmer Joe and started to laugh. Any fear had been replaced by manic joy at getting out of there.

"Fuck this for a game of soldiers!" I said laughing.

"Lets get the fuck out of here," said Smiley.

Back at the base they had heard of our exploits. They had heard us on the radio but thought we were Četniks and they had also heard the gun battle. I wondered why they hadn't sent any kind of back up if they had heard it all? I didn't bother saying anything, what was the point? There was plenty of backslapping and "well dones" on hearing that I had killed some of the enemy. Peter and Terry wanted the full details and wished they had been there, I wished they had been there too. The three Germans exaggerations got bigger and better and Smiley just took the piss out of me and Farmer Joe. We could laugh now that we were relaxed and I, for that night, was top man.

Later, after all the congratulations had died down, only Peter, Terry, Smiley, Farmer Joe and I were left in the kitchen.

"It would have suited them if you lot had got killed out there," said Peter.

"Yeah, I thought that when we tried to get them on the radio," I said.

"Well, at least we won't be here when the Četniks want their revenge," said Smiley.

Peter had organised our getaway; he would go to 106 to get the van tomorrow, and they would give us the transport and a driver, nothing else. When he arrived back we would all break the news to Nico and the rest of them, hopefully they would be OK with it and we could go. Deep down though, we knew they wouldn't be happy and nothing is ever easy.

By now I was drained and exhausted and I went to bed. I lay staring at the ceiling in darkness and listened to Depeche Mode, going over every single moment of the firefight in my head.

10. Fear of a Shitty Death

As I lay in my sleeping bag that night the thoughts of the days events didn't ease off, constantly reliving the two Serbs walking towards me and me opening fire. The fear on Beardy's face, the smirk on Bomber Jacket's face, his shocked expression when my rounds hit his body and their power spinning him round. His body, crumpled on the floor by the doorway, blood soaking through his coat. Like the Iraqi in the jeep, I wanted to know his name, I owed the man that much. I thought about his parents and if he had children, then realised his job was the same as mine and that I really shouldn't care so much but that was what made me who I was.

I slept badly that night, the adrenaline rollercoaster had left me on edge and jumpy, my mind couldn't switch off even though my body was exhausted. The sleep I did manage was filled with the two figures of Bomber Jacket and Beardy walking towards me, laughing. I dreamt I was firing at them, my rifle blazing rounds non stop but I could see the bullets dropping powerlessly from the muzzle, or I would have to check the magazine and realise in a panic that I was firing blank rounds, Bomber Jacket's coat would gradually turn from olive green to almost black as his blood soaked through it, but on he walked, laughing, towards me. I don't know how many times I thought I screamed myself awake before the two of them got to me, but it got to the point where I didn't want to close my eyes. Soaked in the sweat of fear and my heart racing I couldn't help eventually falling into my personal hell of sleep. I had nightmares after seeing the Iraqi, but this was different, it was more personal and real and it wasn't the last time I would have the same nightmare.

I got up as soon as it was daylight, the fear of sleep gone and replaced by the fear of trying to get away from HOS. I walked to the window and looked out over the field and its clearing mist. I could die today, shot in the back and buried in a ditch, the last nineteen and a bit years have brought me to this point and I don't know if I'll see the sun come up again. I didn't feel panic or any overwhelming desire to survive at all costs, I just hoped that I would see tomorrow, maybe it was the exhaustion of yesterday and the thought I'd have to do something similar all over again that was making me think this way. If I were killed then I wouldn't know about it, if I survived then I'd be a happy man. It was strange I didn't feel anything about the possibility of my own death and I thought that maybe I was beginning to turn into another Andreas; a killing machine without any feeling or empathy. I had to get out of there no matter what the risks and at least I wasn't on my own.

I started packing as much of my belongings as I could into my Bergen without it looking too suspicious. I only left my sleeping bag out so that when Tomislav and his men came back they wouldn't notice anything odd and it wouldn't take a second to shove it in the top of the rucksack. I picked up my rifle and attached a magazine. This was my last line of defence and the one thing that made me a soldier, without it I was useless. As quietly as I could I cocked it, chambering a round ready to fire before ensuring the safety catch was on. I never usually walked around camp with a magazine attached, let alone a bullet chambered and ready to fire but today was different, the threat was so much closer and yet undefined, a grey area without any front line. I went outside to the well next door, filling a bowl with ice-cold water before returning to the courtyard. I could see my breath as I heard the stirrings of the others, coughing and farting. I washed in the clean, freezing water hoping it would clear my thoughts and make me feel refreshed. I then had a shave, the razor painfully scraping away the wiry stubble, leaving my face feeling raw. I recalled the time in training, the Geordie Sergeant Headley giving me a bollocking for missing a bit of facial hair. I laughed as I wiped shaving foam from my ears and then began polishing my boots, Gunner Hutt ready for inspection, Sir!

Groggy faces sat in the kitchen over freshly made coffee and the days first cigarette, men were still snorting and scratching. Farmer Joe shovelled handfuls of the dried out corncobs we burned as fuel into the big steel stove. Usually it would be all smiles and jokes as Smiley or Farmer Joe had coughing fits until they were close to being sick, their faces bright red. Not this time though. There was an air of dread in that kitchen along with the ever-present fog of cigarette smoke, men's eyes looked downwards in silent thought.

"Fuckin' hell Si, you off Trooping the Colour or something?" said Smiley.

They must have smelled me before they saw me, all cleanly shaven and deodorised with my shiny Doc Martens and my T-shirt tucked into my combat trousers.

"Some of us have standards Smiley," I said, my shaky voice betraying me.

"This is it boys," said Peter entering the room, leaving the words we didn't need reminding about to sink in.

"I'll go get the bread in a bit, we'll have breakfast, then get ready," said the unflappable Terry.

"I'm ready to go," I said quietly.

"We'll give it an hour or so then I'll sneak off to 106, get the van back and pick you all up then we'll be gone," Peter said, making it all sound so easy. "And make sure we're all ready to go, I'm fucked if I'm coming back for anything."

Everyone glanced around them or at the floor, taking in all the information but not commenting on any "worst case scenario", namely that we all get killed.

"It's a nice day for it," said Farmer Joe. Everyone knew what "it" was.

"Look, it's not too late for anyone to back out, just stay here and say you didn't know anything about it," said Peter addressing the room although it felt like he was looking at me.

I thought about what he had said, but I'd rather follow Peter and Terry wherever they went even if it meant getting killed than turn into the type of people I had seen at here. I'd rather die on my feet than keep living on my knees.

"No, I've come this far with you lot, I'm not turning back now," I said.

"Smiley?" said Peter.

"No, I'm with you," he sighed.

"I'm in," said Terry without hesitation.

"I ain't stayin' with these assholes, hell, we all gotta die sometime. I'm in," said Farmer Joe, who, given the choice, would always take the most dangerous option anyway.

Everyone took deep breaths and the mood lightened slightly with the understanding that we were all in it together. More cigarettes were lit and coffee poured.

"Si, can I have your sleeping bag?" said Terry.

"What?"

"You won't be needing it after today will you, no point it going to waste."

"Fuck off.... I want to be buried in it!" I said, "besides, you've got fuck all that I want.... except maybe your missus, so I'll pass on my condolences when I see her."

"Can I have your boots?" Farmer Joe said, sounding suspiciously serious.

"Fuck off!"

"I wanted his boots!" said Smiley, laughing until he coughed again.

"I'll fight you for them!" said Farmer Joe.

"Right, fuck you all, I'm going to get the bread." I laughed.

I made sure I didn't make eye contact with the few HOS men that managed to be awake, only saying "Hi" to Rommel and Gustav who sat drinking mint tea in the eating area. The bread was warm in my arms and smelled beautiful as I carried it back down the road to our farmhouse, eager to get away from the administration area in case something gave me away. The smell of the freshly baked bread battled with the smell of cigarette smoke in our small kitchen. Peter looked as scruffy as usual but Terry and Smiley had washed and shaved, even comparing moustaches. Farmer Joe walked in combing wet hair. Everyone sat and inhaled deeply the aroma of the bread before opening the soft, warm loaf and spreading jam all over it. I noticed that everyone, like me, was carrying their rifles loaded.

"OK, it's time," said Peter after the bread was all gone and sufficient coffees drank and cigarettes smoked.

"Good luck mate," said Smiley.

"I should be back in an hour or two, I'll drive straight up to the admin building when I get back so I can give them the news, you meet me there when you see the van," Peter said.

"You better be goddam coming back, or I'll be coming to get ya," Farmer Joe said, not joking.

"You know what the Croatians are like; all 'yeah, yeah, in a minute.' And remember the driver is just there to drive, if he thinks it's going to end in shooting he'll be gone," Peter said.

"Farmer Joe's got your gear and if anyone asks us you've just gone into town, we'll be ready for you. Good luck, and see you soon," said Terry.

"Lets do it boys," said Farmer Joe.

Everyone quietly wished Peter good luck and shook his hand before he left the kitchen and the farmhouse and started his walk to the town of Orašje, and 106 Headquarters. The rest of us immediately made ourselves busy, covertly packing and putting away everything we had as well as filling every pocket with hand grenades. Tomislav's shift had returned and were by now all asleep. The farmhouse was quiet and we talked in whispers, not daring to leave the filthy kitchen in case someone saw us acting suspiciously.

* * * *

More coffee and cigarettes, the minutes ticking by slowly. An hour passes and we start to feel on edge. We go through as many different scenarios as we can; shooting our way out, running for it, the danger men we have to avoid, don't make eye contact and don't answer back and for Gods sake don't get one on one - make sure there's a crowd of onlookers, that should make them think twice about shooting you. The more we talk about it the more nervous I become, the truth is we don't know what the fuck is going to happen only that they'll be very pissed off and that they have killed one of their own before so there won't be any search party or investigation for a group of missing foreigners. An hour and a half passes and people start sighing and tapping; visible signs of irritation, I feel sick in the smoky fog, and we all start to wonder if he has done a runner on his own. Then we'd be screwed, trapped here with no transport.

We hear the sound of a clapped-out diesel engine. Everybody looks up at each other. A vehicle is coming down the road, this is it.

Terry goes to the window and watches an orange Volkswagen van drive steadily down the road towards us. The adrenaline is pumping through me again as the van passes the kitchen window and Terry raises his thumb to Peter sitting in the passenger seat.

"The driver don't look too happy," says Terry.

"Lets go give them the bad news guys," says Farmer Joe, taking a deep breath.

My legs feel like jelly as I step out of the kitchen and into the courtyard of our farmhouse, the low sun is bright, making me squint. My rifle is slung across my shoulder and I bring it around to my hip, one hand rests on it, not enough to look threatening but enough for me to be ready. We all nod at each other apprehensively and start the walk out of the farmhouse up the road to the admin building, I know that the only reason I'm so calm is that all the others are with me, leading the way.

"No sudden movements or shouting, lets just be calm," Terry says.

We can already hear shouting from the main farmhouse, the orange van is there doing a three point turn so it faces out and down the road, the driver concentrating more than he needs to. A figure appears, weapon in hand, walking out of the other farmhouse ahead, past the manoeuvring van and down the road straight for us. He's followed by three of the others, all the HOS gangsters, bleary eyed and angry.

"Easy boys," Farmer Joe whispers to us. I hear somebody's safety catch being slowly and quietly moved from "safe" to "auto". The HOS boys are in front of us.

"You want to go huh? We not good enough?" says one of the particularly nasty members of the gang sneering, his face is right in ours and we can smell his breath.

"Here we fucking go," Smiley says as quietly as he can.

"You special man? You fat fuck!"

"Easy lads, we don't want trouble," says Terry in his best Doorman's voice.

I stay at the back saying nothing, being the grey man. Terry has a way with people, easy going and friendly but these guys have guns, which they are starting to wave far too enthusiastically. The nasty one is the only one who can speak any English and the three others just insult us in Croatian, which I can cope with. In the distance we can hear a loud argument in Dutch, it's Peter and the HOS commander, Nico. The four idiots now let us walk past and follow us from behind still dishing out insults and throat-slitting gestures as they laugh, I now see that a couple of them have their rifles pointed towards us.

The farmhouse is a hive of activity when we reach it, people coming out to have a look at what is going on, most of them keeping their distance from the small group of hardcore gangsters and us foreigners. I see the three Germans in a corner looking at us nervously, unable show us that they're friendly. Peter is red faced and shouting like a madman in Dutch at Nico and appears to be getting the upper hand. Nico was never the problem though, the acne-faced Jelko was the real leader of this lot. He was the man responsible for the death of the previous commander and he was the man in charge of all the black market dealings, the morphine and the other criminal activity and using this military unit as his cover. Jelko stood in the middle of the courtyard with a pistol in his hand, I noticed his dirty blond hair and acne-scarred face as he looked in our direction. The van's engine was still running, its driver trying to make himself look as small as possible.

"We ain't gonna shoot our way out of this one," says Farmer Joe exhaling deeply.

Jelko's boys surround us but at enough distance so that they can get a good shot. The non-criminal majority of HOS take a few steps backwards into the shadows, away from the line of any stray bullets. Jelko can see what we're thinking.

"You must hand in your weapons, they belong to us," he says smiling.

"Are you going to let us go? We don't want trouble," says Terry.

"Then why leave? Hand them in," he says finally.

One of his assistants comes towards us taking each of our rifles one by one and unloads them before throwing them on a grassy bank a few feet away, Branko's gun had become part of me. The argument between Peter and Nico stops and Peter turns to see us being disarmed, I see a brief flicker of fear in his eyes as Nico smirks. The four of us are standing in a line facing Jelko in the courtyard. My legs feel like jelly again and I'm now powerless without my rifle and we would be dead before we even had our hands on the grenades in our pockets. There are too many people here though, the HOS headquarters, for them to just gun us down. My mind tries to latch onto anything positive as I look around for friendly faces, if it wasn't for Jelko and half a dozen of his cronies we'd be gone by now, then again if it wasn't for them HOS would be very different and we may have stayed. I make eye contact with the three Germans who in turn look to the floor, Sasha is in a doorway, his collar up around his face and his eyes give nothing away. I'm running out of things to latch onto.

"OK, your uniforms are ours too, you must give them back," says Jelko.

"We'll go get our bags then asshole," says Farmer Joe.

"Easy mate," Smiley whispers.

I thought he wanted us to strip there and then, the ultimate humiliation; first no weapon then no uniform.

"Right then, we'll just go get our stuff and leave all the uniforms in the house if that's OK?" says Terry smiling, coolness personified and diffusing anymore potential tension.

Jelko returns his smile. "Yes, you go."

Peter starts arguing again, now in Croatian as we turn to walk back the way we came. I can hear the tone of Peter's voice behind us, he knows better than to argue with a man like Jelko, I think he's talking to the onlookers, a plea for allies. One of Jelko's henchmen is grilling the driver of the van. We brush past the gangsters that had escorted us at gunpoint up the road. Their spotty faces, pale skin and chipped, yellow teeth making me feel sick.

"This is it boys," says Smiley sighing.

There's a sudden realisation that they have us exactly where they want us; unarmed and about to walk down a deserted road.

"Shit," I say quietly.

With the van behind us we stare down the road we had just walked. It was only a hundred metres back to our farmhouse but the empty road stretched into the distance, on the right hand side were the farmhouses; ours, the one where I did the honour guard for the dead soldier and the one that had once housed Terry and the Mujahedeen. To the left of the road was an overgrown field which ended at a thick forest. The crowd looked on as Jelko lined up alongside his men behind us, still smiling. He had picked up Farmer Joe's rifle and magazine.

There was absolute silence as we started to slowly walk down the empty road, Peter looked on helplessly, he had given up shouting, his pleas falling on deaf ears.

"We gonna run for it?" said Farmer Joe.

We all knew that this was it. Walking down a deserted street with guns pointed to our backs.

"We wouldn't get far," I said pathetically.

"Just keep walking, they won't try anything," said Terry optimistically.

"This is a shitty way to die," said Smiley smoking another last cigarette.

"Goddammit, I never thought it would be like this," said Farmer Joe. "We shoulda put up a fight."

We walk down the road in isolation, waiting for something to happen. I look out over the field and forest to our left and think; that's where I'm going to end up, murdered by dirty drug addicts. Here's where it ends, my dreams of the future suddenly never to be fulfilled. My idealistic hopes killed by a bullet to the back of the head and a shallow grave in a forest. I feel strangely calm as I squint in the sun and awaited death, I'd been a good man or at least I always had good intentions, I reasoned to myself. And I had a strong belief in God, or Allah, or whoever the fuck it was, even though He obviously had a fucking weird sense of humour

"At least we're all together," I said.

"Its been fun boys, its been fun," said Smiley sighing again.

We hear shouting behind us, none of us had turned around yet as we walked down the road, the fear of what we might see putting us off and instead focusing on the quiet road and its adjacent woods.

Here it comes, halfway down the road and he's giving the command to fire.

"C'mon, lets get the fucker over with then," I said.

My mind is clear and calm. I say a silent prayer that it will be quick and in the head and that I hope my parents never find out that this is how it ended.

Someone is running down the road to us.

"Terry, Terry, Terry." It was Marco Tigrić.

Marco runs up behind us and puts one arm around Farmer Joe and the other around Terry as Smiley and I walk slightly in front. We can hear Jelko almost screaming with rage, presumably at Marco Tigrić.

"I walk with you to say goodbye, you good man Terry," said Marco.

"That's very fucking kind of you Marco," said Terry, "you don't have to do this you know."

Now if they wanted to open fire on us they would kill Marco Tigrić, he was risking his life and acne-faced Jelko continued to shout in Croatian to Marco who wasn't listening.

"Marco, I could marry you," said Farmer Joe.

"Lets keep walking, they want to kill you," said Marco, who was smiling as he talked.

"We figured that out," said Terry, smiling back as if they were having a conversation about football.

* * * *

Marco Tigrić carried a lot of influence in the area; he was local, from Domaljevac, was in his late twenties and had previously fought in the Croatian Army where at some point had been captured and tortured by the Serbs, spending time as a POW and losing one of his kidneys in one of their regular beatings. He was the local hard man, which his huge homemade tattoos testified to. Maybe it was because this was his home and he realised that we had come to fight for it, or maybe it was just because he liked Terry that he had risked his life, either way, at that moment he was a heavily tattooed angel in human form. I looked behind us toward The HOS gangsters, who stood, angrily debating their next course of action before Jelko started shouting orders again.

"Fucking hell, get out of jail free," I said.

"We're not out of jail yet mate," said Smiley as we reached our farmhouse.

"Yes, now you make them look stupid and they really want to kill you. They will not try to kill me though," said Marco.

"I admire your confidence," said Terry.

Reaching the farmhouse was met with a huge release of tension. We were, at least temporarily, safe.

"Fucking hell, now what do we do?" I said.

"We could do a runner from here, we're out of sight," said Smiley.

"Must be careful, many of the fields are marsh," said Marco.

"Hey guys, Peter's still up there," said Farmer Joe.

"Then we go back, we'll get our shit together and walk back," said Terry.

"Lets face it, that was their best opportunity to kill us," I said, noticing that everyone was speaking in the fast, machine-gun way people do when the adrenaline is pumping.

"They still will want to," said Marco.

"If we do a runner, Peter's a dead man. We have to go back," said Terry.

"I 'ain't running from those assholes, screw them!" said Farmer Joe.

The thought of running away was tempting if it didn't mean signing Peter's death warrant. I'm sure they wanted us to run, that way Peter could disappear easily and they could hunt us down.

Walking back up that road to look at Jelko and his scum in the eyes was the best option, after all I had just mentally prepared myself for death and it wasn't that bad, and like I had kept telling myself since the train journey from Nuneaton to Southampton; I'd rather die on my feet than keep living on my knees. We were the good guys and I had God, or something, on my side. We rushed around grabbing sleeping bags with shaking hands, stuffing everything we could into rucksacks before getting undressed. I put on my fleece and jeans that I had travelled out here in, then picked up two hand grenades and put them in my zip up pockets. Within minutes everyone was in the courtyard again in jeans or a mixture of camouflage clothing that they had brought with them and civilian clothing, cigarettes were lit with shaking hands.

"Ready then?" said Smiley

"Passports," said Terry, "Just in case."

"What? You expecting a plane out of here?" I said.

"In case we do end up in a ditch. Identification."

There was a seconds silence before everyone started to rummage in their bags again to get passports, which were wrapped in plastic and put down our socks.

"Lets do it guys," said Farmer Joe.

There was no plan this time, we would just walk back with Marco Tigrić and get in the van and hope for the best. Marco stood in front, his arms around Terry and Farmer Joe again, smiling and chatting away like they were long lost friends whilst Smiley and I walked behind. On seeing us reappear, Jelko's men rushed around shouting orders. We walked quickly back up towards the van and as we approached the farmhouse the crowd was still there watching, breathing a collective sigh of relief. I don't think they expected us to reappear, and we saw Peter smile broadly before launching into another heated row with Nico. The three Germans also looked relieved and Norbert started babbling away excitedly to his colleagues, Sasha had pulled his collar down and smiled. The HOS gangsters stood and stared angrily, their momentum had gone, their initial rage and desire for revenge dissipated at Marco Tigrić's intervention. However, they still wanted us dead and just needed another opportunity.

"In the van," Jelko sneered as we reached our transport.

"Fine by us mate," said Smiley.

Marco Tigrić buzzed around us as we gathered around the back of the bright orange VW, the driver turning the ignition and starting the engine again. We waved to everyone in the crowd, making a big gesture, smiling and saying thanks and shaking hands with Marco Tigrić. I made sure I looked at the HOS henchman with the yellow skin and chipped teeth.

"Hvala wanker!" I said and smiled at him.

Jelko and his men weren't sure what to make of our behaviour and went over to Peter to start questioning him. We threw our Bergens into the back and climbed in, I got in first and crouched down behind the drivers seat, Smiley and Farmer Joe sat against one wall and Terry the other. The engine was running and we were all in the van, it felt like the finishing line was in sight. Peter was now outside, near the rear of the van, still arguing, this time with Jelko. Marco Tigrić was also joining in.

"Oh shit," I said quietly.

I had the best view out of the van and saw an expression on Peter's face of a sudden helpless panic as he glanced at us and at the same time the HOS boys smirked and took a step back from the van.

"Get the Bergens in front of you, quick!" I said, as I heard the driver jump out and run around the side of the vehicle shouting at the HOS boys.

They were planning to kill us in the back of the van.

"Fuck, here we go again!" said Smiley.

We were sitting ducks, unarmed and in close proximity to each other in the back of a van and one grenade was all that was needed. I didn't feel the same calmness of staring death in the face as I had when I was walking down the road, I had said my goodbyes and realised that now I didn't want a shitty death, blown to pieces in the back of a van by a junkie with bad skin. I pulled my Bergen tight against my arm, ready to smother any grenade that was thrown in as everybody else did the same, I was overcome by an overwhelming and intense desire to survive.

Waiting. Bracing ourselves. As the arguments continued outside, louder, almost pleading.

"C'mon, you fuckers," I whispered.

People kept their distance but craned their necks to get a better look inside the van and the forthcoming carnage.

"Terry, Terry, Terry!" said Marco Tigrić as he jumped into the rear doorway of the van.

The four of us gave an audible sigh of relief; Marco had put himself in the line of fire yet again. Jelko and his HOS gang looked at each other, irritation and anger visible on their faces. The arguments stopped, Peter was smiling.

"Guys, you gotta get the fuck out of here," whispered Marco.

"No shit mate," said Terry, "we owe you big time Marco."

I still gripped the straps on my rucksack as some of the HOS boys backed away, the momentum and opportunity once again lost. The driver got back into his seat, shouting in Croatian as he did so, Peter answering back and moving to the door.

"You guys owe me a beer," said Marco Tigrić.

"A bit more than a fucking beer mate," said Peter also now standing in the rear doorway. Jelko's acne scarred face sneered at us again, this time it felt less threatening. Marco told him to back off in Croatian, I was glad he was with us and not against us.

"Next time I see you I will kill you," said Jelko.

"You dead men," said the other English speaking HOS gangster as Peter climbed in the back. The driver was now shouting with some urgency, he wanted to get the fuck out of there as much as we did.

Peter said something in Dutch to Nico and gave him the finger, Nico was again in the background and said nothing. We waited until we'd moved off, Marco Tigrić still balancing in the open rear doorway of the VW, until we said our final goodbyes.

"Have a nice day guys!" Peter shouted up the road to Jelko when we reached our original farmhouse. We all smiled sarcastically and waved in unison to Jelko and his gang, aware that he'd have to be a pretty good shot to take us out from here.

"Good luck Marco," Terry said to Marco Tigrić as he jumped down from the van a hundred metres further on.

"Thanks mate, we'd be dead if it wasn't for you," said Peter.

"Don't worry about these assholes, I'll still be here when they're long gone. Good luck yourselves, you're good men," said Marco.

We all quickly shook his hand and thanked him, although it didn't seem enough for what he had done, we owed him our lives.

"Go, go!" he shouted, slapping the side of the van.

The driver didn't need telling twice and accelerated further along the road as we waved our goodbyes to Marco Tigrić and our near death experience. It wasn't until we came to the junction and turned onto the main road through Domaljevac, that the HOS farmhouses were out of view. A collective weight was lifted and smiles of relief broke out. Peter started laughing and soon we all started, shaking our heads in disbelief, the driver turning to look at these laughing foreigners that had almost been murdered.

"How the fuck did we get out of that?" said Smiley.

"Not many people will do that and live to talk about it," said Peter.

"They're real tough guys when they take our weapons away," said Farmer Joe angrily.

"Fucking wankers, I'm glad that's over with," I said, my voice still shaking with fear and adrenaline.

"At least you'd have survived if a grenade had been thrown in, cowering under a pile of rucksacks!" said Terry.

"Fuck you! You were nearest the door, anyway I'm the youngest, and I'm too pretty to die!" I said laughing.

"I could smell your fear!" said Terry.

"That wasn't fear you could smell!" said Smiley.

"OH SHIT!" I said, as faces turned to panicked expressions.

"What the fuck is it?" asked Peter.

"I've left my favourite underpants on the radiator!" I said as faces crumpled into laughter.

"We're not going back for your pants mate!" Smiley said laughing.

"They were my lucky black ones as well."

"They say the first casualty of war is your clean underpants," laughed Terry.

The further away from the farmhouse we got the more relaxed we became, a brush with death making us all realise what it is to be alive. We drove on through Domaljevac and various other villages until it started to get dark, before stopping at a building which must have been the local Headquarters. We picked up another man who was Peter's contact with 106 Brigade and changed driver. The driver leaving slammed the door and began shouting at his boss.

"I guess that wasn't in his job description," said Terry.

"OK guys, you manage to get out," said the 106 commander.

"Only just," said Peter.

"I know, word travels fast out here. We take you to your house, then some of you come back to register."

"We need weapons," said Smiley.

We were acutely aware now of how vulnerable it feels to be unarmed in a warzone.

"Sure, that will have to be tomorrow, it is too late now."

We finally reached our new home in the village of Matiči in darkness. The house was on a street with a grassy field in front and rubble behind. This village was still populated by some civilians although it looked like many houses were abandoned or damaged. The five of us scouted through the house in darkness before returning to the front room which gave the best view of the street, the darkness making us whisper.

"I hear on the radio. Some more guys are in Domaljevac," said the commander after having a brief conversation on his hand held radio. It had been a couple of hours since we had left the HOS farmhouses.

"Jelko and HOS?" Peter said.

"No, they say they are wanting to join you."

"Fuck, I hope it's not some mass exodus," I whispered.

"German?" said the commander listening in to his radio.

"Three of them?" said Farmer Joe, completely unable to whisper.

"Yes, one of the local 104 Brigade commanders in Domaljevac has them."

"Are they OK?" asked Peter.

"Yes, but the commander has heard about today's events also, he wants the Germans gone and doesn't want to make enemies of HOS."

"Right lets go get them," said Farmer Joe.

"We've just got out of one shit storm, let's not get ourselves into another, just go careful," said Smiley.

"They'll be out looking for the Germans as well as trying to find out where we are, so try not to bump into them," I said, not volunteering my services to go back.

"When we come back we'll stand in front of the window with our hands up, if it's anyone else then consider them Jelko and his boys," said Peter.

"And what? Throw stones at them?" said Terry.

In a flurry of activity Smiley, Farmer Joe and Peter jumped in the van along with the commander and a driver who was suddenly wide-eyed with fear. Terry and I waited at the house in darkness. We stood in the middle of the room looking out of the two windows, one that looked down the road and the other that was next to the road itself. Terry and I had often talked into the night about anything that we could think of during our shifts at the front line, today was different, we had almost been killed.

"Funny old day mate," said Terry, I started laughing as Terry tried to keep a straight face. "You should have worn your lucky pants."

"Fucking mental, getting killed by your own side, I mean what's that all about?"

"They're not soldiers, they're a disgrace to the name. At least we're here now, close call though," Terry said seriously, "almost too close."

"Yeah but we're here now to do some proper soldiering," I said.

"I think today was a bit of a wake up call. I've got a wife and kids at home," Terry sighed, "I've been here three months and I reckon I've done my bit."

"I suppose the longer you're out here the greater your chances are of eventually being injured," I said.

"And there won't always be a Marco Tigrić. I'm not leaving tomorrow or anything, I just think the time has nearly come."

For the first time we talked of home and the things we had left behind, I couldn't imagine myself in Bosnia without Terry, he wasn't a risk taker, we had the same surreal sense of humour and he was a voice of common sense in a place full of far too many dreamers, liars and idiots.

"Have you got any hobbies then?" Terry said raising his eyebrows.

"You trying to chat me up? You'll be offering me a sweetie next!" I said.

"No, seriously. Obviously apart from fighting in foreign wars and scaring sheep with your sexual advances."

"I haven't had chance for a while being in the Army and stuff. But, and I know it's a bit gay, I used to collect comics, not the Beano and stuff but 2000AD. Ever heard of it?"

"Yeah! You like Rogue Trooper?"

"I like him but I'm more of a Judge Dredd man myself, and ABC Warriors, D.R and Quinch..."

"Could never get into Judge Dredd, probably because they have different artists doing it."

"I can't believe you're into 2000AD! I always thought Rogue Trooper was a bit of a homo, all that charging around topless in tight trousers - very dodgy. Aha! Now I can see why you like him."

"Bastard. You've ruined it now, I always thought of myself as a bit of a Rogue Trooper."

Terry and I talked quietly in darkness until the early hours about our various favourite Sci-Fi comic characters, whilst at the same time firmly holding on to the hand grenades we had kept. We still half expected a car to pull up sharply with Jelko and his junkie friends jumping out ready to kill us. Eventually the VW van pulled up outside the window and Peter jumped out waving his arms in the air.

"There's a time and a place for aerobics Peter," Terry said.

Smiley and Farmer Joe also got out of the van along with three very relieved looking Germans who babbled excitedly about their great escape. The most welcome sight was the crate of beer that was unloaded courtesy of the 106 commander. We waved goodbye to the van until tomorrow and the seven of us sat in the front room drinking the beer and relaxing in the candlelight. The Germans had just thought, 'fuck it' and quietly left without telling anyone before finding the moderately friendly commander in Domaljevac who, luckily, disliked the criminal activity of HOS almost as much as we did. We all ran through the days events, laughing and joking about it, the tension now gone.

I had somehow got through the last two days. The first was the firefight at the front where, for the first time, I had killed a man. Then today; walking down the road and expecting to die, calmly waiting for the bullet from criminals who were supposed to be on our side. I hoped the rest of my time here wasn't as insane.

Over the next few days we heard that HOS had taken casualties, we hoped that the "good" guys at HOS; the likes of Sasha, Željko Čelik and Marco Tigrić were OK, and Jelko and his scumbag friends were the ones in the firing line. Somehow though we doubted it. Word spreads quickly around here and that includes the Serbs who took advantage of HOS' weakness by giving them a hammering. Unsurprisingly the house at the front finally collapsed after being hit by a tank round almost a week after we left.

11. Strangers

The following morning we woke with heads banging but with smiles on our faces, we were away, though not entirely safe, from Jelko and his idiots and were now with a unit that would use us to our full potential and abilities. We were to be the second Intervention Group for 106 Brigade HVO, and our job was to do reconnaissance and observation of the Serb front as well as some behind the lines mayhem if needed, we couldn't get any more front line, and it was a far cry from sitting in a derelict house for twelve hours a day. This was what we were all here for. After we had found some coffee and got our bearings in the house and its surroundings, Peter and Farmer Joe went off to find uniforms and weapons. I hated being in civilian clothes almost as much as I hated being unarmed. It was a few hours before Peter and Farmer Joe returned in a van.

"Christmas has come early!" said Peter carrying a long crate into the house.

"Ho, ho, ho," said Framer Joe smiling.

"So much for the arms embargo!" said Terry as we all joined in carrying the dozen crates into the house.

After they were all unloaded into the cellar, Peter picked up the top crate and opened the lid, on the side was written 'Made In China.'

"Ooooh, nice!" said Farmer Joe.

"It's still in its grease," I said.

"Fucking typical, always made in China," said Smiley.

Peter unwrapped the rifle, sticky with grease, from its wrapping paper then held up the brand new Chinese made, folding butt AK-47, all black metal with red hardwood grip and stock. It was indeed Christmas, and everyone got to work stripping, cleaning and degreasing the virgin weapons, cocking repeatedly to ensure all the working parts moved smoothly. Not only were there rifles but also Chinese made RPGs and 'Zolya' disposable anti-tank weapons along with crates of ammunition and grenades. We were no longer useless.

Later in the day we were shown around the military stores in the village, with the man in charge saying, "help yourself," before wandering off. Telling a soldier to help himself is asking for trouble, even though there wasn't much in the way of webbing or kit carrying equipment as usual. I grabbed myself a couple of shirts and trousers, a thin coat and a thicker coat with large pockets, I also got a couple of pairs of Yugoslav Army issue underpants, much to Terry's amusement. I had made sure I kept my green ski mask from HOS that I rolled up and used as a "Benny" hat and with arms weighed down with as much as we could carry we returned to the house and immediately got changed. The feeling of clean uniform and a rifle was great, now I was a soldier again, and tried on every piece of kit to see which combination I would be most comfortable in at the front line. Christmas never felt this good.

The house we were stationed in was large and detached, and most importantly it was all ours. The village of Matiči was a quiet, grey front line village just like all the others. The civilian population made the best of their situation whilst the front line was only a few hundred metres south from the outskirts. A corn on the cob burning stove was in the front room where Peter chose to sleep, the three Germans had one of the downstairs bedrooms with Terry and I having the other, Farmer Joe and Smiley slept somewhere upstairs. The house looked like it had been abandoned sometime ago, it had been decorated before being stripped of all furnishings when the owners left. A couple of beds had been left behind, a double bed was in my room although Terry slept on the floor underneath the window whilst I had the bed to myself, "Don't want to start rumours now do we?" Terry said. The house had fitted wardrobes and a small cellar, which now doubled as our armoury. The back yard was a pile of rubble and nobody was sure if it was a demolished house or just debris from the building work that had been interrupted by war. The house next door was a brick shell, the outer structure made before being abandoned without being plastered and glazed. The toilet was an outhouse a hundred feet away beyond the rubble in the back garden and consisted of a small brick shed raised off the ground with a hole in its floor, although most of us just took a shovel to the most hidden patch of greenery before digging a hole to shit in and burying it, which was less hazardous to our health than the toilet.

The following day we were to meet the other Intervention Group who would show us the layout at the front and take us out on patrol. We were getting restless now that we were all ready for action, the fear of HOS now just a memory as we concentrated on our jobs.

"What the fuck is it then?" said Smiley looking at the large green tube that lay on the table.

"It's a Zolya anti-tank weapon," said Peter, "I never used one."

"They're a bit like the British disposable 66mm rocket by the looks of it," I said remembering firing something similar prior to the Gulf.

"How does it work then?" Smiley said.

I clicked off the end caps of the tube and slid the telescopic inner tube out so that it almost doubled in length, Peter started looking at me with a nervous expression.

"Right. When you pull it out all the way it should click into place, that means it's armed and ready. I haven't pulled it out all the way, OK," I said reassuringly, "when it clicks these sights at the top should flick up, you look down the sights then press the tit on the top. Bang. Then chuck it away."

"Where do you put the rocket in?" said Smiley.

"It's already in but isn't armed until the tube is pulled apart and clicks." I showed Smiley the inside of the tube, at the bottom of which the cone of the rocket could be seen.

"Fucking hell," he said looking down the tube," that looks dangerous."

"BANG!!" I shouted, to which Smiley jumped up and off his chair, almost having a heart attack.

"You're in charge of that fucking thing then," Smiley said through a coughing fit.

The leader of the first Intervention Group was called Crny, or Gypsy. He had dark olive skin and jet-black shoulder length hair making him look more like an Native American Indian than an East European Gypsy. There were six others in his group and all of them looked to be about eighteen, though their eyes looked older. They were local lads and knew the area inside out. At Crny's house his men had just woken up and were already chain-smoking on the sofa that doubled as their bed as coffee brewed.

"Welcome, welcome," said Crny, the only one who spoke English, "I'll take you around the front lines then the others will meet us and we go on patrol."

Crny seemed genuinely pleased to see us.

"It is good to have others to share the load," he said in his husky voice.

It was only a five-minute walk down the road to the HVO trenches and it couldn't have been more different than the shattered houses that served as HOS' front lines. Running left to right in front of us was a five foot deep and three feet wide trench, which zigzagged off into the distance. At every other front facing point in the zigzag was a fire position cut into the trench, at every other rear facing point was a bunker. The whole place was reinforced, sandbagged and had branches and logs in front as cover from view. The regular soldiers of 106 Brigade sat in the bunkers drinking coffee and playing cards, Matiči was probably their village. It was fantastically organised and engineered, it was the first sign of professionalism we had seen and we were impressed. At the edge of the field some way in front of the trenches was a hedge then, Crny explained, another small field, another hedge then a field with the Serb bunkers in, in total the Serb lines were just a couple of hundred metres away. The road we stood on went ahead of us into a forest where the hedge was, then continued to a Serb held village a mile away.

"This road is mined, some of the forest is also mined with tripwires. We will show you where they are," Crny said.

Crny introduced us to the men in the bunkers, although they knew foreigners were coming already and as word travels so fast, the Serbs probably did too. Terry and I jumped down into the trench, not only to introduce ourselves but also to have a good look at the position.

"Dobar dan, dobar dan," Terry and I said shaking hands with the men who looked like they had seen it all before. We felt it was important to make an effort to get to know these soldiers even though we were probably bad news to them, bringing the threat of combat with us whereas these guys stayed in this trench happy to defend their own village. After a few minutes our friendly Anglo-Bosnian chat was interrupted when we saw the other members of Crny's team arrive still looking like they had only just got up.

"Benny Hill!" said Terry smiling and waving goodbye to the men in the bunker.

"Benny Hill," the men answered back, waving, quite proud at having learnt a new English word.

Crny walked us out past the line of trenches and onto the road that eventually led to the Serb front line. Everybody was on full alert, our group had never done anything like this before and with my rifle into my shoulder I scanned hedges and trees. The adrenaline was pumping and it felt good even though there was at least thirteen of us going out on a patrol, far too many to try and keep quiet. It was like being back in basic training again although for Crny it seemed to be a stroll in the park.

We stopped and crouched as we neared the first hedge line and Crny pointed out clumps of weeds in the road that covered black plastic mines with their three metal pins protruding upwards. Hardly noticeable unless you were looking for them and they were activated when pressure is released, in other words when you step off the mine and not on it. Crny told us the accompanying story of one of their men treading on one and realising what it was, ended up standing there for hours frozen to the spot until someone came to disarm it. At the hedge line itself where the road entered the small wood Crny pointed out the tripwires that had been laid and armed. These anti-personnel mines flew up into the air when activated before exploding, and they could be set to detonate at different heights; waist or chest height if you wanted to kill people or a few inches off the ground so they only blow someone's foot off, the difference being that it takes several people to give first aid and evacuate an injured man, whereas a dead man can be left if necessary. Peter called them "Poppers," due to the sound they made when they flew up into the air. I wondered what kind of sick bastard invents these things.

We walked carefully around the mines and tripwires and into the small wood and the second hedge line, we were now in no-mans land. On the other side of this hedge a hundred metres away we could see through the trees a row of around a dozen badly camouflaged bunkers. Crny quietly explained that they didn't have trenches only individual bunkers and it was hard to know which were occupied unless they had a fire going inside. We could hear talking and laughter from the Serb lines as well as an engine starting in the distance and plates or tins rattling. I was suddenly totally switched on as more adrenaline pumped through me, I could hear every movement whilst the Germans sounded like elephants crashing through the small forest so I gave them an angry stare. We crouched down and waited, watching the Serb bunkers for any movement or action. I wanted to get people in to some kind of all round defence and explain arcs of fire, just sitting and waiting in no-mans land was against everything I had learnt and made me even more aware of the sounds we were making and how exposed we were if we got "bumped" by an enemy patrol. Nobody else seemed to give a shit though.

Crny had a brief chat with one of his team before splitting us into two groups to go to the edge of the Serb lines and beyond, behind their bunkers. I was lumbered with the Germans, maybe I was seen as some kind of controlling influence after the little firefight in Lijeskovac, either that or just because we were in the same age group. I used hand signals to tell them to shut up, before tapping the side of my head to tell them to stay alert. Terry, Smiley, Farmer Joe and Peter along with Crny and another of his men went first, scurrying back to the road before following the hedge line across the fields. As we waited I tried to explain arcs of fire to the Germans using hand signals, I think I was wasting my time but at least they were quiet. After ten minutes of waiting and listening to the Serb soldiers eat their dinner it was our turn.

One of Crny's men led the way followed by Gustav, myself, Norbert and Rommel, another one of Crny's men stayed at the rear. We skipped over the mines again before scrambling behind the hedge and ran, crouching, across the field parallel to our own trenches. It took us about ten minutes of half jogging, stopping occasionally to regroup, before skidding into a deep, wet ditch almost half a kilometre to the right of the road where we started. We sat in the ditch and got our breath back, before giving the thumbs up sign that we were ready. Using hand signals, the leading scout told us to wait before he slowly walked forwards in the ditch that ran parallel to the road, forwards into the Serb lines to meet up with the other group.

He soon returned and waved us forward, staying in the same line and crouching as low as we could, we quietly plodded through the wet overgrown ditch. Like most of the last couple of days I felt totally unprepared and felt the need to be "cammed up," to have my face covered in camouflage cream and foliage hanging off me to break up my silhouette. I thought it was just meant to be a quick look at the bunkers. We walked for ten metres then stopped to listen before moving slowly forwards again and for once the Germans incessant chatter had stopped, the noises from the Serb lines were now louder and their individual voices could be heard. The ditch became wider and deeper and we met up with the other group who sat against the steep sides of the bank, Terry giving me a thumbs up. Crny waved his arms to attract our attention before pointing to areas on the sides of the bank and in the ditch. Spiky Serb mines could clearly be seen poking out of various bits of undergrowth. I looked around at all the serious faces, silent despite the adrenaline that was fuelling us. The dozen men sat in the cold, damp overgrown hollow surrounded by Serb mines, listening, eyes darting everywhere, breathing shallowly and silently. The scene reminded me of when I was a boy, playing soldiers as a child with my friend Matthew, hiding in building sites and waiting for the other kids who we were playing war with that day to appear then hurling stones or mud at them before running off. I tried not to laugh at the comparison.

Crny waved us forward, thankfully stopping any nervous giggle before it started. The other group stayed as they must have already been up and had a look and our group crawled forwards into another ditch that eventually rose and flattened out until we were at ground level and crawling through wet undergrowth and around tree trunks, occasionally stopping and silently listening. After around twenty minutes of crawling and stopping, the undergrowth became sparse and turned into a forest floor carpeted with pine needles and wet brown leaves. Crny skipped behind a tree and we all followed, each picking individual trees. Crny pointed to the area that we had just gone past. My heart was hammering.

In front of us only twenty metres away was the rear entrance of the Serb bunker at the end of the line. We had gone past the end of their line and were now in the wooded area behind their last bunker. Crny put his finger to his lips before pointing further ahead. Ahead of us a figure with his back to us leant against a tree smoking a cigarette. He wore the dark green camouflage Serb uniform and had his rifle slung over his shoulder. Crny moved forwards closer to the Serb soldier, as if it was some kind of competition, I suddenly thought that Crny was going to kill him and was overcome by a claustrophobic panic. This was no longer a recce mission just to have a look, Crny had the chance to kill a Serb, it wasn't like playing war as a kid anymore and we wouldn't be throwing some mud before running off.

Crny was now ten metres from the Serb soldier and slowly drew a long-bladed knife from its sheath. I suddenly realised I was trapped behind the Serb lines and if the shit hit the fan I would be screwed, 'please don't kill him,' I thought, as my base instinct to run away tried its hardest not to kick in. A voice in the distance shouted to the smoking Serb who in turn laughed and shouted something back. We were wide-eyed and frozen to the spot, there was a few minutes of banter between the two Serb soldiers before he threw his cigarette away and walked off, laughing, away from us and towards his unseen conversation partner, thankfully without looking around. Crny and the rest of us had turned to statues at the sound of this private conversation and Crny, putting his knife back in its sheath, realised it was time to go. My panic slowly eased as we shuffled backwards back the way we had come, my body still screaming at me to run. The Serb would never know how close he came to having his throat cut. We left the area as quietly as we came in and with each step closer to our lines the better I felt.

"How good was that?" said Peter, as we sat eating a spicy stew in the village hall that served as a cookhouse.

"It will be easier when we know the ground better," said Farmer Joe.

"Remember these guys live here and grew up here, they know every blade of grass," said Terry.

"I don't know if I'm up for all that sneaky-beaky shit," I said. "I wasn't prepared for it, we're not the SAS."

"Maybe we should leave the behind the lines stuff to Crny and his boys, they're the experts," said Terry.

"Well I was shitting myself, I can't run as fast as you lot," laughed Smiley.

"We'll be OK don't worry," said Peter.

The following day we met the commander of the area in his headquarters. The commander was tall and imposing, and wore jackboots to enhance the effect, with a holstered pistol at his hip. He must have been in his early forties but had long black hair tied into a ponytail which hung down to the middle of his back. Maps lined the wall of his office with red and blue zigzags and arrows all over them. The commander formally greeted us with coffee before outlining the "big plan", which his assistant and Peter explained and translated. Our job, which is why he agreed to have us, was to direct fire for the artillery, in other words as kind of Special OP's, the job I had wanted in the artillery. Tanks were used as direct-fire artillery here and Peter explained that we had skills in that department; Smiley could drive a tank, I had been in the artillery and Peter bullshitted that he had loads of experience with tanks. The big plan was that we would direct the tank's fire onto the Serb bunkers one by one starting at the furthest left and working our way along the line, meanwhile Crny and his men would attack the Serbs on their flank, where we had been the previous day by the bunker furthest to the right. So with the bunkers destroyed and the Serbs in disarray with Crny flanking them, we would continue the frontal attack and the Serbs would be pushed back. It sounded so easy in theory, and we knew it could be done as we had already been to Crny's forward flanking position, but as is usual in Croatia and Bosnia nobody had a timescale for when the "big plan" would be given the go-ahead, it was always a "soon", or "maybe tomorrow" and until then it would be business as usual. We thanked the commander and promised we wouldn't let him down and Peter asked if we could borrow a tank for a bit. Surprisingly the commander said he would see what he could do.

Word had now got round to other units that there was a group of international volunteers that had formed their own unit together. Groups of foreigners together rarely last too long; people get injured or go home, a groups dynamic changes and people drift apart or off to other units. We were visited one night by a German who must have been in his fifties with badges all over his red beret. He asked us if we wanted to join him but his role was as a regular soldier one of the trenches, Peter knew him and had already warned us that he was a knob anyway. "He didn't fight in Vinkovci," said Peter about the badge on the Germans beret which referred to a battle in Croatia earlier in the year. We had no desire to be regulars in trenches anyway, if we had wanted that kind of routine we could have stayed at HOS. One man who we welcomed was Ivan the Irishman, who we met briefly when we were in HOS.

"I tried to get some of the others to join me, but like you said before - better the devil you know," he said.

"They're welcome whenever they want," said Terry.

"Well I thought you could do with some help and there's not enough Irishmen in your group."

"One rule though Ivan, no silly hats," I said joking about his trademark digger hat.

"Sorry lads, but the hat's part of the deal," he laughed.

Ivan's long ponytailed hair and soft Irish voice hid the fact that he had been in almost constant action for the last six months and knew his stuff. He was another much needed voice of reason and a calming influence, not only that but within minutes of meeting him you would know that you could trust him with your life.

We had a good nine-man team now without personality clashes or any internal aggravation. The three Germans slept in the same room and kept each other company, on one occasion almost blowing the stove up in their room by fuelling it and making it burn until the steel glowed cherry red. When out on patrol however they had started to become more professional, copying what we did and as long as they were not left alone for too long were an excellent asset. Farmer Joe, Smiley and Peter were the older, experienced members of the group. Peter and Farmer Joe often rubbed each other the wrong way but managed to get along and nobody envied Peter in his leadership role, Farmer Joe was happy enough going with the flow as long at it suited him. Smiley, Farmer Joe's comedy partner, was the inscrutable, chain-smoking northerner who got on with it, he was made of stern stuff but any questions about his life back home would be swatted away with a "Nema, nema, polarko." These three smoked like chimneys and liked a drink, often finding some Rakija from somewhere to drink themselves into slurred conversations and slow motion arguments before passing out in the front room. Terry and I, and Ivan when he arrived, liked a few of the sweet Croatian beers but knew that heavy drinking and weaponry surely couldn't be a good cocktail, it was all about control.

Any time not out on patrol was spent doing our own thing; Farmer Joe found a pig was tethered in the rough patch of ground at the back of our house past the toilet and spent much of his time enticing it with leafy green vegetables and the mantra, "you gotta eat your greens," until eventually its owner caught Farmer Joe feeding the pig and screamed at him for making his animal have violent diarrhoea. Peter wandered around doing his leadership thing; trying to scrounge equipment and what could be described as ducking and diving, though we turned a blind eye. He was also making contacts with everyone he could find who were more to do with "business" than friendship. Terry and I, often with Smiley and Ivan, walked into the village if just to say hello to the locals, we were determined not to be the "strangers" in town that they all saw us as, the foreigners that brought the war with them.

"Hello, you must be the Mayor of Bristol," said Terry.

"Da, da, Mayor," said the middle-aged man.

"Dobar dan," I said introducing myself but trying not to laugh.

We were in a small room that served as the communications centre for Matiči. A large radio was propped up on the table against the wall hissing static, the sound occasionally punctuated by someone speaking in rapid-fire Croat. The man was indeed the Mayor, or whatever the Bosnian Croat equivalent was, of the village and another younger man sat smoking next to the radio. The younger man poured us coffee as we admired enviously the long camouflage parkas that the Mayor and his assistant wore. The men spoke no English but attempted to explain their role as a communications centre, proud of their jobs and obviously pleasantly surprised that some of the new foreigners had taken an interest, smiling and nodding constantly at us as we attempted to communicate in two different languages.

"Benny Hill, then," said Terry shaking the Mayor's hand as we left.

"Benny Hill to the Mayor of Bristol," I said also shaking his hand.

"Benny Hill Ingliiski!" said the Mayor of Bristol, clearly well pleased at his unexpected visit.

After around a week of patrolling the Serb lines and getting the lie of the land from Crny and his men, we considered ourselves ready for the "big plan" of attacking the Serb lines. As if on cue and before we could start to get bored, we heard the familiar squeaking rumble of a tank outside the house. We ran outside and watched the T-62 tank roll up the road, menacingly churning out black fumes, its crew waving to us as the long-haired commander and some more of his men followed up behind, the tank turned off onto the field opposite as it reached our house.

"You fucking beauty," said Smiley looking strangely excited.
"I hope you two know what your doing," said Ivan.

"You wouldn't catch me in one of those things," said Farmer Joe.

"Lets go Smiley," Peter said as he ran across the field to the waiting tank.

"Good luck lads," I said, " and be careful of my flowers!"

"And don't press any red buttons for fucks sake," said Terry.

Smiley sat in the driver's seat familiarising himself with the controls, making black fumes bellow from the exhaust as he revved the powerful diesel engine before slowly pulling forward while Peter waited his turn. The tank gained speed and Smiley moved rapidly up the gears, the grassy field instantly turning to mud as the tank accelerated and the tracks ploughed into the earth. Smiley's face was redder than usual, a huge grin spreading from ear to ear as he started to gain confidence, throwing the tank through ninety degree turns at high speed, reversing before turning and spinning into the opposite direction. Smiley was on top form and parked up in front of the commander to a round of applause. Peter also drove the tank, but after Smiley's display, it looked rubbish. The commander and the rest of the men had a ten-minute conference along with Peter and the still grinning Smiley as we watched from the fence by the road. Eventually Peter came running over to us.

"OK lets get ready."

"What for?" said Rommel.

"We're going to test fire it."

"You need us for that?" said Terry.

"At one of the Serb bunkers."

"And we're doing the fire direction? Excellent," said Ivan.

"Lets get ready then."

We were straight into the house and getting our gear on as Smiley drove the tank away to its firing position on some high ground. Physical preparation was also part of my psychological preparation, if my body is ready then so is my mind. I started my ritual of wearing my jacket with the deep pockets, collars up, benny hat on, weapon cocked and ready, magazines and grenades safe, laces tied, and pockets secured with nothing dangling, rattling or looking like it might fall off and I even covered my boots in dust and dirt to eliminate some of the shine. We used a burnt cork to blacken our faces with diagonal tiger stripes. Since the firefight and the trouble leaving HOS I had felt constantly on edge, like something unexpected was about to happen; a grenade through the bedroom window above Terrys bed space as we slept, a stray bullet, a sniper watching me, everything was unpredictable. I felt good this time, prepared as much as I could be.

We were over the tripwires and mines in minutes, then crawling through the hard dirt of an unploughed field along the hedgerow in front of the Serb bunkers until we stopped in the middle of the field against the hedge. It was another clear winter's day without a cloud in the sky and the earth was frozen hard as rock and my hands burned with cold when I scraped the back of them across the dirt as I crawled into position. I was at the rear of the group, the nine of us spread along twenty metres of hedgerow and I turned and faced back the way we had came, my rifle pointing towards the small wood we had just left in case we were flanked by an enemy patrol. The Germans looked at me like I was insane, but I was prepared, it was all part of the training. I could hear the Serb voices again, quieter this time, they were probably huddled in their bunkers against the cold. Peter passed some binoculars down the line so we could all have a look at the Serb bunkers. In the forest behind the bunkers I saw a Serb soldier with a bored expression and a rifle slung over his shoulder hop from foot to foot trying to keep warm, the dark green camouflage and red collar tabs giving him away, as well as his odd-looking Serb square hat.

Peter returned to his position and started whispering into the walkie-talkie, the plan was to destroy one of the bunkers by directing the tanks fire onto it and once destroyed, we were out of there. It was just a matter of how quickly we could get on target.

* * * *

There was a familiar calm that fell across the field, like I first noticed when the MLRS was about to fire in the Gulf, as if everything holds its breath, waiting. I hear the loud boom of our tank firing in the distance behind our lines to my left and feel the oncoming round disturbing the air in front of it and changing the pressure around it as it flies at a supersonic speed, silently over our trenches. I gasp for air as I see a line of twigs and branches in the woods ten metres in front of me snap and fall as the invisible high explosive shell rips through my field of vision ten feet above the ground. Leaves and branches continued to fall in the split second it takes for the shell to cross the hedge and hammer into the woods behind and to the left of the target Serb bunker. I hear the Serb voices, they start to shout and become agitated and I imagine the guy who I had seen through the binoculars diving into the nearest cover, his bored expression now replaced by panic. Peter talks quickly and quietly into the walkie-talkie and I feel my body flatten involuntarily into every groove and frozen rut of the field. The tank fires again, a distant background explosion, then the change in the air pressure as in a second it flies past the woods in front of me, dislodging only a few branches this time before thumping into the ground in front of the bunker and detonating a millisecond after. I can feel the fear returning, would the Serbs be sending out patrols or start firing back with mortars at the unseen observers? I want to become invisible, transparent to the tank rounds that are flying past in front of me. Peter gives instructions again and the tank fires. I feel the tank round coming towards me like a silent train and can do nothing but try and become flatter and melt into the earth, there's a black smudge directly overhead, a flicker in the corner of my eye but close, just a metre above me. The tank round is like the eye of a storm, airless and frozen, a bubble of silence and serenity envelopes it and for a brief moment, me. For an instant I think I am about to die again, sucked into its vacuum, before the smudge disappears. Smoke pours from the end bunker, a direct hit. Peter chatters a way and the tank fires again, it now has its range and it only needs to move a few degrees to the right to hit the next bunker. I close my eyes this time as I feel the gust above me turn into an explosion to the right of me.

My body becomes solid again and I'm a sprinter in his blocks, it's time to go. Whispers and smiles, Peter points at me and I'm glad I'm the first one out, we get to the road and skip over the mines just as the sun is setting. The Serbs fire a few mortars back but they're aiming for our tank's position, which has long gone. It's half-hearted, they're probably more interested in a damage assessment now that the firing has stopped.

* * * *

Smiley stood next to the tank, smiling and smoking as usual. The ground around him was thick, deep mud.

"Bit warm down there boys?" he said, clearly in his element.

"They were a bit close for comfort, Smiley," said Terry.

"What! You were behind me. As usual," I said.

"Hey, I just do the driving lads."

"Was the boss happy?" said Peter.

"The boss was, Crny and his mates didn't look too chuffed though."

Our little test was over and done with and we assumed we had passed with flying colours. So much so that Crny and his team were a little pissed off with the new boys stealing their thunder and over the next few days we got the distinct impression that they wanted nothing to do with us. Ivan, Terry and Myself still went over to their house and made the effort to communicate, but it wasn't easy. Peter made no effort and like Miran before, became positively hostile toward Crny and his team. We were ready and able for the big plan, it was now just the waiting and patrolling which we did every day. Crny and his men laid more tripwires across the road and forest, some were active and some dummies, but this time he neglected to tell us which was which.

"We're what?" said Smiley in disbelief.

"Seriously. That's what the guy is here for," said Peter.

Two uniformed men sat in the front room with serious expressions. They spoke in Croat to Peter who translated for us.

"We're getting paid," said Peter to Smiley.

"Hell, that's a first," said Farmer Joe.

"I wasn't expecting that," said Ivan.

"You can get that new handbag you wanted now Simon," said Terry.

"Yeah, but I've just got nothing to go with it," I said.

"Are we going shopping ladies?" said Ivan.

The money was dished out equally and everyone received 30 Deutschmarks, the equivalent of about £10.

"It's party time tonight guys!" said Farmer Joe. Terry, Ivan and I looked at each other and raised our eyebrows.

The Croat paymasters left with smiles and handshakes and a "Benny Hill!" from Terry.

We pooled half of our money and bought beer and extra food. There were no shops to buy anything worthwhile, and besides we hadn't come here to earn money and being paid felt strange and for me at least seemed slightly wrong. The Croats and Bosnians needed the money, not some crazy foreigners who would spend it all on alcohol. I shoved the rest of the small payment into the bottom of my Bergen and forgot about it.

The rest of the day was spent eating crisps and drinking sweet bottled lager. Everybody was relaxed; smoking and drinking, singing songs in foreign languages and occasionally and momentarily opening up to our separate worlds back home. The drink flowed and the barriers came down; stories of women and wars, farms and universities, countries and languages. There was a whole world in that room but just then, we were like brothers, letting our guard down and opening up with laughter and jokes, the war and the different reasons for each of us being there was forgotten, however briefly. Eventually late into the night the several crates of beer we bought had ran out, and with alcohol induced hugs most of us said our goodnights and left for our rooms to sleep it off. Peter, Smiley and Farmer Joe remained in the front room smoking and talking.

"YOU MOTHERFUCKING SONOFABITCH!!" shouted a drunken Farmer Joe.

I don't know how long I had been asleep, but I was woken to the sounds of a fight outside the door in the corridor, I lay on the bed in my sleeping bag listening to the fracas outside. Terry was already awake and sitting up in his sleeping bag.

"Terry, what the fuck is going on?" I asked.

"I think Joe's been arrested and brought back here, hold on," Terry said as he got up out of his sleeping bag and walked to the door, before going out into the melee. I didn't like it, it was the unpredictability again and I wanted it all to go away. There was a lot of shouting in Croatian from Peter and a strange voice belonging to another man whilst Farmer Joe continued to swear aggressively, interspersed with plenty of "calm downs". I heard Terrys voice trying to calm the situation and soon the noise died down and the struggling stopped, then we heard the strange voice leave.

"He's been caught trying to steal Rakija from someone's still in the village," said Terry returning, "the Military Police arrested him and escorted him back here, that was the MP just going."

"Fucking great, so much for our hearts and minds campaign," I said.

"Makes you wonder why we bother doesn't it."

I put my Walkman on and listened to Depeche Mode to try and drown out any potential noise and zipped up my sleeping bag to my face, cocooned in warmth. It wasn't long before I was woken up again.

"YOU MOTHERFUCKERS!"

"He's at it again," said Terry quietly.

"MOTHERFUCKERS!"

"Fucking hell, if you go mental when you've had a drink then don't fucking drink," I said, by now exhausted and on edge.

"Put the grenades down," we heard Peter say ominously.

Farmer Joe continued his rant at no one in particular. Terry again walked to the door, looking out then coming back into the room.

"He's walking around holding a grenade in each hand by the pin," he said.

We liked Joe immensely, he was slightly mad but weren't we all? And anyway he was our madman and it was our duty to look after him no matter what. Who knows what things he had seen to make him want to blot it out with alcohol.

"We can't let him blow himself up," I said, torn between helping and hiding.

"Fuck it!" said Terry leaving the room again.

I lay listening to Farmer Joe get talked down by Terry, Peter and Smiley, it took half an hour for fatigue to replace Joes drunken rage and he eventually sat drunkenly sobbing at the table to Peter, as Terry returned to the room with two hand grenades.

"I think that's made my mind up Simon," Terry whispered.

"What do you mean?"

"I was going to go soon, but now I want to go straight away. My time's up here."

"What about the big attack? Can't you wait until that's over?" I said hoping Terry would change his mind.

"When? This is Croatia, it's always soon, tomorrow, polarko, polarko. We could wait forever for something that never happens. And when it does happen…No, my times up, I can feel it."

I drifted back off into a few hours of restless sleep. I couldn't imagine Terry not being here, I knew it was coming but didn't know when. He'd been like a big brother to me out here, our shared sense of humour and love for 2000AD comics, Judge Dredd and Rogue Trooper. I felt safe when he was around.

"Ivan's a good bloke, he'll look out for you," said Terry, as we got ready in the morning.

"When are you going?" I asked.

"I reckon the soonest I can go is this Friday, what about you? Do you want to come?"

I thought briefly, but to go now would feel like I had given in and ran away. I felt like I had unfinished business and a job to do, maybe if Ivan wasn't here I would, but not yet. Unlike Terry it didn't feel like it was time yet.

"No, I'm not ready yet. I'll know when it's time don't worry," there was a silent pause. "Do you need any more money? I won't need mine. When I leave I just have to hand myself to the nearest Brit UN camp," I laughed.

"No mate, have a beer on me with it."

Terry broke the news to the others that morning and they looked almost as pissed off as I was. One of our team was leaving despite pleas for him to wait for the big attack, Farmer Joe even apologised for his behaviour. Terry was adamant that his time had run out here. It was less than a week until Terry left and I constantly reminded him that it was a Friday the 13th when he would be leaving. Until then it was routine as usual; we had photos taken for our I.D. cards in the neighbouring village and spent a few days coming up with a name and a design for the sleeve patch for our group, eventually deciding on the "Free Crusaders", with the picture of a Templar Knight designed by Ivan, not for any religious reference but more for the fact that we were an independent group of foreign warriors. Terry went on patrol as a sense of duty to the rest of us but I could sense his reluctance, it was Sods Law that you get injured, or worse, in your last few days.

The day had eventually come for Terry to leave, he had said his goodbyes to the others and we both stood outside, his bags in the doorway.

"Are you sure you want to go today Terry mate, seriously, it's Friday the 13th," I pleaded.

"Got to be done, I'm ready."

"One more day? Saturday the 14th is lucky in some countries," I laughed.

"Look mate, you take care, there are some mad bastards out here and you're a good man. People care about you," Terry said seriously, "you can still come with me out of here you know, it won't make you a coward and nobody will think less of you."

"I'm not ready yet, maybe another month," I said.

"Just keep your head down," said Terry.

"And don't look back," I said.

We embraced each other awkwardly.

"Benny Hill, Terry."

"Benny Hill, Simon."

Terry walked away down the road with his bags containing a letter to my Army friend Pete, along with some hardcore Croatian porn that I had shoved in his holdall when he wasn't looking for customs to find, Terry gave me his British Army magazine pouch. He didn't look back.

"What the fuck is going on?" I said only half awake.

There was a commotion in the front room, I had gone to bed early after a few beers and listened to music, trying to get used to being in the room on my own. I walked into the front room in my JNA issue underpants, the commanders assistant stood at the top of the room. The rest of the team stood listening, only half awake.

"Tomorrow we have to retake a village," said Peter.

The others stood and listened as the man spoke rapidly to Peter.

"There's been a fight and we have to go in to retake a village in the morning," Peter translated. Rommel translated for the Germans.

The commanders assistant nodded and said goodbye, having to go and inform everyone else available in the area to be ready tomorrow to attack the village.

"Right then boys, best get some sleep if it's an early start," said Ivan.

The details were vague but we had to be ready to fight tomorrow and would be picked up in the early hours. I was quite excited at the prospect of real fighting, but it was fucking typical that Terry wasn't here.

12. Paint

Banging and clattering from the hallway woke me up, sounds of weaponry being dropped to the floor accompanied by a "Fucking hell!" along with the usual farting and coughing that could be heard every morning. I suddenly felt sick with apprehension.

I lay in the warm safety of my sleeping bag for several minutes listening to the others preparing themselves for combat. It was still dark and I was alone in that room, I felt Terry's absence stronger than ever. It didn't take long me long to realise that they had forgotten to wake me up. Something though didn't feel right, I lay there and zipped up my sleeping bag until it covered my face as I tried to close my eyes and fall back to sleep, it was impossible, my stomach churned and my heart was racing as the minutes ticked by. I wanted it to go away, I wanted to wake up and they had already gone, then they could come back later and I'd say, "Why the fuck didn't you wake me up?" I had a bad feeling, it wasn't just the fear that I had felt constantly since I had left HOS, it was just an instinctive overwhelmingly bad feeling that I really should stay in bed.

I lay there for ten minutes listening to their noise but it was no good, I couldn't go back to sleep. I unzipped the sleeping bag and got out, the cold hitting me as I sat on the edge of the bed staring at my reflection in the mirror next to the bed. More of the men were up an about, distributing ammunition, filling their pockets with grenades, the Germans talking loudly. Still nobody banged my door, if Terry was here I wouldn't be shitting myself, I thought, if Terry was here I wouldn't have the bad feeling, if Terry was here we'd be out there getting ready. I reasoned with myself that my dread and fear was just because Terry wasn't here.

"Get a fucking grip," I said out loud, "this is what you're here for."

I couldn't stay here, people relied on me and I didn't want to let them down. I stood up and walked to the door with every cell in my body screaming at me not to, the bad feeling almost making me vomit as I turned the handle.

"Fucking hell, we forgot about you," said Smiley.

"No shit," I said.

"Good job you woke up!" said Ivan.

"Any chance of a brew?" I said smiling, standing there in ridiculous Army issue underpants attempting to smile.

"We've got about ten minutes before we get picked up," said Peter.

"I'll get my shit together then," I said.

It never took me long to get ready anyway as I usually had everything to hand in case there was some kind of emergency in the night, those few minutes getting ready made me forget my fears. Back in the kitchen boxes and boxes of bullets were piled high on the table alongside cases of hand grenades. There were different varieties of rounds, green-tipped tracer, red and black tipped armour piercing and the normal round itself, I filled my pockets with boxes of normal rounds then two or three boxes of tracer. Tracer rounds are phosphorous-tipped bullets that burn green as they fly towards a target helping the aim or, depending on where you put them in your magazine, signifying you're almost empty, the standard is that usually every fourth or fifth round should be tracer. And I decided would refill my magazines at the front if I had a spare minute. The remaining pockets I had I filled with half a dozen hand grenades and I was glad I had Terry's ammunition pouch, it saved me having magazines banging around in my leg pockets. Nobody said much, it was a rush to get ourselves prepared and it seemed everyone else was lost in their own thoughts as well. With pockets full and the Kalashnikov feeling reassuringly heavy slung across my back I picked up the Zolya and slung it across my other shoulder.

"I'm ready," I said.

"Have we got everything, we don't know when we'll be back," said Peter ominously.

"Lets just get it on," said Ivan. If he felt fear he hid it well.

"Amen to that," said Farmer Joe, itching to get into the action.

The Germans jabbered away to each other excitedly as everybody surveyed the room, making sure we had everything.

The dawn mist was still clinging to the ground and the sun was just starting to rise as we boarded the lorry, still half asleep and without the black coffee wake up call we were used to. Crny and his men were already in the lorry, along with several other new faces. We stood holding the roof straps as we moved off, swaying and juddering through every pothole and gear change. We were in a convoy of about four trucks, all carrying men armed for the unknown. I looked around me and the faces looked serious and somehow older, there was no joking or laughter now, this was the real thing, this after all was what I had come to do, fighting for a Bosnian village. The thought helped me focus, this is my job, I don't do anything else, it's what I'm here for. The words went over and over in my head trying to convince myself that it was the fear that keeps you alive, but in the pit of my stomach the uneasy feeling remained.

We drove through a few built up areas and villages, all still sleeping, but the nearer we got we noticed the quieter it became. After half an hours drive we reached the edge of another village, the sign said Vidovice. The convoy of trucks were pointed in different directions to park up and we waited, men got out of the cabs and there was a discussion between various commanders. In hushed voices one of them came to the back of each truck, ushering men out into a holding area before pointing them in the general direction of where they were meant to go. It was done quickly and quietly, seventy soldiers standing in a car park would make a good target and we didn't want to hang around. It was our long-haired commander that came to the back of our truck, he simply said, "Come."

We followed him into the part of the village nearest to us, looking around I could see that this wasn't like most of the front line villages we had seen so far, they usually looked like they had been left to crumble for years, with overgrown gardens and thick layers of dust. This one was different, there were lots of unbroken windows and the gardens looked like they had been cared for recently and on one wall I saw a spray painted Serbian cross; graffiti, Serb style. We were in the garage of the nearest house as our long-haired commander spoke to Crny and his men, pointing and talking before they nodded and headed off to the right hand side of the village.

Besides us there were six or seven other men who were already in the garage and by their appearance they had been here since yesterday at least. Unshaven and with a layer of grime and dust, one of them had a fresh bandage around his head, blood seeped through it above his ear. They were wide-eyed and clearly shaken, they wanted out of there more than I did and looked like they were happy to finally see the sunrise and fresh troops, they had done their bit.

From the garage I could see the village was built around one main road, on the other side of the road were farm buildings. The garage we were in was on the outside corner of a sharp bend in the road; to our left the road swayed through the centre of the village, to our right and ahead of us a few hundred metres away the road bisected the last of the farm buildings exiting the village and went through a cornfield to the Serb held village a mile away in the distance. Vidovice looked like it had been evacuated in a hurry only recently; pots and pans lay everywhere, milk carts stood by the side of the road, a building off to the left still smouldered with the occasional red flame flickering from one of the windows and I could see a dog running around wildly, barking at shadows. It seemed like the village itself was holding its breath, awaiting the storm.

The long-haired commander spoke to Peter in Croatian, pointing to the area directly in front of us where the road left the village, Peter nodded away and asked what I assumed were relevant questions.

"In small groups we'll cross the road," Peter said turning to us. "At that farmhouse we'll reorganise and spread out to the left, that's our section," he pointed to the farm buildings to the left of the road that faced the Serb village.

"Talk about front-line troops!" said Smiley raising his eyebrows.

"I bet you wished you had your tank now Smiley," said Ivan.

Our area was every outward facing building from the main road to two hundred metres or so to the left, it was the front of the front. I noticed the man with the bandaged head give me what looked like a knowing smile. If there were to be any action you would bet the main road into the village would be at the centre of it. We skirted around buildings until we were out of sight of the other village in the distance and crouched behind a wall as Peter and

Farmer Joe ran across the road and over a fence to the front-facing farmhouse, then myself, Rommel and Gustav ran across, stumbling over wire fences and hidden lumps of brick. We sounded like a herd of elephants with metal clattering against metal and boxes of ammunition rattling around in our pockets, it took seconds to get to where Peter and Farmer Joe sat crouched by the doorway of the farmhouse but the sweat was dripping off my nose. I was suddenly aware of the smell of shit and rotting food.

"I'm not as fit as I used to be," I said laughing through deep breaths.

"You should start smoking as well!" said Peter, as Ivan and Norbert ran towards us.

"Fucking hell, look at the state of that!" I said pointing to a red-faced Nobby who looked like he was going to be sick.

"OK, I'll take you three to the other end of our line and check out the rest of the area," said Peter to the three Germans. "I'll be back in a minute. This will be our base," he said looking at the rest of us. Rommel translated and I noticed the Germans were totally focused on everything being said. Norbert's face still glowed red from the minor physical exertion.

"See you guys soon," said Farmer Joe.

"Good luck," said Rommel smiling to us.

"Good luck lads," said Ivan.

The four of them scuttled off through a doorway. We were standing in a courtyard area facing towards the building across the road where we had not long came from, behind us was the front room of the farm which faced out to the Serb held village, to our left were the farms out-buildings which stretched for fifty metres before stopping at the main road. On our right were more large agricultural buildings and the door that Peter and the three Germans went into. We each had a look around, getting comfortable with the surroundings. I placed the Zolya against the wall within easy reach and started to empty my pockets of boxes of rounds ready for reloading my magazines, everyone else did the same until it eventually looked like a mini armoury against the wall of the farmhouse.

"Jeeeezus! Would ya' look at that," shouted Farmer Joe.

The door opened out onto a huge modern warehouse, a mesh of broken lighting hung from the ceiling and huge open windows illuminated the scene, the heat and smell radiated out through the doorway. The floor was a mass of wriggling pink skin.

"A Goddam pig farm!"

There were hundreds of them, big ones, small ones, and dead ones being trampled on and eaten. They honked and screeched as they rummaged in the long lines of empty troughs that ran the width of the warehouse, slipping around on their own shit as they barged head down into one another. A dead pig lay on its side near one of the windows, caked in the runny brown mess that flooded the floor as a piglet hammered at what was left of its teats and a couple of others ripped its skin off. The whole scene looked like a sea of giant pink maggots, wriggling and writhing.

The heat from the pigs was overpowering, the sun shining onto the metal roof made it hotter, the stench made me feel sick and the sight of it made me even more uneasy.

"They look like they were well looked after," said Farmer Joe as pigs scuttled away from him.

"The owners must have not long gone," said Ivan.

"I don't like this," said Smiley, echoing my thoughts.

"This is really fucked up," I said, the pigs reminding me of a medieval painting of Hell.

Farmer Joe was away now, into the middle of the pink sea, making the pigs slip and scurry in all directions away from him.

"Ya gotta eat your greens," he was saying to the pigs, waving some sort of rotten leafy vegetable that he had found in front of them.

Smiley, Ivan and I just looked at each other, there were no jokes now, this felt like a mad place and maybe my uneasy feeling was spreading to the others.

"When do you reckon they left?" I said.

"Must have been a couple of days ago, maybe a week by the looks of it," said Ivan.

"Must have been in a hurry as well," said Smiley looking through another doorway. Suddenly a small dog darted out from the room Smiley was looking into and started to yap loudly and irritatingly.

"Fucking hell, I nearly shit myself then!" said Smiley laughing.

The dog didn't stop barking and ran from side to side, stopping at the edge of the courtyard, turning and running back, repeating the pattern over and over again.

"Stroke him," said Smiley as he lit another cigarette.

"It's fucking mental," I said.

"He might be rabid," said Farmer Joe reappearing, still with the rotten green vegetable in hand.

"Must be the farmer's pet, it's too small to be a working dog," said Ivan opening a tin of processed meat.

We watched as the dog ran up and down in the same direction, yapping constantly.

"Here boy!" said Ivan holding out some of the tinned meat.

"He might not understand you if he speaks Croatian!" I said smiling.

The dog paused from its yapping and jumped a few paces towards Ivan, then immediately jumped back again, its eyes fixed on Ivan and the slice of meat.

"If he goes for you we'll have to shoot it," said Smiley matter-of-factly.

"It's not his fault he's here." Ivan was holding out the food as far as he could and at the same time trying not to startle the dog.

With one jump the dog grabbed the ham and jumped back again, then started to repeat its previous pattern of running up and down, this time with the piece of ham hanging out of its mouth, never going further than the courtyard and always in a perfectly straight line.

"Why doesn't he just eat it?" said Smiley.

The dog then ran over to a pile of what looked like ashes, and started digging, then when it must have been deep enough, he dropped the ham into the ashes and buried it.

"What the fuck was that about?" I said.

The sad faces around me said it all and with that the dog started running up and down again. We didn't give it any more food, we didn't want to see a repeat performance.

The low November sun seemed to burn into everything, the heat from the pigs barn was like the blast from an oven, bright sunlight made every surface reflect and shine, we were hot and anywhere else it would have been a beautiful day considering it was the verge of winter, the smell of a weeks worth of pig shit being slowly heated up reminded us where we were.

"This is starting to get a bit surreal," said Ivan looking to the road.

Through the heat haze I could see what Ivan was looking at, a large figure came running towards us.

"Fucking hell it's a cow!" said Smiley.

"Is this Doctor Doolittle or what?" I said.

"We could do without all the animals in the area coming to check us out," said Ivan.

The cow staggered towards us, occasionally stopping and taking a few steps sideways, mooing so loudly it almost sounded like a scream and all the time waving its head from side to side, the dog was unimpressed by the new visitor and continued its yapping and mindless running.

"Now what the fuck do we do?" said Smiley.

"It's just a cow," Farmer Joe said.

The black and white cow stood six feet away from us, staggering from side to side, its head nodding repeatedly, violently mooing at us. It was one of the saddest things I had ever seen and it looked like the others felt the same way.

"Maybe we should shoot it, put it out of its misery," said Farmer Joe.

"You can't do that," Ivan said sternly.

"It's not his fault he's shell-shocked," I said feeling sorry for the mad cow.

"If we started putting all the animals out of their misery we'd be here all fucking day," said Smiley over the incessant din of barking and mooing.

"It's a she anyway," said Ivan correcting me.

The cow started running in circles, still mooing and throwing its head around.

Four heavily armed men watched, sad faced, a mad cow and dog run around in circles, with the smell and screeches of a hundred pigs nearby. It was, as Ivan said, getting surreal. After a few minutes of watching the cow in silence Ivan said in a quiet voice.

"Maybe we should shoot it."

The cow staggered left and right a few more times before heading to the road and breaking into a gallop back the way she came.

"Thank God for that," said Ivan, "must have heard me."

The dog snapped out of its routine and chased after the cow, eventually disappearing behind the other farm buildings, its yapping gradually getting quieter, although we could still hear it in the distance.

"This is shit," I said quietly.

"We've spent the last twenty minutes being freaked out by mad animals," said Ivan, "lets get it together."

"I don't see how we can get across that cornfield without taking casualties," said Joe thankfully changing the subject.

"Hold on, are we attacking that village or defending this one?" I had just realised I didn't know what we were here for.

"I thought we were counter-attacking that one," said Ivan. "Peter is refusing to talk to Crny, otherwise we would know."

"Is that one of theirs, or one of ours that they've took over?" said Smiley.

"No, wasn't it that this village is ours but they took it over, you saw the Serb graffiti everywhere, then we took it back," I said, not sure if I was making sense.

"Then why the fuck are we here if the village has already been retaken," said Joe.

"Unless they took both villages and we retook this one but not the other one?" said Smiley.

"You can't just take two villages that quickly can you? By the time they took the first one we'd have reinforcements in this one," said Ivan.

"If that one is theirs then we can't retake it, because we never had it in the first place," I said.

"The bloke last night definitely said retake," said Smiley.

"There didn't seemed enough guys around here this morning that looked like they had retaken this one," said Ivan. "They must have come from that one."

"So both these villages are ours? If the Serbs had reached this one so recently then you'd think they would have more guys here defending them. I don't get it," said Farmer Joe. Nobody really did.

"Maybe this is a Serb village and we're waiting for them to retake it?" said Smiley.

Ivan shrugged his shoulders. "We'll ask Peter, or find Crny, when he gets back." Nobody could be arsed with this conversation anymore.

Everyone looked confused and none the wiser as to why we were here, the only thing we knew was that the village in the distance was held by the Serbs, Vidovice was ours, until anything changed, we would wait and see what we were told. I had been in this country long enough now not to think about what was going on, but to just get on and do it. There would be a good tactical reason for us being there, you just had to hope you get out of it the other side, unlike the animals. We had switched off and were standing with our backs against the farmhouse wall, Smiley and Joe chain-smoked as we stood with faces squinting in the sun, the only sound was the mad dog barking in the distance, and the occasional too loud screech of a pig. It was good to forget for just one minute that we were there to risk our lives and kill other people, although at least that was the one thing we were sure of.

"Smiley! Joe!" Peter had appeared and was shouting from the other end of the pig warehouse.

"Gotta go boys," said Farmer Joe waving as he entered the house of pigs.

"Fucking hell, here we go then," Smiley said apprehensively.

"Good luck mate," I said to Smiley, Farmer Joe was already halfway through the sea of pig shit.

"You too lads, see you soon," said Smiley.

We watched these two middle aged men slip through the filth and scurrying pigs to Peter on the other side, Peter gave us a thumbs up and then they were gone.

"Just the two of us then," I said.

"Very cosy!" said Ivan. " Shall we retire to the lounge?"

"That would be splendid old chap," I was glad I was with Ivan.

The room was indeed some kind of front room, through the glassless window stood the unharvested brown cornfield rippling gently and a mile away in the distance was the village held by the Serbs. Squatting down out of view we made our way across the room to the dark red sofa with its back to the window, we slouched down on the damp seating so that our heads couldn't be seen.

"Some fuckers nicked the telly!" I regretted it as soon as I said it.

The room looked like it had been recently burgled. Clothes and personal possessions were strewn across the soaking wet carpet, newly made holes in the roof had let last nights rain in and anything of value had been taken. The Serbs that entered this village made sure they looted everything they could; searching through drawers and cupboards, smashing mirrors and picture frames in the process, even the sofa had been slashed open in the search for valuables. What they couldn't take, they destroyed. Clothes that were once worn by the farmer and his family spewed out of drawers, a week ago the farmer would have sat here watching the TV hoping the war didn't come too close, leaving this farm would have meant giving up everything as the family couldn't take their livestock with them.

"Do you think they'll ever come back?" said Ivan.

"The farmer? Could you imagine coming back to this?" I said.

"It's all so personal and recent, I mean, is there any need to just trash the place?"

"And this would have been all they had," I said catching myself rummaging through a drawer.

"Makes me fucking sick, the dirty bastards," said Ivan.

Amongst the wet indecipherable paperwork and nineteen-seventies style shirts in the drawer I found a single Polaroid photograph. A couple in their forties or fifties stood either side of a young man in uniform. The uniform was the old Yugoslav National Army so it must have been their son doing his National Service, the picture looked like it was from the seventies or eighties. It was hard to make out what they all looked like exactly but I could see they were all smiling in the sunshine, the parents proud of their son, the son proud in his new uniform. I handed it to Ivan.

"Fucking depressing isn't it," I said angrily.

"I wonder what they're doing now?" said Ivan inspecting the photo in detail.

The son would be in his thirties at least now, maybe he once helped run the farm or maybe he was still a soldier. What was once a treasured memory was now just another piece of litter in a house that over the next few months would probably become another derelict front line building, furniture used for firewood, old clothing used as toilet paper and inevitably the washing machine or cooker used as a makeshift barricade. There would be nothing for the family to come back to, their home had now been raped and murdered. Without a word Ivan passed me back the photo, I glanced at it again before carefully placing it back in the drawer.

Ivan began to carve on the stock of his Kalashnikov with a tool of some kind he found on the floor. I started to empty my magazines and refill them, inserting tracer rounds along with the normal rounds, we were both distracting ourselves from the fact that we were in someone's home.

After a few minutes Ivan had carved "Eire" onto the wooden stock of his rifle in perfect capital letters as I continued to refill my magazines. When I had finished filling the magazine I carved "Angel of Death" onto the stock of my Kalashnikov. We were starting to get bored now and felt like intruders in that room, as bad as the Serbs. Occasionally we looked over to see the Serb held village in the distance, the only movement was the gently swaying cornfield.

Ivan and I chatted for a while, I took the piss out of his "digger" style hat, which made him look like an Australian soldier the way it was pinned up on one side but he said it had got him this far and wouldn't swap it for anything. Ivan was only a year or two older than me and had been here at least six months. He had seen and been involved in plenty of fighting but he was quiet and polite and saw no need to go on about what he had done and most importantly, he was here for the same reasons as me; partly through a sense of adventure but mostly to stand up and make a difference. I saw he was passionate about what was right and wrong, and truly believed that the people he'd never met, like the farmer and his family, were worth risking your life for.

"If it wasn't for people like us there would be more homeless farmers and ethnic cleansing, I can walk with my head held high, someone once said that the only thing necessary for the triumph of evil is for good men to do nothing," he said.

"Good men? At HOS I wasn't sure if we were the good guys or the bad guys," I said.

"No. You came to Bosnia to make a difference, you left HOS to make a difference and now your sitting here at the front and today hopefully, we'll make a difference," he said. I wished I had his conviction.

We heard movement outside.

"Anybody home?" Farmer Joe said poking his head through the doorway.

"What's going on?" said Ivan as we got up and shuffled our way to the doorway and into the courtyard again, out of sight of the other village.

"We're only the other side of this barn and the Germans are only another hundred metres further on," said Smiley wiping pig shit from his boots.

"Nothings gonna happen until the rest of the reinforcements arrive, thought we'd go find ourselves some food," said Farmer Joe.

"What's Peter doing?" I asked.

"The usual; going around talking to everyone like he's the big man," said Smiley.

"Asshole thinks he's in charge of the Green Berets!" spat Joe.

"Are you going to get some fucking food then or what?" said Smiley. The comedy double act was back, I didn't envy Smiley being with Farmer Joe, he was a maniac at the best of times.

"When's it all going to start then?" asked Ivan.

"They'll be sending out patrols soon to test the Serb defences, then, who knows?" said Joe.

"I'm up for some of that," Ivan said. I kept my mouth shut, as across the road I could see the mad cow again, staggering from side to side, mooing loudly.

"I'll come with you Joe," I volunteered myself.

"I'm staying here, I'm knackered already," said Smiley lighting another cigarette.

"I might go and see if I can find Peter, see when the patrols are going out," said Ivan.

"You're not leaving me on my own!" said Smiley.

We ran back the way we came in, over the fence then across the road, not as wary as the first time now that we were more familiar with the surroundings and more relaxed. We thought we'd start our hunt for food at the garage area where we came in, usually bread is baked fresh every morning then given out at the front immediately along with jam, fruit or whatever else is available and we always made sure we took some of the tins of meatballs with us, but the fresh bread was delicious. At the garage area the commanders were busy discussing the forthcoming events and we made sure we didn't interrupt them.

"Jeez, these guys are still here," said Joe referring to the men we saw this morning that had obviously been here all night at least.

"Lets just get the food and fuck off," I said.

"Had it pretty rough, huh?" said Farmer Joe to one of the unshaven soldiers.

The man nodded and made lots of explosion sounds along with "tromblon" (rifle grenade), "bomba" (mortar), "Srpski" (Serbian), and "grenad" (rocket propelled grenade), ending his description with a loud sigh and shake of the head. You didn't need to understand Croatian to know they'd had a pretty shit time of it.

"Lets get going Joe." I felt nervous around these guys and didn't want to be noticed by our commanders in case they had a particularly dangerous task to be carried out, if they did then Farmer Joe would be the first to volunteer. Trying to hurry things along, I put my fingers to my mouth in the universal sign for food and nodded to the unshaven man. He smiled and walked over to a box in the corner. The box was full of bread, the man picked a loaf up and snapped it in half with a crunch and shrugged his shoulders, it was yesterdays food.

"Hvala, dobro," I thanked him and said "good", also shrugging my shoulders. I wasn't going to complain.

I shoved a couple of the stale loaves in my jacket and Farmer Joe did the same and thanking them, we left, glad to be away.

"Lets go and have a look round, they won't miss us for a minute," I said.

"Sure," said Farmer Joe. "At least the bread won't go stale!"

We plodded up the road until we were almost opposite the house we saw ablaze earlier on and saw a few other soldiers milling around, getting into positions and having a cigarette. In the distance we could hear the rumble of an armoured vehicle approaching.

"Sounds like the cavalry's arriving," said Farmer Joe.

"Best get back in a minute then," I said.

At the end of the road we saw the armoured personnel carrier come round the corner and head towards us, its tracks squeaking and growling, a long line of infantrymen followed behind it. I glanced through the window of the house next to me.

"Fucking hell, look at that!" I said.

"What?" said Joe.

The house had been left for some time; it might even have once been a shop front as the window was huge, though no glass was left. It was grey and dusty inside; there were no obvious signs that the room had been used for anything in particular. In the middle of the grey floor in stark contrast to its surroundings was a large crimson puddle of liquid.

"All that blood!" I said wondering if whoever owned it was still alive.

Joe had a good look at the pool of red liquid; I noticed now that it had footprints in and smeared marks where someone must have been dragged. There was even the sickly metallic smell of blood.

"That ain't blood," said Farmer Joe confidently.

"What?" I said, not quite understanding what he meant.

The pool had absorbed the dust on the floor and was a greyish-red around the edges, the centre of the puddle was a dark red, almost black.

"It ain't blood, I've seen it before in 'Nam. And that ain't blood."

It was a good couple of pints worth and I was no Doctor but I was sure it was blood. In the warmth of the room flies flew in zigzags above the pool of claret.

"What do you mean it's not blood? Of course it's blood," I said, confused as to what else it could be.

"I'm tellin' ya, that ain't blood!" Joe was adamant.

"We're in the middle of a warzone, it's a derelict house and there's a fucking big red puddle on the floor, what the fuck else can it be?" I said wondering if Joe was just saying it to put me at ease and make me feel better.

"It's paint. Blood don't look like that."

"Paint!"

I didn't believe this. I wasn't sure I heard him properly.

"Paint?"

"Yep, that's paint all right. I know the difference between paint and blood, that's paint."

"Paint?" I repeated. "What's someone doing out here with a pot of red paint?" I said.

"Don't know," he said.

"Were they doing a spot of decorating before being ethnically cleansed?"

"Don't know how or why, I'm just telling ya, it's paint." Joe looked convinced that it was paint, and his face was telling me that he didn't like arguments, he was right, that was the end of it. Here was a Vietnam veteran telling me that the big red pool of liquid on the floor of a derelict house in a front line village of war-torn Northern Bosnia was, in fact, paint. Joe was shaking his head.

"But you can see the boot prints in it, the drag marks…"

The deafening rumble of the armoured personnel carrier stopped any further talking, its tracks squeaking loudly on the paved road, I had been too carried away with my insane conversation with an equally bizarre friend to notice the vehicle was right next to us. I turned and looked.

The APC's commander and driver had their heads out and were shouting at everyone and each other, the vehicle seemed huge and out of place, with its heavy metal armour and stubby cannon mounted on the turret rumbling through this village. The back doors were open and I could see men hunched inside, smoking and laughing. Behind the armoured vehicle and stretching down the road as far as I could see were a line of hundreds of men walking to the front in single file; all heavily armed with different weapons, and wearing various makeshift uniforms. It looked like some of them were in fancy dress; with bowler hats, bandannas, woolly overcoats and Vietnam-era U.S. helmets in abundance. Just as I was staring at a man in a white cowboy hat, the mad cow appeared and ran in front of the APC, the commander shouted from his turret and the cow darted from the front of his vehicle, mooing at him before galloping past the soldiers in the direction they had come from down the road. The man in the cowboy hat didn't even notice, behind him flames flickered red through the window of the blackened building. The mad cow ran down the road to our left mooing wildly on his way out of the village.

"We'd better get back," said Farmer Joe.

"Couldn't agree more. Lets get the fuck out of here," I said tearing my eyes away from the strange scene that was in front of me. The uneasy feeling had come back, this was a bad place, I could feel it.

We ran across the road, cutting in between the procession of soldiers, the bread crumbling in our jackets as we jumped the fences. Groups of soldiers were taking up positions and we shouted, "It's OK we're English" to them as we passed as if that made it perfectly normal. We could hear more armoured vehicles driving into their positions around the village.

Ivan and Smiley were still there, Ivan was checking for any movement from the other village, Smiley squatted next to our mini armoury having a cigarette.

"You took your time, it's going to kick off soon," said Smiley.

"You gotta see the amount of guys they got coming in," said Farmer Joe.

"We heard the tanks," Ivan said still looking out over the cornfield.

"It's gonna be a helluva day today!" said Joe

"They've only got yesterdays bread," I said brandishing one of the long loaves from inside my jacket.

"It'll have to do I suppose, but I'll have to complain to the management," said Smiley.

"Right, I'm going to find Peter and see when the patrols are going out," said Ivan.

"Take these for the Germans," I said handing Ivan two loaves of stale bread. "See you soon."

"I'll be straight back as soon as I find out what's going on," Ivan said as he entered the warehouse, sending pigs squealing in the opposite direction.

Farmer Joe put the bread on top of our ammunition dump and lit another cigarette.

"Well, it looks like we're gonna have a party," said Joe smiling.

"And we still don't know what the plan is," I said.

"It doesn't matter, this is Bosnia, nothing ever goes to plan anyway," said Smiley.

We stood around for ten minutes psychologically preparing ourselves for the kick-off but talking about nothing in particular. I was as ready as I could be and was glad I had my friends around me. Tanks and armoured personnel carriers noisily rumbled into unseen positions nearby, men shouted to each other to our rear, confirming their locations to each other. The three of us checked our magazines were safe, weapons cocked and ready to fire, pockets done up so nothing can spill out. I took the end caps and handle off the Zolya so that I just had to pull it apart until it clicked then fire, I hoped I didn't have to use it but as I was the only one who had a vague idea about how it worked I would have to at some point. I'd look pretty stupid if we had a major battle and I came back never having fired it.

I started to look for a decent fire position for the Zolya, when suddenly something out of the corner of my eye made me look round. I turned quickly to see a small puff of dust or smoke from the floor about twenty metres away along the wall from where we were standing.

"What the fuck was th…"

13. Angel of Death

In an instant I was doubled up in pain. It was as if a sledgehammer had violently and without warning hit me in the belly, I dropped to my knees and gripped my stomach as I struggled to breathe.

My head was between my knees when the pain kicked in. A violent burning, stinging sensation above my left hip, I fought for breath, my eyes shut tight against the pain. I didn't know what was going on but I knew something had hit me like a giant punch in the stomach. I automatically tried to feel the area with my left hand but the magazine pouch that Terry had given me was in the way, I could feel the spring from the magazine poking out of the pouch, it was red hot. I sensed the others were shouting and moving quickly, a hand was gripping my shoulder. I wanted them to be careful, my insides could be hanging out but the only noise I could make was a low groan as I fought for air.

"Can you move?" Smiley was crouching down next to me.

I managed to get to my feet whilst still bent double and with my arms wrapped around my waist, my breath came in short gasps. Smiley and Farmer Joe guided me into a doorway and pushed me to the floor. I sat with my back against the interior wall, my knees against my chest, groaning. Smiley squatted next to me, Joe stood by the doorway on high alert, it looked like the courtyard area was out of bounds from now on. My head spun with panic and I wondered if I was dying, I was scared to look at my waist in case I saw my intestines spilling out, maybe me being bent over or my belt were the only things keeping them in so I didn't want to move. It felt like it was on fire.

"Fu…cking…hell," I managed to speak in between gasps of air.

"Put your legs down, you've been winded, deep breaths, stay calm," said Smiley, his voice shaking.

I did feel strangely calm which wasn't right, but I could feel the pain. It was shock. I could have massive injuries but was feeling OK. Slowly and reluctantly I stretched out my left leg, looking to the ceiling I breathed easier but still in gasps.

"It looks OK," said Smiley looking at my waist, the shaking voice now gone.

"Goddam motherfuckers," said a raging Farmer Joe, still scanning the courtyard.

"What…was…it?" I said as if it mattered.

"Rifle grenade, that's why we didn't hear it coming. You OK?" said Joe.

"Du…nno…mate…hurts…like…fuck," I said gasping.

"Nothings hanging out anyway," said Smiley.

I looked down at Terry's magazine pouch, the green canvas was shredded and the spring from one of my magazines poked out of the top. I couldn't see any blood or ripped clothing and a sense of relief washed over me. I gently undid my belt and as I did so the release of pressure almost made me crap in my pants, I was doing everything in a shaky slow motion as I knew the shock could mask serious injuries. I looked at the area above my left hip where the pouch was, my jacket had a couple of small tears but there were no dark patches of blood, Smiley watched every movement. I unzipped my jacket and slowly lifted up my shirt to look at the area of impact. There was a circular wound about three inches in diameter which started seeping dark red blood, that was a good sign, if it was squirting blood then it would have been deep, probably with shrapnel in, this bled slowly but heavily.

"You are one lucky son of a bitch," said Farmer Joe looking at my magazine pouch. "Looks like Terry saved your ass."

I slowly inspected the pouch, it was made of thick canvas and had several small tears in it. I rummaged around in the pouch, taking out each item one by one as they were still hot from the energy of the flying shrapnel. Loose bullets filled the bottom of the pouch. I took out the springless magazine, the side of which had two or three jagged holes in it and still rattling around inside it I could see the shrapnel, twisted pieces of thin razor sharp metal between one and two inches long. My leather belt also had a piece of shrapnel still embedded in it. Everything was hot to touch.

"Fuck me!" I said as Smiley watched in amazement as I fished out the pieces of shrapnel with shaking hands.

"Somebody smiled on you today," he said laughing.

"Take him to the medic and get him checked out, there could be shrapnel in there. I'll go and tell the others," Farmer Joe said to Smiley.

Joe pointed out to Smiley where the nearest group of reinforcements were congregated and thankfully they were only the other side of the fence. My breathing had eased but my hip felt like it was on fire, the sting when clothing touched it almost unbearable. I noticed my whole body was shaking.

"Well, that's me out of here boys," I said forcing myself to exhale.

"The first weapon fired in anger today and you're on the end of it, I don't know if you're lucky or unlucky!" said Smiley.

I zipped up my jacket halfway, making sure all my clothing was as loose as possible, and refastened my belt as slowly and as carefully as I could. Every movement brought a sharp burning pain, making me suck in air through gritted teeth.

"You ain't outta here yet," said Farmer Joe looking for more telltale puffs of smoke and dust.

We were still at the front and another tromblon could land in the area at any time, the medic would be another hundred metres away. I was useless here in pain and the shock was beginning to wear off.

"Ready then?" Smiley asked, obviously dreading the hundred-metre sprint and the added danger of falling rifle grenades.

I attempted to take a few deep breaths as I tried to stand up using the doorframe as support. I was still almost bent double, my left arm gripping my waist, my right arm holding my Kalashnikov.

"OK…Ready."

"See you back at the house, say Hi to the Nurses for me!" said Farmer Joe smiling.

My run was more of a drunken stagger, every footstep felt like I was ripping open the skin on my hip and I was growling in pain as I ran. Smiley's hand gripped the material on my jacket at the shoulder, half dragging and half pushing me forward, he didn't want to hang about though I could hear him wheezing hard. I threw myself over the fence and dropped to the floor letting out a yelp of pain, Smiley's hand grabbed me, pulling me up to my feet and throwing me toward the buildings in front. I was over a foot taller than Smiley and it took immense effort for him to drag and pull me to the building. I staggered through half closed eyes towards the large doorway ahead of me

"Done it!" Smiley sounded like he was going to have a heart attack.

There must have been at least twenty men in the open plan ground floor of the building. They sat smoking or drinking coffee as they talked quietly.

"Need a medic!" Smiley shouted, still dragging me through the room.

The building was different from the other farmhouse, this had been abandoned a long time ago, there were no carpets or possessions in there, only soldiers lining the walls. The men's eyes widened as they saw me, some stood to have a look then smiled as they saw I wasn't too badly hurt, some patted me on the back and I noticed their chatter become louder and more animated at seeing the first casualty of the day. The man I saw earlier with the white cowboy hat was there with a cigarette dangling from his mouth, he smiled and nodded at me as if we were old friends now. The shock of the impact from the rifle grenade had worn off and was now replaced by an adrenaline high.

I was buzzing, I was the man with the red badge of courage, I was alive and I had cheated death. If it wasn't for the full magazine pouch and leather belt I'd either be dead or shitting in a bag for the rest of my life, fifteen minutes ago God had smiled on me and I could feel it. I started to laugh manically. Men scurried around me as Smiley pulled me towards an exit and propped me up against a doorway. I stood leaning against the door frame looking out to the porch, grinning like a drunken idiot. A couple of metres opposite was an identical door. Between the two doors was a concrete floor and roof, to my right the porchway opened out and the concrete floor stopped after several metres, giving way to a grassed area and the main road beyond.

On the grassed area men sat around a smouldering fire; boiling water in a can. I propped my rifle up against the wall and with some effort, managed to stand up straight, the pain had now become a violent sting, though my breathing was almost back to normal. The men were looking at me and talking excitedly in Croatian as I gently took off my belt, the HVO soldiers looked at the magazine pouch in amazement, pointing and laughing in disbelief as it was handed around to the delight of the small crowd.

"Tromblon," Smiley said, informing them it was a rifle grenade.

One of the men had come over, gesturing at me to lift my shirt up.

"Polarko, polarko," slowly, he said.

I winced as I unzipped my jacket then lifted up my shirt, blood had smeared across my stomach under my clothing and the man took a good look at the dark blood oozing out of the wound.

"Think is OK," said the man nodding.

"What the fuck have you been doing?" It was Peter's voice from behind me.

"Can't leave you alone for five minutes," said a breathless Ivan.

"I know! Who's going to fire the Zolya now?" said Smiley, who sounded almost as happy as I was to hear Peter and Ivan.

Ivan put his hand on my shoulder and Peter closely inspected my hip whilst smoking a cigarette. I no longer felt any fear, only relief that they were all there, with my friends around me I felt safe.

"Good to see you. I can't believe it, I was one lucky bastard," I said.

"I know mate, Farmer Joe told us," said Ivan.

One of the Croats handed Peter the belt and shredded pouch, shaking his head and smiling as he did so. Peter took the punctured magazine out, looked at it and started laughing.

"Yep. You are one lucky bastard!" he laughed.

As Peter started to issue commands in Croatian, another face appeared in the opposite doorway. A short fat man was wearing a Vietnam era U.S. helmet and held in his hand a large bottle of Brandy, this was the commander of the group and he handed Peter the bottle. The men started filling in the commander on my injury and he shook his head and laughed, this was my fifteen minutes of fame.

"This is your medal from Bosnia," the Croat medic said smiling as he handed Peter a dressing from a large bag.

Peter undid the cap from the bottle of Brandy and soaked the pad in the liquid.

"This is going to fucking hurt," he said, "you might need a drink."

Peter handed me the Brandy and I immediately took a long gulp.

"Fucking hell," I said as the Brandy's warmth burned down to my stomach. "Better than Rakija though...OK...go for it!"

Peter pressed the wet dressing directly onto the wound, the sting making my legs feel weak as he gently dabbed and cleaned the area, each touch making me want to scream.

"Doesn't look like anything's still in there," he said wiping away blood from the area in case there were other puncture wounds he hadn't seen. Peter threw away the blood soaked pad and poured more Brandy on another.

"Keep this on it," he said pressing the dressing hard onto the hole in my side, the pain almost made me scream. The Croat with the medical bag got out some surgical tape and stuck the pad against my hip. I took another gulp of the Brandy.

"We've gotta go, some of us have work to do," Peter laughed.

Ivan, Peter and Smiley decided that Smiley would stay with me and they would see us all later.

"See you back at the house, and smarten yourself up you scruffy bastard," laughed Ivan.

"Be careful lads," I said. And they were gone.

"You know, I had a bad feeling about today," I said to Smiley.

"I have that feeling everyday," said Smiley lighting a cigarette.

"No, proper bad, like when I wasn't woken up this morning, I was tempted to stay in bed."

"Tell me next time then for fucks sake," said Smiley, "Look, don't read too much into it, you were hit but you were lucky, next time it might be different."

The adrenaline was still coursing through me, making me feel invincible and Smiley was doing his best to keep me in touch with reality.

"I'm as glad as you are to get out of this fucking place," said Smiley.

The men still milled around the boiling water, chatting in the sunshine, a couple of them had gone inside the building on hearing I was hit by a rifle grenade and a new tension filled the air. I was beginning to feel exhausted and wanted to be out of there as soon as possible. As I looked at the men brewing coffee in the sunshine and the road that disappeared through the village to safety in the distance, I suddenly felt drained and tired and the realisation hit me that I'd had enough. No more mad cows or men in cowboy hats or pigs or slivers of jagged metal or bad feelings or cheating death. No, that was it, I didn't want to push my luck any more, my time here in Bosnia had run out and I had done my bit. It was like Terry had said - you instinctively know when it's time to go. God must have given me a break in that split second of the shrapnel being stopped by a magazine pouch given to me by someone the day before. It was time to go home and I could feel that I was no longer invincible, I was scared. I watched as the remaining flowers were rocked by the gentle breeze which brought the smell of diesel fumes with it. My hands were shaking violently.

A deep rumble from further up the road focused everyone's attention.

"Fuck me. Here we go again," said Smiley rolling his eyes as a few more of the men scurried into the safety of the house.

A tank appeared at the far end of the road, going at quite a speed, it was obvious it wasn't just manoeuvring into a safe position. The sun glinted off the glass periscopes on the turret, dirty smoke squirted out from the exhaust as it changed up the gears and I could hear the familiar loud squeak of track on paved road. I still leant against the doorway with my rifle and belt in a pile on the floor, my jacket open and my trousers undone at the waist with my hand pressing the pad into my painfully stinging hip. The tank came closer at speed, it had been spray painted all dark greens, browns and black and on the side of the turret the letters HVO were printed in large yellow paint alongside a painted Croat red and white squared panel. The tank commander and his driver both had their heads out of the vehicle looking in the direction of the Serb village as they sped onwards, their faces stern and hard, eyes focused on the enemy village in front. I could sense an evil fear coming back and felt sick, the closer the fifty tons of metal war machine got the worse I felt, it was bringing my bad feeling with it in all its noise and fumes and oily steel.

It was almost opposite us when the tank commander shouted to his crew, his eyes still focused on the village a mile in the distance. The tank changed down the gears and slowly juddered before gently rocking forward on its tracks to a halt. It was right next to us on the road only twenty metres away, facing the Serb held village down the road.

"Don't tell me it's going to fire from there!" said Smiley.

The tank was guaranteed to draw enemy fire and although it could reverse back up the road at speed to safety, we couldn't.

"Fucking hell, I think I've had enough for one morning," I said watching the exposed tank commander scan for targets using his binoculars.

"Best just enjoy the show," said Smiley in a tone of resignation.

As if on cue the driver and commander ducked down into the tank and slammed shut their hatches. The engine revved loudly sending a black plume of fumes into the air as the turret rotated slowly to the left with a loud whir, the tanks gun gently swaying up and down. Less than thirty seconds later the movement stopped.

The World stopped for a few seconds, holding its breath, the waiting.

Red flame jetted out of the gun as the tank rocked back on its tracks in a cloud of dust.

-BOOM-

The sound wave reached us, ear-splittingly loud. The ground trembled, the pressure change made us gasp for air and loose bricks and timbers fell from nearby houses. The hardcore of soldiers that remained in the grassed area watched, cheering like spectators at a football match.

The tank's engines revved violently, again pouring out more dirty black diesel smoke, the gun swayed onto its target, the first one would have found its range. Another seconds pause, a moments calm.

-BOOM-

The earth jumped in time to the flame spurting from the gun, there were fewer debris falling from houses this time. Everyone was watching, amazed at the power of this massive dirty machine.

The engine, the smoke, its gun moving imperceptibly onto its distant target again. A pause, a jet of flame.

-BOOM-

An earth tremor, a shockwave, the cheering.

"I wouldn't want to be on the end of that," I said to Smiley.

"I'd rather be in the fucking thing," he replied.

Seconds after the tank fired its third round, we could all hear a faint whistling and the cheering was cut short. The whistling got louder and louder as it came closer, over our heads a black smudge flew through the sky, the pitch of the whistle became deeper before the smudge dropped hard into a building out of sight much further up the road to our right, the whistling ending in an almost inaudible explosion. The sound muffled by the walls of buildings. Dust and dirt were thrown in to the air and a wall fell down, the soldiers spoke animatedly to each other discussing whether to head for cover. It was the inevitable retaliation, a Serb mortar trying to hit the tank. It probably needed to be a direct hit to destroy the tank but it would be enough to make the tank back off and at the same time maybe take a few infantry casualties.

I watched the mortar shell fall and the tank fire with the strange detachment of a man who had come so close to death already today, I felt like an objective observer, I had already pulled the short straw and it was now somebody else's turn. I wanted to be away from this place but had become transfixed by the sights and sounds, the pressure wave as the tank fired, the whistling and screeching mortars, louder, closer, the men cheering. The power of the tank firing its rounds that flew faster than the speed of sound and the explosive power of the Serb heavy mortars. The soldiers were cheering like madmen, aware now that the tank was in a duel with a mortar, one would back down or be destroyed. The tank was exposed and it had to fire as many rounds as it could before the mortar found its range.

-BOOM-

The tank paused for a second, not correcting its aim now. Another mortar came screeching over to the right of us. I craned my neck, looking around the wall of the house and I could clearly see the mortar fly through the air, a spinning dark blur. It fell harmlessly away to our right again in a puff of smoke and debris.

"Fucking miles away!" I said to Smiley.

There was more incoming whistling of mortars, now several of them flying through the air, the single range-finding mortar rounds had now become a barrage.

-BOOM-

The tank rocked back on its tracks, black smoke now poured non stop from the exhaust and the throttle down so the engine revved on high constantly.

The whistling again, louder this time. Serb mortars were raining down around us and their impacts sounded like a steady rumble of nearby thunder. Most of the remaining soldiers scattered for cover, running past me into the house or crouching behind the nearest wall, some still watched the proceedings, as hypnotised as I was.

"Where the fuck are our mortars?" I said.

-BOOM-

The whistling became a loud screeching, over our heads. A flurry of screaming black smudges began hitting the buildings nearer to us, the ground rumbling with each impact. I watched the dark objects become bigger as our eyes tried to follow them and we watched one thump into the ground opposite us. A cloud of brown dust and dirt, grey smoke, debris and shrapnel flew up. There was the sound of pieces of metal hitting the tanks armour. It was only forty metres away on the edge of the courtyard near to the road.

"They're getting closer," said Smiley.

-BOOM-

The tank rocked back on its tracks for the last time. It was time for them to go, the barrage of mortar fire was too close and too heavy. The exhaust churned out thick black fumes as the driver put the tank into reverse gear, the hatches flew up simultaneously and the driver and his commander appeared, the commander hammering his fist against the turret, shouting as he looked at the road behind him. Then he turned to us and raised his fist in a salute, the soldiers cheered and saluted him back.

The whistling of another mortar came again, louder and louder and it seemed to be flying through the air forever, soldiers looked up, more ran for cover. This one was a deafening scream as it flew over our heads, there was frantic activity as men darted behind the nearest wall, throwing themselves to the floor at the last minute. I seemed to watch the events unfold in slow motion in front of me passively, oblivious to danger, I took a step forward to get a better look.

"That one's coming closer," I said, stating the obvious.

Out of the corner of my eye I caught sight of the blur of the mortar round as it dropped, hammering into the centre of the grassed area just five metres away.

There was a yellow flash followed by a grey burst of smoke, a plume of dirt sprayed upwards and outwards, a millisecond later there was a huge metallic bang, like a single ring on a school bell. Then silence.

* * * *

Suddenly everything slows down, I feel like I'm moving in mud and my thoughts are filled with fog.

A red-hot blast of air blows through me like the opening of an oven door, rocking me sideways, the sudden change of pressure tightens my chest. I can't breathe, my head feels like it will explode. Men run in slow motion in the dust and smoke, their mouths are moving but no sound comes out, eyes are wide in panic. To the left of me I see Smiley stagger into the wall then fall down out of sight, everything is shrouded in a red-brown fog of dirt and dust and the silence is replaced by a gentle metallic ringing in my ears. The dirty fog seems to envelop my brain, something isn't right, that was too close, I must get into cover, why is Smiley sitting down? Figures dart past me like shadows through the doorway into the building.

Move. Got to move.

I try to move through the invisible mud that surrounds me, but can't feel anything, there is no pain, it is as if my whole body has become numb. I can feel a grinding, crunching sensation from inside my body.

"Oh Fuck. Oh Fuck." I think I am hobbling a couple of steps forwards.

The dirty fog starts to settle, covering everything in a red-brown film of dust. It's no good trying to walk, my legs feel cold and they suddenly give way. I have almost reached the opposite wall but slowly fall onto my left side before rolling onto my back. I look up at the small entrance area, I am at the foot of the wall with my right shoulder up against it, my head pointing out to the road, I can see the sky from here and the wall and doorway where I had stood a lifetime ago is to my left. I can hear muffled voices above the ringing in my ears, the courtyard is deserted but a couple of blurry figures can be seen running in various directions.

I look down at my legs and try to wiggle my toes, my left leg is fine but my right leg - nothing. Why am I lying down? I bend my knees to have another look and sit up slightly, my right knee seems to curve instead of bending at an angle. Shouldn't I be getting under cover? My trousers are darker and I touch them carefully, they're wet and warm. Where is everyone? I think I must have pissed myself. Am I OK? I look at my fingers and see they are smeared in blood.

Then it starts.

A gently pulsing fountain appears, pumping deep red blood six inches into the air from the inside of my curved right knee. I watch the blood squirt slowly into the air in time with my heartbeat. This isn't right. Doesn't it smell horrible? I must stop the flow, I place my hand on the wound and the blood is hot and sticky. I draw my hand away and look at it. Purple-red blood covers my hand and arm, tacky and smeared, sticking my fingers to one another. It looks nothing like paint. I realise I'm injured, but I'm not in pain although I feel a bit cold. It isn't a huge spray of crimson, it is a gentle pumping of hot, red, sticky liquid and I watch it half fascinated, half horrified. I can smell it now; metallic, warm and sickly, gagging at the back of my throat. I look around me and see that it seems to be on everything, the wall, the floor, somebody's rifle, the stuff that makes me live is flooding out and being trodden into the dirt. It keeps on flowing, pumping out what was keeping me alive. There's fucking loads of it, disgusting and sickly smelling like freshly butchered meat, I'm in my own horror movie and I want to move but I can't, I don't know where to go. I can't think straight. Have I just been blown up? Why am I shivering?

"Uh…Help," the words sound pathetic, almost inaudible.

I can see more shadows running, moving in my peripheral vision. More shouting.

"Help." A bit louder, but still pathetic.

The blood is forming a warm pool around my feet and legs, soaking up the dust and making the liquid look black and dirty. I give up trying to stem the flow which is gradually slowing, the blood only pumping a few inches into the air and lay back, looking at the sky and my sticky, blood smeared hand. My panic subsides. I stop shivering.

I know I have something seriously wrong with my leg, but all I can think of is the mess. I see soldiers invade my vision. Of all the places I'd rather be and here I am, with blood pissing out of me. I said I'd had enough, that I was going to go home now and this is what you do. Were you listening? Do you care? I'm one of the good guys, remember? It's me you bastard! I don't feel so cold anymore.

"I want to go home now."

My blood is everywhere. Dark and sticky; the smell of it chokes me and men around me tread and slip in it, leaving footprints and smear marks all over the floor. I can't see my blood fountain anymore, the pumping has slowed along with my heartbeat. Everything is muffled and the only colour is the red-black liquid everywhere.

I said I was tired of it. Tired. So fucking tired.

"Home now please."

Slowly I turn my head sideways, there are more men and some vehicles. Do they know I'm here? My body is numb and warm, I quite like this feeling. My vision is blurred and I have spots in front of my eyes.

I sense a scruffy looking unshaven man touching me, the top of my leg, the inside of my elbow. White material is being wrapped around me covering my right leg, the whiteness looks out of place here in the dirt and blood, a dark patch immediately appears. A clear liquid-filled plastic bag hovers above my head. I have no peripheral vision.

"I think I've had enough of this now."

A whisper. Ssshhhhhh.

I watch my body being tugged, injected, moved and talked to as I lay there, a ragged man in a river of his own blood. It doesn't feel like me any more. My body is warm and comfortable and it feels like I'm in my sleeping bag, cosy and warm. There isn't a cloud in that blue sky and I am being wrapped in the most beautiful warm duvet. I close my eyes.

I don't care now. Can you hear me? Am I dying?

Sleep now. So tired. Ssshhhh.

Sleep now.

A sweet, warm darkness holds me and nothing matters, only sleep.

"WAKEUPMOTHERFUCKERDONTDOTHISTOME!"

No.

Got to sleep, so tired.

"WAKEUPMOTHERFUCKERNOTYETYOUBASTARD"

Need to sleep. Wrap me in the warmth. Leave me. I'm tired.

"YOURENOTGONNADIEHERENOTYETNOTHERE."

Leave me.

"SIMONYOURENOTREADYYETMOTHERFUCKER."

I'm not ready.

I can't die here. The warmth has gone. This isn't how it ends.

My face is being slapped as I force my eyes open.

"YESSSSSYOUMOTHERFUCKERSTAYAWAKE,"
Peter's voice.

"You've got to hold on Simon, you had us worried there, were all here for you."

I open my eyes and see people all around me, my blood is smeared everywhere; on hands, boots and faces. Everyone looks sad and I feel cold. I close my eyes again but the warmth has gone forever, Peter shouts at me to keep my eyes open.

* * * *

I look around me, men stand, staring at the mess that is me, thanking God it isn't them. I can see Peter and the three Germans, they must have heard I was badly hurt and come to see me and I wave weakly to them. Peter is kneeling next to me.

"Thanks for coming," I said in a whisper.

The Germans have tears in their eyes. I look at the scruffy medic that has stopped the bleeding and saved my life.

"Hvala," I said to him.

"Is OK, no problem, you go home now," he said.

"You think you've got it bad, Smiley's got shrapnel through both his arse cheeks!" Peter smiled.

I managed a smile as I looked around me. I was already on a stretcher stained with my blood, a thick white bandage was strapped tightly from the top of my thigh almost to my ankle, the second medic held a bag of fluid in the air which attached to my right arm. My clothes were dark, ragged and wet and I noticed the medics clothes were covered in it as well. The floor looked like a horrific oil spill, footprints and drag marks surrounded the stretcher, blood smeared on every surface. On the grass almost exactly where the mortar landed an ambulance had been parked, an old fashioned Citroen estate, its rear doors open ready for the next customer. I was cold now, the sleepy warmth had gone and I wondered if opening my eyes to this horror was a mistake, I could be asleep now embraced in warmth where nothing would matter. Now I'm cold, sticky and dirty with my own blood, in a place that now looks like an abattoir.

I'm alive but it feels like hell.

Peter, Norbert, Rommel and Gustav all held a part of the stretcher, and then on the medics cue, gently lifted me to waist height.

"You'll be OK Simon. We see you soon," said Rommel.

"We'll come and see you in the Hospital. Keep fighting," Peter said.

The faces were serious, frightened, grown men trying hard not to show emotions and at the same time there was a kindness I had never witnessed. They all took turns to grip my left hand tightly, tears streamed down Norbert's face as he said something in German. I didn't know what to say to them, I didn't have the energy.

As they slid me feet first into the Citroen I held onto Gustav, the others let go of the stretcher and watched as the medics secured it into place.

"Simon, ist OK, ist OK," Gustav said. I gripped Gustav's sleeve as hard as I could, I didn't want to let go and I didn't want the journey into the unknown.

Peter took my fingers away from the Gustav's sleeve.

"I can't do this," I said

"You'll be OK," Peter said.

"I don't want to do this anymore," I said.

Smiley spoke to the others as I lay on my left hand side, facing inwards, my head almost outside the rear of the car, the bag of fluid suspended from the ceiling.

"Go, Go!" said the scruffy medic gesturing to Smiley, aware that more mortars could fall at any time.

Smiley winced as he shuffled to the car and was clearly in pain as he got in and squatted next to me.

"How's your arse?" I said to Smiley.

"Stings a bit mate. You just relax."

The ambulance pulled away and got onto the road as quickly as it could, I watched my friends standing with fists clenched in salute, their faces stony and emotionless as they became smaller as we got further away. I did my best to wave back as we rounded the corner and out of sight, my head bouncing off the stretcher in time with the potholes in the road.

I saw the parked up tank, its engine revved loudly as we passed and I watched it pull out and go back towards the front in the opposite direction to us.

"No smoke! No smoke!" said the blood-covered medic driving.

Smiley had lit a cigarette in the back of the ambulance.

"FUCK OFF!" said Smiley.

"You can't smoke in an ambulance mate," I said almost inaudibly.

"Put your head down and relax, you need to rest," Smiley said in the quietest, gentlest tone of voice I'd ever heard.

The long grass still swayed in the diesel filled breeze, the sky was still a light blue, the sun was higher now making the shadows smaller. It was Saturday 14th November 1992 at about Midday. My body rocked and bounced with the hydraulic suspension as I lay down watching puffs of smoke from another incoming mortar barrage appear in between the receding buildings. As the front line got further and further away I closed my eyes, not caring whether I ever opened them again.

14. The Puppet

I woke up surrounded by masked faces. I was lying on a steel table at the bottom of which near my feet was a plughole. There must have been ten people around the table, wearing white uniforms and surgical masks and hats. This was a Hospital room and it was clean with boxes of surgical equipment on shelves lining the walls.

"Not the boots," I said, raising my head to see two Nurses at each of my feet gently cutting through the leather of my Doc Martens with thick surgical scissors.

The Nurses stopped and looked at each other as two tall men to my right who had previously been whispering whilst looking at the bandaging on my leg, looked up.

"Ingliiski," said one of the masked Nurses, looking at the men.

"You are English?" said one of the men.

"Yes, HVO," I said.

"Relax, we will take care of you."

The Nurses buzzed around me each cutting through different sections of my clothing, gently lifting away the matted, blood soaked rags piece by piece. I could feel my pockets were already empty of ammunition and grenades. Soon I was almost stripped of my uniform, my Yugoslav Army issue underpants on display and it felt like they were stripping me of my identity and dignity as the pile of blood soaked uniform grew bigger. Trickles of blood ran down the steel tray and emptied down the plughole. The small crowd gently pulled and prodded me and the last remnants of uniform were snipped away and lifted off, there was no energy left and my almost naked body was lifeless and white, the red smears of blood covering it in stark contrast.

"Don't cut the watch," I pleaded with the Nurse who held my wrist aloft. My watch was a birthday present from my parents and it was all I had to hang on to.

"Please. Not the fucking watch!"

The Nurse looked at the two men and after a whispered conversation in Croatian, she smiled at me with her eyes before undoing the strap and placing it carefully into a plastic bag. There were more whispered conversations between the two men, obviously about how to deal with the thick white bandage around my leg and what they thought was underneath it.

Thankfully, I passed out into a dreamless sleep before they reached any conclusion.

A tube was being pulled out through my mouth as I opened my eyes, I could feel the long slimy tube coming up from my stomach making me gag and I automatically tried to swallow as it passed through my oesophagus. A Nurse was on standby with a cardboard bowl, placing it under my chin as the end of the tube was finally pulled out through my mouth. I vomited hard, a thick grey sludge soon filled the bowl and the Nurse wiped my mouth with a tissue. I lay back down on the bed as she disposed of the tube and sludge filled bowl, another Nurse adjusted the flow of liquids being fed into my arms.

I was in the corner of a large grey room, partitioned off by wheeled curtain screens. I didn't know where I was or what I was doing here, my thoughts are all jumbled and confused. How long had I been here? Snapshots of blurred memories flash in my mind, disappearing just as I try to hold onto them. I was a soldier and I was lying on the floor. And the blood, lots of blood. My leg was hurt. The window to my right lets the watery light in, rain taps on the window and runs down the pane of glass. The Nurse finally finishes checking the drip and leaves with a nod and a smile.

I lay on the bed aware of the unfamiliar cold white sheets, bags of liquid hung from tall stands around my bed, a mass of tubes were attached to my body, feeding me and draining me of fluid. I looked down at the bottom of the bed where both of my feet stuck out from the end of the sheet, I noticed my right foot was a greyish colour, but at least it was still there. My body ached and stung everywhere, even my left leg that I thought was undamaged, my arms felt dead due to the constant insertion of needles and feeding tubes into my arms and the back of my hand making them numb. A man in the bed next to me groaned loudly through the curtain partition as if he was trying to get words out that would never come.

I looked at the ceiling unable to summon the energy to move, I was like a broken puppet with plastic tubes instead of string holding my arms. I closed my eyes again hoping that I would wake up, all time and reality had been distorted, brief snapshots of events jumped into my head; the ambulance, the steel slab, my watch, the tube down my throat. I drift in and out of consciousness. Nothing was continuous, it was like having a weird dream but you're not sure if you're awake and it's real or you're asleep and dreaming. I kept my eyes tightly shut. It seemed like only minutes ago I was watching the grass sway under the clear skies.

There must have been a dozen of them around me this time, talking quietly in Croatian, I could hear the word "Ingliiski" and they looked more interested in the Bulldog and Union Jack tattoo on my right arm than with what the Doctor in charge was saying. The sunlight was brighter now and the rain had stopped. A Nurse took down an empty bag of blood from the tall metal stand next to my bed and put a fresh one on as the man who I assumed was the Doctor ushered the other white coated people out on seeing I had woke up.

"Sorry to disturb you," he said, his English perfect.

"It's OK," I could hardly speak, my voice hoarse and sore.

"We almost lost you. You lost so much blood," he said, as I recalled the soldiers slipping around in my blood.

"Am I OK?"

"You need lots of blood, but Croatian blood is good," he smiled. "We also managed to save your leg."

He gently lifted the sheet from the side of my leg, it still seemed to have the same bandage but sticking out from the side were five steel rods all joined together by one vertical bar, the joins were adjustable screws and reminded me of Meccano. The rods started at my knee and finished at the top of my thigh.

"Each of these bars is screwed into a piece of bone, this other bar holds it all together."

It was broken in five places from my kneecap to mid-thigh and must have been difficult to repair but they had somehow managed to fix it all together, some of the rods were just inches away from one another.

"The area behind your knee was also destroyed which is why you lost so much blood." It was too much to take in and he must have seen my eyes start to glaze over. "I will see you later, the Nurse will help you with the pain."

I didn't need the Nurse, I passed out again. I don't know how many times I drifted in and out but it always seemed to be daytime. The pain of movement always waking me up. I was drained, my survival instinct had kept me from dying but it didn't prepare me for this. I was disorientated and in agony, the slightest movement caused a tug from a drip or the catheter and my leg would crunch and grind, the broken pieces of bone rubbing against each other despite the external metal frame. I had no sense of time or place, just a partitioned grey room and pain, lots of pain. Every time a Nurse with a needle approached I wondered on which attempt they would hit the collapsed vein.

I woke up in agony again, this time it was my stomach that was hard and swollen, I felt as though I would burst because the pressure was so unbearable.

"Nurse," I attempted to shout, my voice a gravelly whisper.

A Nurse rushed in immediately and I pointed to my swollen abdomen. The Nurse touched the hardness of my belly then checked the bag that hung down from the side of my bed that drained my bladder. It was empty, the Nurse rushed off to get the Doctor. I looked under the sheets at the tube coming from my penis, it was the first time I'd even checked it was still there and I noticed my pubic hair had been partly shaved and a large stitched incision was on the right hand side, as I was checking myself the Doctor came in with several Nurses. The female Doctor checked me over, pressing my rock-solid urine-filled bladder as gently as she could whilst checking the empty bag. The Doctor barked orders and the Nurses scurried around the bed.

Within minutes I was on the steel slab again, now naked apart from the tubes that were attached to every limb and appendage and the metal ladder-like frame that jutted from my thigh. The medical staff surrounding the metal bed spoke quickly to each other through surgical masks. They didn't speak to me and only gave me an occasional glance until the speaking finally stopped dead with nods of agreement. Now they all stared down at me, pathetic and naked on the giant steel tray. Nurses gently held my shoulders and arms, another held my left leg. They were pinning me down. The Doctor placed one hand on my painful abdomen above my half shaved pubic hair, the other hand gripped the catheter at the end of my penis, she then looked at me and nodded. I nodded back. I should have felt fear, but felt nothing, my emotions long since exhausted and replaced by confusion. It took some effort from the Doctor, but the long thin wire-like tube slid out gradually. It felt like my insides were coming with it as I gritted my teeth and growled my way through the pain. The catheter bent its way out and with every inch the burning sensation increased. I could feel the Nurses struggling to keep my shoulders against the bed, every sinew and muscle in my neck stretched almost until they snapped as I tried not to scream.

As the Doctors arm came fully back, catheter in hand, there was an explosion. Red-hot orange-red piss spurted out from my penis, burning like a river of acid over my chest and stomach. I had never screamed up until that point. My body tensed involuntarily against the gushing agony from my penis, my upper body raised from the bed as more Nurses came to press down on my shoulders. Nurses closed their eyes and turned away. I screamed until all the dark burning piss was drained from my bladder. It took some time.

I was panting and shaking now, I had never known pain like that. Nurses opened their eyes and looked at me in a mixture of disgust and sympathy, the Doctor nodded to me, I nodded back, still trembling. The acidic, stinking urine was carefully mopped up so that none soaked into the bandaging, then they washed me down by hand. As gently as they could, I was lifted onto my clean white bed, the grinding of the bones in my thigh now just a distraction and pushed to my space in the corner, shaking and exhausted. I told them I'd piss into one of the cardboard bowls from now on and I think they were relieved.

After seeing the sight of my half shaved pubic hair I made an effort to assess myself. I had to lift the single white sheet as slowly and as carefully as I could so as not do knock any of the drips in the inside of my arms or the tap in the back of my hand, and had to make sure the sheet didn't catch on one of the bars sticking out of my femur. The stitch at the top of my right leg where my pubic hair had been shaved must have been where they clamped the artery to stop the blood flow during the operation, my left leg had a huge rectangle of padded material stuck down with surgical tape. It ran up the inside of my thigh from my knee to my groin and the area of skin around it was dead and numb, I didn't have a clue why it was there but at least now I knew why my left leg was so painful. My right leg just felt like a piece of meat attached to my hip, there was no feeling apart from the crunching of bone and my blue-grey foot already looked dead. Another square of padded material was taped down above my left hip which was my original shrapnel wound, the one where I thought I was lucky to be alive. I thought about the explosions. Was I lucky to be alive? Being blown up in two separate occasions on the same day would be considered pretty fucking unlucky. I remembered the feeling I had that morning; an overwhelming fear, an uneasy feeling. I thought back to what Smiley said about not reading too much into it, it just happened, tough shit.

The Nurse gently slid a needle in and out of the back of my hand, she looked at me apologetically as I winced with each insertion. It couldn't be easy trying to find my veins as they had all collapsed when I bled out, so she finally gave up and smiled at me before leaving to get another Nurse. The sites in my arms were sore and matted with congealed blood, there was a site on my right hand which they used to shoot antibiotics or pain relief into which always felt like a golf ball being forced down a hosepipe and that too was sore and covered with the red jelly-like blood.

The Nurse returned with a new, miserable-looking female Doctor; she was short with mousy brown hair and a large nose and reminded me of an English teacher I had at school, she never smiled either.

"We have a problem finding somewhere for injection, yes," said the Doctor smiling.

"Afraid so," I said with a sigh.

The Doctor scrutinised the back of my hand.

"Mmm, maybe one more try? Is OK?" she said.

"Go for it," I said, what choice did I have, the stuff had to go in somewhere and I was beginning to get used to the feeling of needles being slid into my skin.

The Doctor held my hand with the palm facing down, and gently prodded with the fingers of her other hand trying to find where "X" marked the spot and when satisfied that she had found the location, out came the needle. She slid the needle in as slowly as she could until she frowned.

"Is no good," she said, slowly withdrawing the needle.

She looked deep in thought. "We have to put this in, is for to stop infection," she said waving the long needle, "we may have to use your…erm…" She was pointing at the side of her neck, not knowing the word "Jugular Vein" in Croatian. Fucking fantastic. Now they wanted to stick a tube in the vein in my neck, this wasn't something I could prepare myself for and the very idea of it filled me with horror.

The female Doctor had found another Doctor and a couple of Nurses, which seemed to be happening a lot with me, maybe next time they would just come in a group and get the discussions over and done with before the pinning down and the start of the pain. The Doctors had a long discussion about the next step, the back of my hand was inspected again and the new Doctor had a good look at the existing sites with a shake of the head, then more talk which included the word "neck", followed by nods of agreement all round. He was older with greying hair and a serious face hidden beneath the wrinkles of a heavy smoker.

"OK, this man in charge. He say is only way to get fluid in. We don't like to do this. It can be very uncomfortable," said the female Doctor, her hand on my shoulder as she said the last sentence. "Is OK?" she said.

I took a deep breath, "Is OK," I nodded, though I was very far from OK. I was about to have a fucking long needle stuck into the side of my neck, though by now I was just a passive recipient of everything they threw at me without question or explanation. I didn't like it but what choice did I have. The Nurses went to each side of the bed and undid bolts on the side of the frame before lowering the top half of the bed until I was completely horizontal.

"Now you go back so more blood," she said.

I didn't have a clue what she meant until the same Nurses turned another lever on the frame of the bed and slowly tilted me so that the whole bed was at an angle with my head lower than my feet. Blood started to hiss in my ears as the male Doctor unwrapped a new sterile needle from its packaging. It was bigger and longer than the one meant for my hand.

Inside I was screaming. I was uncomfortable and in constant pain and now a huge needle was about to be pushed into a vein in my neck. Why is this happening to me? I thought about the warm comfort I felt as I lay bleeding to death, when? A few days ago? A week ago? Yesterday? I had opened my eyes as Peter had slapped me, I wasn't ready to die and yet here I am not feeling like I'm alive. It felt like I was in between life and death, just existing, in limbo. I took a few deep breaths as the needle got ever closer in his hand, getting bigger and bigger.

"Maybe uncomfortable, you must relax."

My head was turned away now so he could see his target, and I couldn't see the needle. Relax she says! Easier said than done. I grit my teeth as the needle touches my skin. The initial sting of the large bore needle piercing my flesh and a trickle of warm blood runs up the back of my neck into my hair. I exhale slowly as the needle is pushed in and downward towards my chest, I feel like my ribs are going to explode and my collarbone is about to snap.

"Is done now, OK."

"OK," I only wanted to whisper, it felt like the needle had gone into my heart, there was a sharp pain in my chest and I could only breathe shallowly. I was too scared to move my head in case the needle was pushed deeper in.

Nurses move quickly but gently, returning the bed to almost its original position as the two Doctors clean and secure the tap that sticks up from the right hand side of my neck. I lay like a statue, frozen in the fear of movement and pain. The bag of opaque yellow liquid is finally hooked up to my neck, another drip, another string for the puppet.

"Not long. OK," she says.

"OK," I whisper not daring to move my eyes.

The Doctors and Nurses clear up before leaving. It seems they can't get out of there quick enough and nobody looks at me. I'm on my own again, staring at the curtain partition to my left, the man on the other side groans like a drunk attempting to speak. I don't know how long I lay there immobile, listening to the man trying to scream, staring at the aqua blue curtain partition. Every twitch of my body, every breath, was agony. My leg was shattered and dead, parts of my body sliced open and stitched back together and the drips and tubes were ropes tying me down. I wanted to scream so loudly that I lost my voice, scream until it was all better. I wanted to cry, just to start weeping and not stop. If I close my eyes I can dream I'm running and if I could run I'd never stop, taking big deep gulps of fresh air as my legs and arms pumped away, the sound of my boots hammering the pavement. God, make it stop. The tears wouldn't come, and like the man in the bed next to me I couldn't scream. I lay there, a body, testament to the human beings ability to survive anything God throws at them. Staring at the curtain, listening to the man groaning as I struggled for breath and pinned to my bed by stuff that kept me alive, I wished I were dead. Still the tears wouldn't come.

I don't know how long they had that thing in my neck for, it felt like eternity but it could have been minutes as I was still drifting in and out of consciousness thanks to the constant sedation. Eventually I could take no more, I thought I was going to have a heart attack as the pain in my chest was so great.

"Boli, yako boli," I said hoarsely, attempting to indicate my chest.

My Croatian had improved, I could now say "Nurse" (Sestro), "pain" (boli), and "big pain" (yako boli), which were just about all the words I needed at the time. The Doctor understood and again went for a posse of other medical staff.

"Your breathing not good?" said the female Doctor, I was starting to like her because she was a constant presence, a little bit of familiarity even though she never smiled unless she was giving me bad news. I tried to point without bending my elbows to the various parts of me that hurt; my collarbone and my chest, the tap in my neck was more of a serious irritation compared to my chest pain.

"You have enough in now, we can take it out," she said as a Nurse handed her some latex gloves.

The bed remained in the same position this time as I turned and looked at the curtain again, by now I knew every fold and stain. The needle slid out gently as blood trickled down my neck and chest and onto the white sheets. Almost immediately I could breathe properly and took some deep breaths, letting my chest expand as I gulped in air.

"Hvala," I said.

I now had a drip in each arm and a tap on the back of my right hand for the injections that I regularly had. I had also, after a few mishaps, learned to urinate into the bowl they gave me. I was feeling better, probably because I had got used to my situation but also the Nurses would often look in to say "Dobar Dan Simon" to me. I didn't feel so alone now, maybe because I was the foreign stranger that had come all this way was the only reason they wanted to look, though I didn't mind being the freak show as long as I saw a smiling face. One of the patients gave me a copy of the International Herald Tribune and I tried to read every word, though the words became jumbled after only a few sentences and the young Muslim with his arm in plaster insisted on sitting with me as I read it, but it felt good, almost like I had a visitor. I discovered I was in Slavonski Brod, one of the largest towns on the River Sava and the first stop for casualty evacuation, soon I would be going to a Hospital in Zagreb and the groaner in the bed the other side of the curtain partition had a brain injury thanks to a Serb Mortar. I found out that I had been in this Hospital just four days. Now that my thinking was less confused I was looking forward to getting better; I thought a few months of Hospital then I'd be up and about again. I even debated to myself whether I should return to the front or hand myself in to the British Army and go home.

On one occasion I woke to see a hand-written sign pinned to the curtain, which read: "UNPA ZONA" - UN Zone. A Nurse came in to take my piss-pot away; she was the unlucky one.

"Nema UNPROFOR!" I said pointing at the sign.

"Sto Shest Brigada Hah Vey Oh!" not UNPROFOR, 106 Brigade HVO, I said angrily.

The poor girl looked bewildered and ripped the sign down and took it, and my piss-pot out with her. I felt a bit guilty at having a go at her. After a few minutes the female Doctor came back.

"Hello Simon," she said, "the sign was a...erm...you say joke?"

"OK, I am HVO, your Army, not UN," I said, "please say sorry for me, I didn't mean to shout at the Nurse."

"Yes, she is crying, very upset because was only joke," she smiled, "we know you are with our Army."

Now I felt like a complete wanker. They were entitled to their joke, after all I can go home to Britain and away from this war, they live it every day. The Nurse came back in later on with another empty pot for me, her eyes were red. I didn't know the Croatian for "Sorry" so I placed my hand on my heart, smiled and said sorry in English, she smiled back. I still felt like a wanker.

"Later, you go Zagreb," said a smiling Nurse.

"Today?" I couldn't believe it.

"Yes, today."

I smiled, I wanted a change of scenery more than anything else, but I would be further from the front and the soldier I was, and may never see the faces of my friends again. It was also a step into the unknown, here they had patched me up and stabilised me, in Zagreb I had to get better. I would also have to inform the Embassy that I was an AWOL British Soldier and hand myself in. I had thought about staying in Croatia, despite the war I had fallen in love with the place and its people, Jelko and his scum friends were the exception to the rule. Deep down though I knew I had to go back, I had family that must be worried sick and the Army would probably give me a slap on the wrist and it would be back to normal. In reality I didn't belong here, I would always be a "stranger."

A group of Nurses came in, chattering away to each other, smiling and laughing.

"You are busy man today Simon, you have visitors," said the Nurse.

The Nurses took the brakes off the bed and pushed it along with all my drips, down a corridor. It was the first time I had seen outside the grey room apart from the room with the metal bed. I saw the groaner, his head bandaged and surrounded by drips and bags that disappeared into his arms and up his nose, he looked only slightly older than me. At the end of the corridor a group of figures stood behind a door talking to a Doctor, I recognised a hat. The Nurses pushed me into a space at the end of a corridor and applied the brakes, still smiling and chatting.

"Not long, soon you go, only three friends allowed, sorry." And away she went with her happy colleagues.

After the last few days of semi-consciousness and lying immobile on the bed I was confused, it was all too much to take in. Was I asleep again?

"We forgot the fucking grapes," Smiley's northern accent had never sounded so good.

"You're lucky, I'm off to Zagreb today," I said still bewildered.

"We thought we'd better come as soon as we heard you were stable," said Ivan.

"You had us all worried you bastard," said Peter.

"The Doctor said they nearly lost you," said Ivan.

There was smalltalk about my injuries and the shrapnel going through Smiley's arse cheeks, it was all a blur but I was glad they were there so we could say goodbye properly.

"We've brought all your stuff, but they said you can't take it, there's no room in the ambulance," said Peter.

"Don't worry about it, split it amongst yourselves," I said.

"We gave your passport to the Doctor, it'll go with your files."

I can't remember what we talked about, mostly about how crap I looked and a hundred jokes about Smiley's war wound. I was just happy to see their faces, smiling and joking like nothing had happened as if we were back in the house. I could see Farmer Joe and the three Germans standing behind the door.

"What a waste of a day," Smiley said quietly.

"Gustav went a bit apeshit when we got back to the house, unloaded three magazines into a wall," said Peter.

"After you were hit we just wanted out of there. We watched their incoming mortars and it looked like hell on earth watching them throw everything they had at the village, everything was shredded," Ivan said. "Another guy died on the patrol we went out on. Turns out that one of our mortars had a misfire and the round got stuck in the tube so the position had to be evacuated which is why we had no mortar cover. Apparently we were there to retake the village and cut the road to Brčko, if we could cut the road we would have cut the Serb supply lines to the Brčko pocket. It didn't happen."

I was glad Ivan told me the background to the days events, It was a pivotal moment for all of us when I got hit. Some had never seen a casualty, let alone one that was a friend and the reality of it had hit home. This part of my life was over now, I knew I would probably never see these men again but at the same time never forget them and they would never forget me, even if it was for all the wrong reasons.

"Time to go, sorry," said the Nurse returning with her gang.

"I'll look you up when you get back," said Ivan.

"Say Hi, to the others for me," I said.

"Get yourself better, we need you back," said Peter only half joking.

"Take it easy mate, we're thinking of you," said Smiley.

"Keep your heads down and stay safe. I'll see you again sometime," I said. From behind the door Farmer Joe and the Germans smiled and gave me the thumbs up, the three others smiled and waved their goodbyes as the Nurses wheeled me past the groaning man and back into my little corner of Slavonski Brod.

"We will come back soon, when ambulance is ready," the smiley Nurse said.

It wasn't long before they came for me. I said "Hvala" to everybody I saw, I wanted them to know I was thankful for what they had done for me and though I did not know their names, I would always remember what they had done. Doctors and Nurses waved goodbye, some even said "Goodbye Simon," the miserable female Doctor picked up the folder containing my medical notes and came with the group of Nurses, escorting me outside. The ambulance was the same type of old Citroen estate with hydraulic suspension that I had travelled in when I first was injured, easy I thought, a few hours watching the Croatian landscape go by, then the big city.

The breeze was cold on my skin and the sky was grey, but still brighter than my room in the Hospital. Slavonski Brod looked like Orašje, a communist-era grey, with all the ground floor windows and doors sandbagged or with large timbers covering them, the difference here though was that all the shops were open and cars buzzed around the streets whilst people put up umbrellas against the steady drizzle. I closed my eyes and felt the rain on my face, clean and cold, licking my lips to taste it. The Nurses were in no mood to hang around to get rained on. Unsmiling Doctor handed the folder of notes to the Nurse that would be travelling with me, trying not to get them wet from the rain, then turned to me and said.

"Good Luck Simon."

"Hvala," I said smiling.

The Nurses slid me into the ambulance head first, clipping the bags of fluid onto hooks in the ceiling, the metal frame on my right leg brushing the inside of the ambulance wall, I squealed as my leg crunched as they pushed me as far as they could towards the wall, leaving man-size space to my left. I should have known nothing would be easy.

"I very sorry, soon in Zagreb," said the escorting Nurse as another gang of medical staff pushed a bed towards us.

"Oh fuck! You're joking!" I said.

It was the groaner. Tubes still flowed out of his nose, arms and from under his bed sheet, though there was no bandage around his head now. A bag of urine was placed near to his feet as he too was pushed up alongside me, his eyes closed, asleep or unconscious. I didn't care as long as he stayed that way. The Nurses waved their goodbyes and ran back inside the Hospital. The escorting Nurse gave me a tablet to help me sleep for the journey.

"Not long, just sleep and we will be there," she said closing the rear door and climbing in alongside the driver.

It would have been claustrophobic at the best of times, but here I was, side by side with a man with a brain injury amid a tangle of tubes, it felt like a giant coffin. I did my best to nudge away from the side of the car, my ultimate fear was of the metal frame on my leg hitting against the interior steel wall of the ambulance. The car pulled away from the Hospital and drove through the streets of Slavonski Brod until hitting the motorway. The man next to me was once handsome and young looking but now his jet black hair was shaved and a long red scar ran from his ear across the top of his head to the other side, on his forehead and around his eye the jagged shrapnel scars were still raw and new.

I don't know how long we had been driving when I was woken by the groaner, he moaned pathetically, reminding me of the mad cow I had seen in Vidovice. His eyes were half open and his arms flailed around in slow motion. I patted his arms away from me and used my left leg as a shield as his body moved as fast and as hard as his damaged brain would allow, I was afraid he would rip the tubes from my arms or a sudden spasm would push me in to the side of the car, my external frame taking the full force. His hand went beneath his bedsheet before grasping something, his arm strained against the tube that drained his bladder.

"Sestro! Sestro!" I shouted to the Nurse up front.

She turned around and saw what was going on, there was a quick conversation with the driver and the ambulance pulled sharply onto the hard shoulder. Before we came to a stop there was a loud "snap" as he pulled the catheter from his penis, his arm waved around again, now with the unattached piss tube in his hand. Cold urine splashed across my face and chest as I fought to keep his arm down and away from my drips and me. His groaning became louder and more forceful, his brain searching for words it could never find. The Nurse already had the syringe in her hand as the rear door was flung open. Within ten seconds he was asleep again.

"I am so sorry," she said mopping up the spilt piss.

"It's OK," I said, relieved that I had got out of it unscathed apart from being covered in another mans urine.

I turned my head away as the Nurse quickly reattached the catheter, the man deserved some dignity. The Nurse gave me another tablet and when she was satisfied everything was secure, we drove away again.

I didn't fall asleep straight away this time, I was still nervous of the groaner who I now felt immensely sorry for and at the same time realised how lucky I was. Was he trapped in his own brain, aware of everything but unable to express anything? Or was he just a vegetable who a couple of months ago was running through fields with a rifle just as I was? I wondered if he would have been better off dead, a martyr for his village. I lay looking up and out of the window, the rain making diagonal rivers in the glass as I watched the grey skies occasionally blocked by the sides of green hills or mountains. It was getting dark as I fell asleep again.

The back door opened and the inside of the ambulance was flooded with the glow of orange streetlights. The Nurse put the interior light on and I saw that the groaner was still out of it. A cluster of Doctors and Nurses stood at the rear of the vehicle, papers were handed over and conversations about the journey were had before the groaner was slid out.

"Good luck mate," I said to him quietly as he was carried away.

The Nurses slid me out onto a bed, my leg grinding at the movement, I noticed there were fewer sandbags here and it was the first time I had seen the night since I had been injured.

"Sorry for the journey," said the Nurse as I lay on the wheeled bed.

"No problem, hvala," I said waving.

"Goodbye and good luck," she said as she climbed back into the passenger seat.

The Nurses wheeled me into the new Hospital. They chatted away before one of them noticed the Bulldog tattoo on my arm.

"Ingliiski?" one of the Nurses said.

"Da, HVO," I said wanting to make sure they knew I was one of them.

The Hospital looked modern and clean, all the lights worked and the smell of industrial strength cleaning fluid filled the air. The Doctor was flicking through my notes as we reached the lift, the Nurses were still laughing and talking quietly. One of them looked down at me, laughed and said,

"Welcome to Zagreb!"

As the lift ascended it suddenly dawned on me that I had forgotten to ask for my watch back.

Terry, Smiley and Myself in the same front line house.

A Picture of the Serb lines, the bridge (with the rails) clearly visible.
The left hand house is the one that "Beardy" and "Bomber Jacket"
attempted to take cover in.

A view from the upstairs fire position, this is the wall that almost caved in when the Serb Heavy Machine Gun opened up at me.

Below: After a shift at the front.

Above: The house immediately behind the front line. It was this position that Norbert, Rommel and myself ran to when we heard the tanks engine.

HOS' International group posing in front of the River Sava whilst visiting the town of Orašje. L-R: Mahmood (Turkey), Terry (England), Myself, Peter (Holland) and Smiley (England). Kneeling down is Želko Čelik (Croatia)

Below: Farmer Joe (USA)

Right: Marco Tigrić (Croatia)

Peter (in camouflage uniform) pays his respects at the funeral of Andreas Bühner (Germany), on the right of the picture is the Hungarian Elias Laszlo.

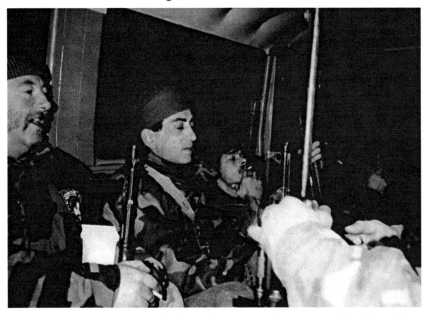

A picture of us cramped inside the van on the way to the front line, L-R: Smiley, Mahmood and Farmer Joe.

Sasha (Slovenia) and Myself.

Farmer Joe and Peter enjoying coffee and cigarettes at the front line
positions.

The USDDR Ceremony for fallen foreign volunteers in Vinkovci, Croatia, November 2008. I am third from the left, Ivan the Irishman wears the eyepatch.

The end of a long journey. My moment of reflection, Vinkovci, 2008.

15. Pain and Prayers

They wheeled me into a room with four other beds all in a line next to each other, my bed was opposite the door, the furthest bed was next to the window on the far wall. It was dark and most of the other patients were asleep but I could see the man in the bed next to mine. He was an elderly man, bald and with no teeth but as tall as me, his eyes were sunken and his breath came in rasps. It was strange being around civilians after all this time in a military atmosphere. And I was still pissed off about my watch.

"You sleep now, we see you in the morning," said one of the Nurses after replacing a bag of fluid and injecting me with something.

I stayed awake for some time, I was thirsty and the sounds of the other patients so close to me would take some getting used to, all I had known up until that point was my own little world of pain and discomfort. God I missed my Walkman.

The Nurses woke us up early the next morning, checking fluids and talking quietly. The winter sun streamed through the window at the end of the room reflecting brightly off the white paintwork. The old man next to me hadn't moved, his breathing still loud and shallow. The patient nearest the window laughed and joked with the Nurses, he was in his early twenties and had a full leg plaster, I heard the word "Ingliiski" and they looked over, I nodded to them and smiled. A Doctor came in to check us all over along with the Nurses and there were serious faces when they looked at the old man.

"So, you're are the Englishman," said the Doctor looking at my notes.

"Yes," I replied as the Nurses looked at the tattoo, it seemed it had become my replacement passport.

"We will change your bandages today and see how much it has healed, what is this?" he said looking at my chest.

I had been scratching my chest all night, it was itchy but I had thought no more about it, but looking down I saw large red blotches covering me.

"It's a bit itchy," I said feeling like a bit of a idiot. After everything that had happened a reaction to the medicine was the least of my worries.

The Doctor scribbled something down on my notes and spoke to the Nurse.

"You have an allergic reaction to the medicine from last night, we will change it, no problem," he said as he turned for the door and left.

A while later Nurses appeared again, this time with a large trolley full of trays. So much had happened since yesterday I was still struggling to take everything in, my brain was only just starting to catch up with the events that had started just a week ago with the mortar explosion. There were fewer drips in my arm and although the pain was there, it was less constant, just the sharp pain of the stretching stitches in my left leg when I moved and an uncomfortable grind when I accidentally moved my right leg. I had forgotten to ask why I had my left leg sliced open and stitched back together and I desperately needed to shave, the weeks worth of facial hair was itchy and made me feel grotty.

A tray of bread and jam was placed on my bedside table and I suddenly realised I hadn't eaten or even felt hungry for a week. I stared at the plate, the bread was fresh and warm but the jam reminded me of blood. I still didn't feel hungry but the drips must still be doing their job, I nibbled at the bread though swallowing food seemed strange and uncomfortable, my belly immediately felt full.

"Dobar Dan." It was the man nearest the window, sitting upright and waving to me.

"Dobar Dan," I replied, waving back over the two other sleeping patients in between us.

He said some questions in Croatian that I didn't understand, I shook my head and looked confused.

"Armija?" he said.

"Da HVO," I said realising that he was asking me if I was a soldier, up until that point I had thought it was obvious but I was amongst civilians now.

"Dobro, dobro," he said, then pointed to his leg and shrugged his shoulders.

"Srpski bomba," I said, assuming he wanted to know how I was injured.

The man gave a pained expression and shook his head.

"Ingliiski. HVO. Dobro, dobro," he said smiling and clasping his hands together and shaking them, he was well pleased. I was the man again.

Two Nurses entering the room cut our tricky conversation short as they began fussing around my bed, they saw the almost untouched food. The Nurse asked me something in Croatian and smiled.

"Ingliiski!" said the man by the window to the two Nurses.

An expression of realisation spread across their faces as the man continued to tell them everything he knew about me though I only understood the words "Srpski Bomba." The Nurses smiled, all the Nurses I had met so far in Croatia seemed to be beautiful and this girl was no exception, her long dark hair in a ponytail and her eyes warm and smiling. She pointed to the food and frowned and shook her head.

"No Dobro?" she asked.

"Dobro, dobro," I said making sure she didn't take offence at my not eating it. I then pointed to my belly making a rounded shape.

"Ah!" she nodded and smiled again before moving the table out of the way. She tried to explain something else to me, pointing at my leg as she did so, I nodded and smiled like an idiot as if I understood. The brakes on the bed were taken off and the two Nurses pushed me out of the room.

A young blonde female Doctor dressed in surgical scrubs was waiting at the doorway to the room. The room looked like a consultation room, boxes of files and paperwork filled the walls, there were two large windows and it had carpets and a desk that sat piled messily with medical notes in one corner. The Doctor gave the

Nurses instructions and I saw a wheelchair standing ominously in the centre of the room next to my now secure bed.

"We will get you on the chair and change your bandages," said the Doctor.

This didn't feel good, I didn't feel ready to be sitting in a wheelchair. I knew my leg wasn't right, it felt dead and lifeless, my foot had got pinker but was still more like a piece of dead meat attached to me but the Doctors all said it was OK and that "this is normal." I also kept forgetting to ask questions as I had fallen into the role of "patient". The three of them managed to support my leg as I shuffled across the bed towards the chair, with each movement there was a crunch and grind of bone, I was sweating with the effort although strangely pleased with myself that I was even slightly mobile. I finally made it painfully to the chair, bending my left leg slowly to the floor, stitches stretching uncomfortably as I felt the warm carpet beneath my foot, my right leg sticking out in front of me on a thin metal support attached to the chair. I felt dizzy and sick, and noticing how pale I had gone the Doctor offered me a glass of water. The Nurses pushed the bed out of the room as I began to get my breath back.

"Can you lift your leg?" said the Doctor holding my foot.

"No, too painful, no feeling," I said, hoping she would say that it's OK, it's normal.

She turned her attention to the other bandages and pads on the rest of my body and slowly and carefully revealed each one. My hip wound was now a gigantic dark red scab, at the top of my right thigh next to my regrowing pubic hair was an incision about two inches long sown together with a thick catgut stitch also two inches long. I watched amazed as she pulled and tugged at the pad on my left leg. The pad revealed a cut that ran in a perfectly straight line down the inside of my thigh from just above my knee to just short of my groin, this was sewn together with the same thick catgut, here though the stitches were about three inches long and three inches apart and there were sixteen of them in total, thick linear scabs formed around the cut and the stitches. I gently touched the skin around the wound, it was numb and my leg seemed to be dented all the way down the inside of my thigh. The Doctor had the scissors out and started to gently snip the bandage on my right leg starting from the outside of my leg at the ankle, I breathed deeply awaiting the moment of truth. I winced as she reached the metal rods protruding from the bandage but she delicately cut her way through around each pin before continuing up the outer thigh. I exhaled deeply, that was step one over with, what worried me more was that I didn't feel anything. She started on the inside of my leg, cutting away, slowly and gently, my leg still resting on the metal support.

"OK, now we see," she said smiling confidently.

She held my foot and gently raised my leg, the broken bones moaning at the pressure. The Doctor started lifting the section of bandage away from the underside of my leg, I tried to peer over and see but the leg itself was in the way. I felt something suddenly sag, as if my calf muscle had dropped and was held on by an elastic band. I felt no pain, but it was most definitely not OK or normal.

The colour suddenly drained from the Doctor's face. The confident smile had gone and had been replaced by the ashen face of someone who was about to throw up. I could smell meat, but not fresh meat.

"That didn't feel right," I said raising my eyebrows and smiling.

The Doctor placed the bandage along with what must have been muscle and ligaments back against the underside of my leg and lowered it onto the support, my leg was now encased again, her hands were shaking, that wasn't what she was expecting. I was only glad I couldn't feel anything or see the extent of the damage.

"You have an infection," she said, still looking as if she was going to vomit. "We will dress the leg, but you will have to go to another Hospital where they are better at this."

"Nema problema," I said. It wasn't a problem, I knew my leg wasn't healing correctly and I knew by now that nothing ever goes to plan.

It was visiting time when I woke up in my room with the three other patients. Looking down I could see my bandages were clean and fresh, a new bag of liquid hung above me feeding me with what I assumed were antibiotics. Next to me the old man's family stood or sat around his bed, there were several generations of them, some wept, some held his hands. They must have been told he wouldn't be around long. My friend by the window also had some of his family with him, it looked like his parents and wife or sister. The room was quite crowded.

"Dobar dan Ingliiski!" the man by the window shouted.

"Dobar dan," I replied waving, not wanting to have a conversation above the family that would probably be seeing the old man for the last time. The man chatted away excitedly to his parents who nodded in understanding with serious faces, the family constantly looked over in my direction. Near the end of visiting time the man's three relatives walked over to me. They stood at the end of my bed smiling, not quite knowing what to say as the Mother held my hand.

"Hvala," she said. "Hvala."

I nodded and smiled. The warmth of their gesture and the strange softness of her hands made my eyes fill with tears, it was the first time anyone had said thank you to me.

I would be going to the other Hospital tomorrow where they would be better equipped to deal with this infection so I spent the evening admiring the needlework on my left thigh as I had still forgotten to ask why it was there. I had a conversation with the man by the window that consisted mainly of mime and sound effects, I think he wanted to hear all the war stories but it was all so new and real I found it too difficult to describe. Eventually we both gave up, the darkness not helping with the game of charades.

I slept my usual disturbed sleep, the nightmares had started since I had left HOS and it always consisted of the two Četniks running towards me and I fire at them but I can see the bullets missing their target. I woke with a jump in the middle of the darkness and I was desperate for a drink. The old man next to me had a bottle of untouched pear juice on his table, his breathing was the quietest I had heard it and he hadn't moved in all the time I had been in the Hospital. I watched him for ages, strangely fascinated by the old man and scared shitless he would suddenly wake up if I had a quick gulp of his juice. After some time the man exhaled deeply and noisily, then didn't inhale. That was it, he had stopped breathing, I had just watched this elderly man die and now he was just a body. It was worrying that I found nothing strange or odd anymore, the unusual had become normal. I picked up the old man's pear juice thinking he wouldn't need it anymore anyway and took a long gulp before gagging, realising it was actually undiluted squash.

I arrived at the new Hospital at around midday and it was a hive of activity, Doctors and Nurses buzzed around through the maze of corridors and rooms. My new room had the same layout as the previous one with four beds side by side, I was nearest the door again only this time on the wall next to me was a sink and a mirror. The other patients in the room were all much older than me, I could see the man nearest the window had had his leg amputated, though as a result of some age related problem rather than combat, they all slept or were unconscious. The Nurses left me and within minutes a man in his thirties in a wheelchair pushed himself into the room and sat near the end of my bed.

"Dobar dan," he introduced himself, he also had a metal pins in his leg, but sticking out of his shin.

"You are the Englishman, yes? I am pleased to meet you."

"Yes, Simon, 106 HVO."

We talked for a while about our injuries. He was in the Bosnian Army, the ABiH, and was the victim of a Serb RPG. I noticed a beautiful gold crescent and star hanging from a chain around his neck.

"From my wife," he said noticing me looking at it, "you are Muslim?"

"Er...no," I said slightly embarrassed.

"Is OK, were are all brothers," he smiled.

A female Doctor walked into the room, her hair scraped back into a ponytail, she had a serious expression and looked far too young to be a Doctor. The Doctor and the man in the wheelchair talked and smiled to each other.

"Here is the best Doctor in Zagreb, I will see you later," he said wheeling towards the exit and the noisy corridor. The Doctor smiled.

"Hello Simon, we have seen many injuries like this and we will make it better," she said looking me up and down. "Is there anything we can do for you?"

My mind raced, since my injury I had just been on the receiving end of everything, nobody had asked me what I wanted.

"I need to contact the British Embassy," I said.

"That is no problem. We will also try and find you some books in English, we will look after you."

"Thank you, how long before I'm better do you think?"

"Who knows? We must get rid of the infection first."

"Why is this scar here?" I said referring to the sixteen stitches in my left leg. I was remembering all the questions I had been meaning to ask.

"Here they have taken some of the vein from that leg and put it here where your other one was destroyed," she said looking through her notes and pointing to the area behind my right knee.

She explained that my leg would need dressing daily and I'd have plenty of strong antibiotics, she also said I had had enough blood and that would be one less bag of fluid going into me, even though I had by now got used to the tubes and drips constantly attached to me.

"You have so much blood you are Croatian now," she said smiling. "We will see you later."

The food came around soon after and for once I actually felt hungry. The food didn't look up to much but I had eaten worse and only managed to finish half of it before feeling full. I no longer felt disorientated, from now on I would try to sleep at night and stay awake during daylight, I also knew where I was and, more importantly, what was happening to me. Later that evening the same female Doctor came round with another Doctor and a couple of Nurses.

"Hello again, we will change your dressing now, OK," she said donning latex gloves as one of the Nurses injected painkillers into the tap in my hand.

"OK, lets do it," I said feeling confident and immediately light headed.

She snipped away just like the previous Doctor had done, down each side from ankle to hip. I was pleased to be laying down so nothing fell out this time, I still didn't feel anything, not even the crunch of bone as she cut her way around metal rods, there was only the dull ache of blood attempting to circulate through my leg. The Doctors talked quietly to each other as the Nurses watched, holding bags for the old bandages to go into and trays for the scissors.

"We will gently peel off the bandage, OK."

She gently lifted the area around the cut in the bandage, first an inch, then another, occasionally I would flinch as dried blood was stuck to the bandage as it was peeled. She then tried to peel a bit further on the area around my calf.

"NO, NO," I blurted out. The bandage was stuck fast against my leg, it wasn't stuck against skin, it was dry bandage stuck to bare muscle and nerve endings. The sudden pain was intense.

"OK, painful yes."

"Yes, don't pull that anymore, please," I was starting to panic.

She slowly lifted the bandage as far as it would go before peering underneath, then letting the other Doctor have a look. They talked in hushed voices to each other as the patient next to me tried not to look.

"Simon, we will have to give you anaesthetic to change your bandage, the skin has split because of the infection and the dressing has stuck to the flesh."

"Anaesthetic. Dobro, yako boli," I said.

They gave me the general anaesthetic and changed the bandages, I could cope with the anaesthetised, pain-free dressing changes. The following morning the Doctors did their rounds and I was glad to see the female Doctor again. In charge of the gang of Doctors was a grey haired man with a moustache, he was tall and had a permanently angry sneer, barking orders at Nurses and patients alike. They started at the end of the room with the one-legged patient nearest the window.

The head man barked his orders to the female Doctor, who in turn tried to explain something back but was cut short. The Doctor started to unwrap the bandages on the stump of the elderly patient as the rest of the posse hurried to put down notes and put on latex gloves. A rotten stench filled the room as the man's stump was unwrapped, making the rest of us gag and turn away. The grey haired Doctor barked more orders and trays and bowls were brought in and I was trying not to look, I didn't want him even noticing me let alone shouting at me. The patient was semi-conscious and started to groan, the smell of rotting meat almost unbearable. I looked up to see the Doctor squeezing the patient's stump which was open around the mid-thigh, the Doctor was pushing out rotten flesh from the wound, a thick lime green mush with lumps the size of pineapple chunks slopped into a metal tray. The man groaned as the bowl filled with the rotten green stew, I turned away, I had seen enough. There was more groaning and squeezing before the trays of rotten meat were taken away and the window opened slightly, the winter chill far more bearable than the stench of gangrenous flesh. Only when the man's stump was dressed could we then look up.

The Doctors eventually got to me and the female Doctor filled him in on my condition and my progress so far. I was scared of him, he was the exact opposite of the nice English-speaking woman Doctor.

"You have lots of our blood," he said.

"Yes, hvala," I said, wondering if he wanted it all back or something?

They talked for a minute and the grey haired Doctor grunted his acknowledgement. All the time I was waiting for him to rip off my bandages or rattle the metal frame on my leg just to make sure it was tight enough. He nodded, grunted again, and thankfully left, allowing me to breathe normally again. The woman Doctor came back into the room.

"Sorry you had to see that, he is a very good Doctor," she said before leaving again.

The Bosnian in the wheelchair came to see me later on, bringing a couple of his friends. The oldest of the three was also in a wheelchair with metal pins in his lower leg, but his right arm was missing above the elbow making him struggle to push the chair, much to the amusement of the other two. He had been injured by a hand grenade, blowing his arm clean off and shattering his leg at the same time. The youngest was about eighteen and had a tube that ran from beneath his tee shirt to his stomach contents that he carried around in a clear bag with a wire handle, he had been shot in the stomach by a sniper. All of them were Bosnian Muslims. We talked for ages even though it was only the Bosnian I had met first that spoke broken English, taking the piss out of the grey haired Doctor, "Doctor Death" the eldest one called him, laughing through the gaps in his teeth. It was good to be around people who had been through the same thing as I had and probably had the same bad dreams, they all thanked "Allah" that they were alive. I wished I could have their faith. We were all family, like my friends still at 106, Terry, or Pete from the Gulf. Never having to talk about everything we'd seen or done because each of us, in some way, already knew.

I had a shave for the first time since my injury. It was the first time I'd had a shave with a cutthroat razor and the first time anyone had done it for me, it was the best shave I've ever had. I had regular bed baths as well now, the Nurses scrubbing me down with an alcohol solution before giving me the cloth to clean my privates. I was beginning to feel positive again and the staff were fantastic. I had a book donated to me by one of the Doctors and even though it was about the ancient Aztecs I still attempted to read it but found myself tiring quickly. The Bosnian with his see-through handbag stomach somehow would manage to find a broadsheet newspaper in English every so often and pass it to me with a huge grin as if to say "mission accomplished". The Physiotherapist came by every day, a woman in her fifties with a big greying beehive hairdo. She would smile as she massaged my right foot, her expression more of hope than expectation as my swollen foot was still a pink-grey colour and completely numb. All I could do was shake my head and shrug my shoulders as she continued resolutely massaging the dead foot for ten minutes. She would always say "maybe tomorrow" as she left, probably the only English she knew, a bit like my "yako boli." A visit from the English speaking female Doctor would always make me feel better as she would always tell me what was going on and what was happening to me, it felt as if she never left the place as she always seemed to be on duty.

I had only been there a few days and my infection worsened, I suddenly felt cold, really cold to the point where I was shivering.

"Sestro, sestro," I said, my teeth chattering.

The Nurse was dishing out the food and came rushing into the room.

"Vruche, yako vruche," I told her I was cold.

"Vruche?" the Nurse asked before realising that I was actually shivering.

A Doctor and another Nurse came in carrying blankets, the Doctor took my temperature as the Nurse placed blankets over me. No amount of blankets made me any warmer and there were around ten blankets weighing me down before the shivering stopped. I lay with my face snuggled into the blankets trying to keep warm. The Nurse stayed with me as the Doctor left, twenty minutes later I was getting hotter and the blankets were took off one by one until it was just a white sheet, and me.

"Hladno, hladno," Hot, hot.

Sweat was pouring off me and a fan was brought in and turned up to full speed. Another twenty minutes and my temperature dropped and on came the blankets, another twenty minutes, blankets off, fan on. I don't know how long that went on for, only that the Nurse was with me the whole time.

The days were a constant round of waking up in the morning where I wasn't allowed to eat before having a general anaesthetic, then waking in the evening from the general anaesthetic where they would then try and make me eat something, but I still felt queasy from the anaesthetic and wasn't hungry enough. As a result of the constant anaesthetics I could see I was losing weight rapidly and my ribs were starting to show, my arms had lost all their muscle. Every evening people would try and make me swallow some of the food, but I couldn't face it, even the Bosnians were worried about me. The pain was still there, always a "malo boli" (small pain), or "yako boli" (big pain).

"Simon, this is a man who had the same injury as you," the female Doctor showed in a huge man in Croat Army uniform.

"How you doin' mate," said the man with an East Midlands accent. "She's a brilliant Doctor isn't she?"

He was in his early forties, his hair thinning and with a beard, he limped along with a walking stick.

"She said I should come and see you, same thing happened to me a year ago, Serb mortar totally fucked my leg but the Doctors saved it," he said, showing me his leg, which seemed to be one large red dented mess of scar tissue and skin grafts.

We talked for a while and it turned out he now lived in Zagreb with a Croatian girl and considered himself Croatian. We talked for some time before I grew tired.

"Why would I want to go back to England after everything these people did for me," he said. "And besides, have you seen these Croatian women!"

I had to agree with him there.

At visiting time I was always pointed out to the families by other patients, I wasn't sure whether it was because I was the English volunteer and a bit of a novelty or because I had no visitors due to being so far from home. People would always come to say hello or shake my hand, Bosnian Muslim and Croatian Catholic families always said they would pray for me. Their kindness touched me and I never felt alone or wished I were home, this felt like home and despite the pain, I was quite happy. It only lasted a short time, the reality of my situation was always ready to bring me back down to earth.

"Simon, you have another visitor." The nice female Doctor escorted in a dishevelled looking woman with half-moon glasses. Two visits in two days, I was Mr Popular.

"Hello Simon, I'm from the British Consulate," said the woman who was Croatian but spoke English.

We went through my details; name, address, next of kin, phone numbers. All the time she looked at me with a face that seemed to say "I've seen it all before and you've only yourself to blame."

"You will have to pay to be flown back as you have no insurance."

I hesitated before I said it, it would be the point of no return again and everything would change from now on.

"I'm a British Soldier, I'm Absent Without Leave."

That got a reaction. She looked over her glasses at me, there was another sigh. More details; the date I went AWOL, rank, number, and unit.

"I will get in touch with your next of kin and the military. As you are AWOL, you belong to the Army."

I wondered if I had made the right decision, but it was too late now anyway.

I knew I was dangerously underweight and it must have been hard enough for my body to fight the infection as it was even without me not eating. At the Doctor's rounds every morning I would try my hardest to be the grey man and go unnoticed to "Doctor Death", the thought of what he might do to me filled me with fear but the female Doctor would always fight my corner and be answered in grunts by the seriously dislikeable man and every day they would move on to the next room. I knew eventually it would be my turn for him do whatever the fuck he felt like doing to me that day, but so far I had got away with it. This morning he looked like he was in a really bad mood, arguing the toss with the other Doctors and looking angrily at the other three patients who, like me, were all trying their hardest to become invisible.

They reached my bed. And the barking of orders continued as he looked me up and down and flicked through my notes aggressively. The female Doctor pleaded my case again, this time louder and more forceful, they were on the verge of a full-scale row as the other Doctors and Nurses tried not to make eye contact with either of them and at the same time trying to become as invisible as me. The shouting stopped, the staff looked at each other nervously. Female Doctor looked at me and she was shaking with anger, she didn't need to say anything.

"Oh shit," I said out loud. It was my turn.

* * * *

Orders are barked again and medical equipment brought in at double quick time, Nurses take their positions around my bed wearing surgical masks.

"We have to change your bandages without anaesthetic, you are losing too much weight," she says holding my hand. I don't want to let go.

"Please don't, please," I don't know what else to say. Sometimes the fear of pain is worse than the pain itself. She lets go of my hand and puts on her surgical mask. Two Nurses have one hand on each of my shoulders, pressing down, their other hand holds mine. I can tell by their eyes that none of them want this to happen, the next fifteen minutes would probably ruin their day. Nurses not involved in pinning me down or holding metal trays pretend to be busy, not looking over at me because they know they will hear it, they don't want to see it.

"Please don't, please," I repeat it over and over. I had for so long just lay there as they got on with whatever it was they wanted to do to me, this though felt different.

"Shhhh."

"I'm begging you, please." I said I had enough.

"Please, no."

"NO. NO. NO. Please don't."

I beg and plead pathetically to the grey haired Doctor who never listened when people begged in Croatian. Nurses look away or close their eyes tightly. My now skinny body is exposed, my muscles are tensed, I grit my teeth trying not to give the Doctor the satisfaction of hearing me scream, he has already heard me beg.

"Please no," I beg one more time. Tears are already spilling from my eyes.

The tearing of bandages starts. It sounds and feels like Velcro being torn apart, dry bandage stuck to bare wet muscle and exposed nerve endings. The pain is indescribable. Why me?

I scream as loudly and as violently as I can.

The Nurse calls for help. I am almost breaking her fingers. More Nurses pin me down.

"NO…GOD…PLEASE."

The sheet falls from the bed. My pathetic body is naked.

Screaming.

Screaming.

Nurses shut their eyes tightly. One wipes a tear.

Screaming.

It stops. No more. The Nurses ease their grip and rub their crushed hands. The grey haired Doctor is the only one to look me in the eyes.

I am shaking, the violence of the experience has drained me. The tears rolling down my cheeks feel freezing cold, I breathe through sobs.

* * * *

The sheet was put back on the bed, covering my body. Doctor Death left the room, not before shouting at a crying Nurse.

"I'm so sorry," said the female Doctor. "I'll be back soon."

The gang of medical staff left me, some of the Nurses quietly apologised in Croatian as they tidied away. I struggled to get myself back together, lying there looking at the ceiling as tears soaked into the pillow by my ears, my bony ribs rising and falling as I gulped in air. I was so cold, shivering, my hands trembling. The dull ache in my leg was now a hard pulsing throb of pain. I stared at the white ceiling panels, focusing on the pattern for an eternity, blanking out everything else as my sobbing subsided. I must have fallen asleep.

My eyes flicked open to see my English speaking Bosnian friend sitting at the end of the bed in his chair, silently waiting for me to open my eyes.

"You OK Simon?" he whispered.

"Yes mate. Yako, yako, yako boli," I whispered back.

"Your shout. Many people in Hospital hear," he said furrowing his brow. Hearing another man's scream when you're in Hospital is witnessing another man's pain, I could imagine it must be horrifying.

"You will be OK. No problem," he said holding my hand.

"Doctore, yabente pitchko matre," I said. I wasn't sure what it meant but I did know it was the worst group of swear words in the Croatian language. The other patients in the room overheard and started laughing my Bosnian friend was slightly taken aback but smiled.

"Shhh," he said as the female Doctor entered the room and the patients attempted to stifle their laughter. "Simon. No problem. OK?"

"OK," I said to the back of his wheelchair as he left.

The Doctor must have heard what I said but didn't comment.

"How are you now Simon?" she said.

"Yako boli. Doctor no dobro!" I said even though I think she already knew how I felt about the grey haired Doctor. She smiled and looked down at my leg, up until that point I had forgotten it was unwrapped of bandages. I slowly sat up dreading what I would see.

I looked down at my calf that seemed to be the most painful area and saw that either side of my shin was a bright red mass. My calf muscle was the size and shape of a deflated football and had split the skin either size of my shin as it expanded with the infection. The muscle and tendons were bright red and shiny with moisture, throughout the red mass small white threads of nerve endings wriggled their way to the surface, parts of the exposed and bloody flesh were silvery grey, almost like fish scales.

"OK Simon, you can see where the infection is around your lower leg," she said waving her pen around in the general direction.

"It doesn't look good," I said.

"Your bones are healing and blood is circulating down to your foot, so we know the vein transplant worked," she pointed to my grey-pink foot.

"Right. Now the bad news," I said.

"This grey coloured meat is actually dead," she said as she jabbed it gently with her pen, I flinched thinking it would hurt. "It is dead so it doesn't hurt, every time we change your dressing we have to shave this dead flesh off to stop it spreading," she went on, "the red part of the leg," she held the pen above my calf.

"NO!" I shouted, thinking she was about to jab the living part of the infected calf.

"It's OK, I'm not going to touch this, it would hurt."

"Good!" I smiled.

"We need to keep as much living meat as possible but at the same time get rid of the dead meat to keep it clean. Eventually the infection will go and your leg can heal properly."

"It will take some time though," I said.

"A week maybe," she said placing her pen back into her pocket.

I looked at the leg, it was my leg but was just a bloody, infected mess and a constant source of unbearable pain, I couldn't go through having my dressings ripped off by Doctor Death again nor could my body cope with daily general anaesthetics.

"Can you take it off?" I asked.

"What? Your leg?"

"Yes."

"Only if we cannot save it."

"No. I want you to take it off, it's no good."

"You want us to amputate?"

"Yes, get rid of it."

"We can save your leg, only when we know we cannot save it will we amputate."

"But it's no good."

"It will be OK," she said, confident that my leg would heal.

I didn't have her confidence.

My leg was redressed under general anaesthetic so the tearing off of my bandages by Doctor Death was completely unnecessary anyway, which was probably why the female Doctor argued so vehemently with him. The next couple of days were an easy routine of waking before Doctors rounds, then the anaesthetic. They must have been speeding things up or giving me less of the sleeping juice because I no longer felt as groggy when I woke up, I also managed to eat a little, though it was still not enough.

I don't know how long it was since the explosion, two weeks or three weeks? During that time I still hadn't had a crap. I hadn't needed one. This particular morning I did and I wasn't looking forward to it, it meant getting my body at the right angle so I didn't get covered in my own shit whilst trying not to make the bones in my leg crunch.

"Sestro, sestro," I called over a Nurse then pointed down below and blew a raspberry.

"Ah, dobro!" I was glad she was so pleased I needed a shit.

She brought in a bedpan and helped me manoeuvre it into position, my dignity was out of the window now that I could feel my insides cramping, this wasn't going to hang about. In position, I held onto the handle above my bed and pulled myself up so that my backside was slightly above the bed and resting gently on the bedpan.

"OOOOWWWWWWW!" my insides were tensing.

This was the biggest thing I'd ever done, it was literally the size of a small log. When it was halfway out I took some deep breaths, it couldn't stay there, half in and half out. I gritted my teeth and tensed up again, pushing this time.

"Fucking hell, that's better," I exhaled with relief as I saw the gigantic log.

I thought I had shit some blood until I moved the bedpan.

* * * *

The area of bandage around the back of my knee is bright crimson. Between my legs I watch the sheet turn from dry and white to wet and scarlet as it soaks up all the liquid, red-black puddles form in the folds of the sheet underneath me and I can hear dripping from my bed to the floor.

"Sestro, sestro!"

Her smiling face changes when she sees the blood, she immediately turns and runs for assistance, shouting down the corridor as she goes. I can smell that gagging, metallic, sickly smell of fresh blood again. In seconds they swarm around me, shouting, injections, latex gloves being snapped on. The bottom half of my bed is now wet and bright scarlet. I know I'm bleeding out again but this time there is no shock of a mortar explosion to confuse my senses. It's out of my hands.

Here we go again.

My vision blurs. I feel myself become light headed. I'm sleepy again. Not here, after all I've been through.

I'm so tired again. Sleep now.

My bed is being pushed down the corridor to theatre, the Nurses remind me of a bobsleigh team. The Hospital's usual smell of disinfectant is overpowered by the fresh meat stench of my blood. There's another drip in my arm that wasn't there before. Female Doctor is here, shouting, telling me it's going to be OK. I have no peripheral vision. The bed has never felt so comfortable, with its soft pillows and cool sheets. Everything is so clean and bright and people in white surround me.

I can hear the splash of my blood onto the clean, polished corridor floor.

Not now, not yet, that would be unfair.

Who ever said it was fair?

"It's going to be OK, Simon," a whisper.

Sssshhhh, sleep now. Sleep.

* * * *

16. Something Lost

It didn't feel like I was dead, not that I knew what that felt like. I wasn't light headed anymore and at the same time I wasn't asleep. My head was facing left and I could feel the sensation of tubes everywhere, one of my eyes was half open and I could see my left arm stretched out and taped down onto a board or support, tubes entered the arm and back of my hand and there was a clip of some kind on the end of my finger.

* * * *

I can hear talking, a simple conversation, the giving of instructions. The clatter of metal instruments being dropped into a metal tray, the bleeping of a monitor in time with my heartbeat, my body being pulled or moved in some way. I try to shout but not even my lips move, I attempt to move my arm but there is nothing, it's like I am trapped inside myself, paralysed and unable to tell the world I am awake. I watch the Nurse at the end of my left arm, it's the only thing I can do as I hear a crunching sound and feel my body being tugged in a downward direction. I feel like I am so small, pure consciousness or soul, I am a spirit inside the body of a man. There is no feeling, only a view from an eye half-closed, a wiggling tongue, a twitching finger. Nothing else but the external sounds.

Panic is setting in. I don't want to be like this. Scream. Move. Anything.

I hear the whining sound of a small electrical saw. My tongue moves and I try to move every single cell in my body. I see my finger on my left hand move, the first finger, I try to make it tap as loudly and as fast as possible but it's all slow motion. My tongue licks my lips like a madman, but it feels like someone elses tongue, someone elses lips. The talking continues, louder to compensate for the saw as my finger taps slowly away. I hear a slopping sound, then the sound of the saw blade coming into contact with something and I sense my body move as the saw grinds through bone.

Turn me off.

Wake up. Go to sleep.

Turn me off.

I can't take any more.

The thought of existing like this, it's not sleeping, not dreaming but not awake. I'm just the view from an eyeball and a tapping finger.

I want to close my eyes and go to sleep, but I'm awake and it just won't go away, the tapping continues, as does the sawing. I don't know if this is real, all I am is a spark of awareness trapped inside the body of a broken soldier.

God, turn me off, flick the fucking switch.

I scream as loudly as I can. There is nothing.

My tongue can feel the tube down my throat, the dry cracked lips.

Scream. Kill me. I've had enough.

Turn me off.

There's a quick conversation from the Nurse at the end of my left arm, a syringe of opaque liquid is forced into my hand.

Turn.

Me.

Off.

A tube is being pulled from my mouth and I gag as it goes past my throat and the back of my tongue. I wretch but don't vomit. I've done this before, I can remember. I was a soldier. I've been blown up and they tried to fix it. A Nurse stands in the semi-darkness with a cardboard bowl in her hands, she looks relieved I haven't thrown up. Am I in Slavonski Brod or Zagreb? I no longer know what real is. Has this all been a weird dream? Maybe I'm dead and this is my punishment, to relive the last two horrific weeks over and over again in a surreal eternal loop; the burning piss, the tubes, the ambulance, Doctor Death. I close my eyes and all I hear is the repetitive bleeping of machines.

Turn me off.

* * * *

It's daytime. Everything is white and sunlight bounces off sheet and curtain, dazzling me. I am awake, or at least it feels like it. I feel good, some of the pain is gone and has been replaced by a bruising ache and tingling. I look down. Something's wrong, I can't see my leg but I can feel it so it should be there, where is it? The Nurse sees me wake up in confusion, she is in her thirties and wears a white Nurses uniform, not the light blue I had become used to.

"Your leg gone now," she said using a chopping motion with her hand on her thigh.

I place my hands face down where my leg should be as if feeling on the ground for a lost contact lens. Everything is white. Again I wonder if I may be dead. Or still in Slavonski Brod.

"Dobro," I smile at the Nurse. "Dobro." And start to laugh.

It takes a while for me to stop feeling the space where my leg once was. I'm relieved it's gone, it was rotten and dead, damaged beyond repair and a constant source of pain. No more daily anaesthetics or exposed nerve endings or crunching, shattered bone held together by steel pins. All I have to do is heal and I can move around and eat. The bags of blood are here again, emptying more of the stuff into me, replacing the blood I lost when I had a shit. Bags of fluid and bleeping machines surround me, monitoring and feeding me. My left leg sticks out looking surreal and lonely. I'm not sure about anything anymore, only that right now I'm lying on a bed with a body part missing.

It takes a day or so to get my bearings again and I'm surprised by my own attitude to my missing limb, my other leg literally looks odd, poking out on its own. My head spins, I'm happy it's gone.

The room is larger than before, in the far corner near the door is a Nurses station which consists of a desk and a pile of medical folders. Opposite me is another patient hooked up to machines and bags of fluid, I can only just make out that it's an elderly woman, her curly grey hair sticks out from the soft pillows and the window next to her illuminates the scene. The bed to my left is empty, the machines next to it silent. Every so often the Intensive Care Nurses come to check on the status of the bleeping machines and the levels of liquid in the bags, they smile at me and attempt conversation happy in the knowledge that I will be one of the few patients that won't die in here.

"Hello Simon how are you?" It was my friend the female Doctor. Her hair scraped back as always, she looked younger than the Nurses.

"Dobar dan Doctore!" I was genuinely happy to see her.

"We had to amputate your leg because we couldn't repair the vein again, it broke because of the pressure when you....er…" She struggled for the words "had a shit". "I am very sorry," she said after abandoning the attempt to find the right word. Her expression was one of genuine remorse.

"No problem, it's much better now. No more 'Yako Boli!' Thank you Doctor, it's OK," she smiled at the "yako boli" bit. I was smiling and giving the thumbs up, after all, I had asked her to cut the thing off anyway.

"How are you feeling?" she asked.

"Fine. I feel good, when can I get back?"

"Tomorrow if you feel OK, you will be back in your room, your friends miss you," she smiled.

I could hear him trying to tiptoe around the bed.

"BOO!" I sat up and flicked my eyes open, he almost dropped his stomach.

"Shhh!" the Nurses looked over sternly.

The Bosnian boy with his stomach in a bag was trying not to laugh, his stomach in one hand and a newspaper in the other.

"Dobro?" he asked.

"Dobro, dobro," I smiled back with a thumbs up. I noticed him look at the space where my leg should have been with a sad expression. It was strange how people seemed to treat my lost leg like the death of a person, maybe I should mourn its passing, then again it caused me nothing but pain and I was glad it was gone. I knew early on that it would never heal correctly. Bosnian boy gave me the paper and tiptoed out again, waving goodbye. I read the paper cover to cover but it seemed to take me forever as I was still weak and got tired easily, the words turning into a jumble of letters by the end of every paragraph.

I noticed the bleeping of the old lady's machine slow down. The lights from the street cast a dim orange glow over her bed, I could hear cars in the dark city below. The Nurses station had a light permanently on above it and they dozed or did paperwork half-heartedly, there were always at least two of them on duty all the time. The gaps between beeps were becoming longer now and a Nurse took notice, looking up from the papers on her desk. The old lady didn't move as the two Nurses moved the short distance to her bed where they checked the lines and the machine to see if the machinery was wrong or there was a blockage in a tube. There wasn't any external thing wrong with the lady, she was just dying. The bleeping had stopped without me realising. The Nurse physically checked her pulse before looking seriously at the other Nurse, they had done this hundreds of times before in this room and they didn't bother with any more resuscitation. She was dead. The Nurses moved quickly removing the drips and machines attached to the lady and once they were gone it just looked like she was sleeping. The Nurses covered her face with her sheet. Again I felt nothing.

The morning came and the covered body of the old lady being wheeled out woke me up. There was a new patient in the room occupying the bed next to me, still with the same tubes and machines attached, he was old and had both legs amputated and I couldn't help thinking he wouldn't be around long and immediately felt sorry for the Nurses constantly watching people come in to die. I sat up and stared out of the window, I could only see rooftops and grey sky and occasionally I could hear the frantic movement of Zagreb traffic below the window, a reminder that the real world still went on without me.

In a short space of time I had got used to the absence of my leg, it looked like it had been cut off mid thigh and they would have had to use the last break of bone as the end of my leg. The stump was sore and thick and heavy with bandages wrapped around it, it had been sewn together from left to right, joining the thigh muscle at the front with the muscle at the back of my leg and at each end of the stitched together scar I could feel a tube poking out, this drained away excess blood and I assumed it went all the way though my stump. I tried to move it but the muscles obviously hadn't had time to get used to their new position and it felt like it weighed a ton. I could still feel my right foot, a tingling sensation in my non-existent toes was the usual feeling, a general sense of it just "being there". Sometimes it could be painful, a sensation of boiling water being poured down my leg or a stabbing on the bottom of my foot, pins and needles, cramp, all sensations that I could do nothing about, it was my brain sending messages to nerve endings that were no longer there and occasionally my stump would spasm and twitch as the nerve endings received an electrical impulse. It wasn't unbearable, although I had only been an amputee a couple of days.

"Hello Simon, time to go." Female Doctor had come in with a couple of the Nurses I recognised. The Intensive Care Nurses hurriedly handed over paperwork whilst chatting to the female Doctor, over to my bed they came, detaching the machine from my finger and securing the bags of fluid.

"Hvala," I said to the two of them, I was pretty sure they didn't hear that very often and they certainly wouldn't be hearing it from their new patient. They waved as I was pushed back to my ward.

I had the same bed space as before, next to the sink and a couple of the patients in the room, including the gangrenous amputee, had been moved elsewhere and replaced by new faces. I sat up on my bed and bent my left leg flat onto the bed as if I was sitting cross-legged, the stitches stinging in disapproval. I gently experimented with my newfound ability to move, using my hands to lift myself and turn sideways, my arms shook and sweat dripped off my nose, I was weak. I turned and faced the mirror to my right, wondering if I could stand.

I held the sink with both hands and lowered my leg from the bed to the floor, the ground was cold under my foot and I felt like I was climbing Everest as I heaved myself upright, the physical exertion coupled with the need to achieve the incredible. All I was doing was standing but to me it was a statement, a great big "Fuck You! I'm Back!" My knee shook, it felt as if the stitches on my stump were coming undone and the meat inside would fall out onto the floor, sweat ran into my eyes as I looked into the mirror.

It was was the first time I had seen myself in several weeks and it was still me, albeit a hollow, weak version. My eyes were sunken and dark, my cheekbones and collarbones jutted out sharply, my hair had grown out to a fuzzy mess. The soldier was gone.

"No, Simon, no...Sestro!" it was my Bosnian friend in the wheelchair, "Sestro!"

Female Doctor came running into the room and immediately grabbed me by the arms and guided me down onto the bed.

"You are not ready to stand like this, you just have a major operation, you are very weak. What happens if you fall?" Her worried tone turned to anger at the last sentence.

"I'm sorry, I just wanted to move."

"Maybe in a few days you have a wheelchair, but for now...bed."

I never thought I could fall, I had made the first step on the road back to being me and it felt fucking great, my body was alive with the physical activity and my brain in overdrive at the thought of the coming weeks, months, years?

"You must be careful, you are not better yet, very thin, first day you big man, but now...," my Bosnian friend pinched his cheeks in.

I sat in my version of the cross-legged position on the bed, still on a high at the mere thought that I was mobile and relatively pain free, the three Bosnians sat with me around the bed talking in an English-Croat, sign language mix of communication. They could see the relief on my face and were happy for me, though they too felt the sadness of losing a limb like it was losing a member of the family.

"Owww," I yelped as my stump twitched, flicking up into the air with an electrical impulse. "You fucker!" I held the top of the stump, hoping there wouldn't be a series of impulses.

The older Bosnian laughed uncontrollably, his head thrown back showing his gap-toothed smile, before waving the stump of his arm at me.

"He say he feels his hand all the time and has the jumping," the other Bosnian explained to me after talking to One-Arm.

Suddenly I was feeling exhausted, I hadn't done any exercise for some time and just standing up felt like I had done a marathon. The Bosnians noticed and left me to sleep, One-Arm waved his stump at me and cackled again.

Later that same day I cheekily asked one of the Nurses for a wheelchair but she shook her head and smiled, they must all have had an advance warning that I'd want a chair but it was worth a go, I was itching to get mobile.

"Simon, you have a visitor." Female Doctor showed a man in through the door. He was tall, fit and wore uniform, with a blond moustache that reminded me of Terry. I felt dread as soon as I saw him, the uniform was the smart, neatly pressed camouflage outfit of the British Army and on his head was the light blue beret of the UN, on his arm he wore three stripes and a crown of a Staff Sergeant. The usual hustle and bustle of the corridor had disappeared and the other patients in the room looked at this tall serious looking man with some kind of awe as he sat down in the chair next to my bed.

"I came the other day but they said you'd just had it amputated. I suppose you know who I am," he said with the air of a man who would rather be elsewhere. He went on before I could say anything. "You've been a silly boy but you're ours so we'll get you back and sort you out. I have to remind you that you are now under arrest, I'm not going to do all the formal bollocks, you don't need it and you're hardly going to run off are you?" It was the first one-legged joke I'd heard, you have to admire the British sense of humour.

"No Staff," I was slightly taken aback by the sudden seriousness of it all. "I just want to get back home."

"We'll do that, the Doctor said in a week or two when your stitches are out you can go. Apparently you're lucky to be alive."

"Yep, pretty lucky."

We went through details again about name, rank, number, unit and next of kin.

"I'll see you in a week or two then," he said and off he went.

In that brief conversation he had made me feel like a prisoner already, I was under arrest and I'd been a silly boy, and in taking my name, rank, number and unit, he had stripped me of something and left me with a hollow feeling. Before, I had been Simon the Ingliiski of The Free Crusaders, 106 Brigade HVO, one of the strangers, injured and almost killed by a Serb mortar, people had said thank you and Doctors saved my life, I was no longer just a foreigner, I felt I belonged here.

That was all gone, now I was just a "silly boy". For the first time I thought about my future, I would be a one-legged ex-soldier in a country that didn't care. I had to focus on getting better, that was my first priority, then see what the future would bring.

The ward seemed a happier place now, full of conversation and people milling about. It was as if my leg had took a big black cloud that was hanging over me with it and even the visits of Doctor Death didn't scare me, after all, what else could he do, but he still looked as if he was waiting to pounce on an unsuspecting patient and barked orders to Nurses and Doctors alike.

"OK we take some stitches out now," female Doctor said placing scissors and a metal tray on my bed.

"What, they haven't healed yet!" I said in a panic.

"No, these ones are ready," she smiled and pointed to the sixteen stitches running down the inside of my left thigh.

The stitches were huge and dislodged the thin scabs that clung to them as they were pulled through the skin, the scar itself was a thick red and black line of scabs and newly formed scar tissue, as each stitch was removed it left a red scabby line where it had cut into the skin. When she had finished it looked like a child had drawn a railway track down my thigh and painted it red and black. The skin around the scar was still numb.

"Dobro, now we see your stump tomorrow, then a week or two your stitches come out, then you go home," she smiled.

The following day the dressing was changed on my stump. It was the first time I had seen it in the flesh and it surprised me how neat it was. The Doctor told me that the last break of my leg was what they had to use as a guide for amputation, though they left plenty of "meat" as a cushion for when I had an artificial leg fitted. The stump was curved and rounded, eight of the large catgut stitches knitted the skin and meat together horizontally and there were two scabby holes on my outer thigh where the top two metal pins of the external frame had stuck out holding the broken bone together. The end of a large diameter clear plastic tube poked out of each end of the scar.

"This we will take out soon," the Doctor said pointing at the tube.

I remembered a mole I had on the back of my thigh and one particularly deep scar on my knee amongst all the other scars caused by a boyhood of climbing trees, playing on building sites and playing football in the playground. Now all gone.

The Nurses eventually gave in, they must have been sick of me nagging them and they could see that I was eating and generally getting better, I was raring to go. It was wheelchair time. I must have looked quite a sight, a skinny man in "lost-property" mismatching pyjamas. Thankfully I only had the bags of fluid at night, so I could bend my arms at the elbow for the first time. The Nurse pushed me up and down the corridor a few times, I was trying to take in the unfamiliar view and I was moving nowhere in particular instead of being rushed into theatre or an ambulance. I gave a huge beaming smile to Nurses and patients alike who in turn smiled at me or put a hand on my shoulder.

"OK, OK, I go," I said to the Nurse.

"Slowly. I come with you," she said, clearly worried.

I pushed the chair along the corridor, it felt heavy and I could see my biceps trembling, I was sweating after only a few metres. I went past other rooms, mirror images of my own and at the last room before the stairwell I saw one of the Bosnians.

"Simon!" One-Arm waved with his remaining hand.

"HEY! HEY! HEY!" I shouted as I pushed myself into the room.

"Slowly," the Nurse trailing me said.

"Dobar dan, Dobar dan, Dobar dan," I said to the room with a huge grin.

My Bosnian friend ushered me in, introducing me to the other patients one old guy they called "Elton John" because of his glasses, another "Ustaše" as he was a Croatian soldier during World War Two. I shook their hands like they were old friends, they had all already heard about the Ingliiski, most of them said they heard my scream. I tried to take in all the new sights and the feeling of movement and after two or three weeks in a bed it was overwhelming, visitors started arriving and I took that as an excuse to leave, some of the visitors recognised me and said hello. The Nurse said goodbye for me and pushed me, still grinning and waving, out of the room. I didn't want to go back to my bed yet even though I felt exhausted, I wanted to be left by a window so I could just look out onto the world and the Nurse seemed to understand and pushed me back down the corridor to another room.

"Stay here, no leave, I come back for you soon," the Nurse said pointing at me, obviously I should have been taken back to my bed.

"OK. Hvala," I said grinning.

The room was some kind of visitors room or smoking room, ashtrays were full and the fog of strong Croatian cigarettes hung in the air, I could see the streets a few floors below. The smell reminded me of Peter, Joe, Smiley and the others, I missed them and part of me missed the constant fear. As a casualty I lay on the bed and waited for things to happen to me, at the front I at least had some measure of control, I had a gun, I was a somebody. I could prepare for the unpredictability of combat but as a casualty I couldn't prepare for what I knew was going to happen. I suddenly felt very lonely in that room, something was lost that I could never get back, not just my leg, but part of me, the man I was had changed and I had saw someone else in the mirror when I stood up. I would never hold a gun again or feel the same way as I did only a few weeks ago. My thoughts were interrupted as a group of people entered the room, it looked like a family on a visit talking loudly as they walked in.

"Simon!" it was the Bosnian boy and his stomach in the see-through bag.

"Dobar dan," I said quietly, not wanting to intrude on his visiting time. I knew his family must have come some distance to Zagreb just to see him. The boy spoke to his family, obviously explaining all about me to them as I could hear the words "Ingliiski" and "bomba", he had his Mother, Father, teenage Sister and a little Brother with him. I smiled politely at the family as they looked over during the conversation.

"Come, come," said the Father walking towards me, the family behind him smiled at me. I wasn't sure what was going on so I just smiled back like an idiot. The Father grabbed my hand with both of his and shook it passionately whilst saying something in Croatian then grabbed the wheelchair and pushed me over to his family who were now seated at the table and chairs. I was quite honoured that he wanted me to be part of his family visit but I still felt like I was intruding. There was a pause as the Father closed his eyes, Bosnian boy smiled at me and whispered,

"Is OK."

The Father held his hands out open in front of him, his palms upward and with his eyes closed and his head tilted up towards the sky, he started to sing.

It was the Islamic call to prayer and it sounded beautiful. Reminding me of the Gulf, the expanse of desert and the giant disc of the sun burning the morning mist away. The rest of the family looked out of the corner of their eyes at me and smiled, sensing I wasn't used to this. I held my hands out, palms upwards along with the rest of the family and just listened to his voice in prayer, carried away by the moment.

The following few days were much the same, I would eat anything and everything they gave me to eat, always fresh bread in the morning, and always a cooked meal. Croatian cooking mainly consisted of boiled stuff that looked like it tasted - bland. I ate the stuff anyway and even attempted to explain what bacon was but to no avail. I felt better just by being mobile, talking to the other patients and medical staff, some who wanted to improve their English, some just wanted to talk, I simply wanted the company of friends as I whizzed around the corridor and into various rooms. I would sometimes leave the ward and was allowed to go as far as the stairwell, it was a bit more than a stairwell, it was the main stairs for the whole Hospital and the stairs themselves were the width of my room. I would sit in the corner facing the stairs watching medical staff in various uniforms go up and down, at mealtimes the stairs were full of people moving upstairs or downstairs at once, it looked like an escalator with people shoulder to shoulder moving at the same speed. Some would look over to me sitting in the corner, smile, and continue their journey.

One night came the moment I had been dreading.

"Simon, you have a phone call," the Nurse said taking the brakes off the wheelchair.

It would be my parents who had phoned the Hospital to speak to me. What do I say? How do I explain? The Nurse pushed me up the corridor to the dark, smoky, visitors room. The female Doctor had the phone to her ear and had been speaking in English to my parents.

"Ah, here he is," she said handing me the phone.

I took the phone carefully, a very real link to my very real world, I was still unsure of what to say as the Doctor told me I had five minutes and left the room.

"Hello?" I said hoping we'd been cut off or they had the wrong patient.

"Simon, thank God you're OK," it was my Dad.

"I'm fine…look I'm sorry I worried you…I'm all right now though."

"What happened? The Embassy said you had trod on a mine…what did you think you were doing?"

"It was a mortar, I was blown up…."

The longer the conversation went on the longer the uncomfortable silences became. My Dad was just like me, he didn't know what to say either and the fact that I was OK was all he needed at the minute, not the details or the whys?

"Here's your Mum," he said, his voice shaking.

"You had us so worried...are they looking after you?" she said. I remembered that wherever I was in the world or whatever I was doing she would always ask if I was looking after my teeth.

"I'm OK, staff are really good here, really looking after me, you know I've had my leg amputated don't you?" I had to say it or we would spend the next five minutes making the polite smalltalk that we were so good at without actually finding anything out.

"Yes...the lady Doctor said..." The uncomfortable silences, the polite smalltalk again.

"Some of you friends are here," she said handing the phone over.

"How are you mate?" It was my civilian friend Matthew. The boy who lived a few doors down the road from me, the boy I used to play soldiers with.

It's hard to have a grown up conversation with your friends. It's usually women, booze and football. I didn't expect them to ask how my life was with a newfound disability, all I wanted to ask them was what's everyone been up to. The conversation with my friends was as difficult as it was with my parents, with a lot of long silences.

"As long as you're OK mate, we'll see you soon, here's your Mum again," said Matthew.

The female Doctor entered the room saw me and tapped her watch, smiling apologetically.

"I've got to go now Mum, my times up."

"Yes, that's five minutes I suppose. You take care of yourself, the Embassy said they would tell us when your coming back, I think you will be going to an Army Hospital in London, we'll visit you there."

"OK Mum, it'll only be another week or so, so I'll see you then."

"You take care then, bye," I could hear her start to cry.

"Bye Mum."

The next week passed all too quickly, I enjoyed the company of my Bosnian friends and the Croatian Doctors and Nurses, but I also knew it couldn't go on forever. I didn't really belong here. The female Doctor checked my stump.

"Your leg is good now, tomorrow you will be going, the man from your Army called to asked when you are ready," she said smiling.

"Oh...OK," I suddenly felt deflated.

"You don't want to go? It is your home, you have Mother and Father, they are very worried."

"I like it here."

"But it is not your home. You have done your job for us and we thank you. Now you must return home."

She carefully removed the stitches that sealed my leg, they were like the ones taken from my thigh, crusty and long, leaving a jagged red smile across the length of my stump.

"You still have stitches inside that will dissolve, they will keep you in Hospital for a while in England but you will soon be walking," she looked at me smiling. "We will miss you, I hope you remember us well we are not all like the bad Doctor that changed your dressing."

"I know. Hvala."

That night I did my rounds of the ward, telling my Bosnian friends I would be going the following day. They couldn't understand why I was under arrest or that I faced punishment.

"You stay here? You can come and stay with us in Bihač," the English speaking one said, if only it was that easy.

There was nothing left for them to repair now, the only pain I had was the phantom limb pain, my non-existent foot tingling or the feeling of boiling water on my calf, my stump would jerk with the electrical impulse sent by my brain to nerves that were no longer there and sometimes the twitching would go on and on, exhausting me as I gritted my teeth through pain I had no control over. The bags of fluid had all gone and I must be classed as officially Croatian I had had so much of their blood, there was no infection in the stitches and no longer any requirement for medication, it was now a matter of rehabilitation. I knew the rehabilitation didn't just mean learning to walk again, it meant adjusting to a new life. I had no comprehension of just how new that life would be or how long my rehabilitation would take and I still had a naïve notion that I would be back in Croatia in a few months time with a new leg, fighting at the front. Rehabilitation meant returning home to family and friends and the Army's punishment, if I had stayed in Croatia I would still be an AWOL British soldier and that would mean never returning home without being arrested anyway, I might as well get it over with and besides, I had put my parents through enough for one lifetime.

The tall Staff Sergeant drew everyones attention again as he walked through the ward with another Doctor, still immaculate in his combat gear and blue beret. I had gathered up what possessions I had been given which consisted of a small washbag containing travel sized wash kit and toothbrush and the mismatching pyjamas; stripy bottoms and a polka dot shirt of different colours.

"Ready then mate?" asked the Staff Sergeant.

"Yep, can I just say goodbye to everyone."

"Two minutes, I'll be in the corridor."

I pushed myself up the corridor and past the visitor's room towards the staff room, I wanted to remember every face in every room, to take a piece of them with me forever. The room was full of Nurses and Doctors, the Physiotherapist was there, all were smoking and drinking coffee.

"I go now. Goodbye. Hvala" I couldn't remember the Croatian for Goodbye.

"Goodbye, good luck," one of the Nurses said smiling, I smiled at the faces I recognised, realising that despite everything I was just another patient.

I said goodbye to everyone I saw even if they wondered who the hell I was. The three Bosnians shook my hand and wished me well I thanked them for their friendship and their family's prayers.

The Staff Sergeant put his coat over my shoulders. "It's cold outside," he said. I suddenly felt like I was someone else's property wearing that coat.

"What's the date by the way?" I asked.

"December thirteenth," he said. I had been a casualty exactly a month.

He pushed me into the lift as the three Bosnians came into the corridor and as they watched me leave they clenched their fists in salute.

I held my fist to them as the door hissed closed, I then realised that this was the end of an episode in my life and the start of a new one. I looked downwards at the combat jacket enveloping me as the lift descended and started to cry. These were the tears that wouldn't come in Slavonski Brod and now they flooded out. Tears of every emotion came streaming down my face in powerful sobs before dripping from my chin, as I realised that I didn't know any of their names.

17. Coming Home

I was sedated and strapped to the floor of an Army Hercules Transport aircraft all the way back, it was draughty and noisy so the RAF Nurse escort didn't attempt to make conversation. After a few hours we landed in the UK where an ambulance was waiting with yet another military Nurse escort. I was unstrapped and carried to the ambulance, secured for another journey. This Nurse didn't attempt conversation either, I had no idea where I was going and every one I had encountered, however briefly, had treated me like a large parcel that had to be delivered somewhere. Nobody spoke to me on arrival at the Hospital, I was sat in a wheelchair and pushed through immaculate corridors lined with hundreds of military pictures hanging on walls before ending up in a single room.

The room had its own sink and mirror and a large window opposite, the curtains were drawn and the light above the mirror had been turned on for me, giving the room a warm yellow glow in the darkness, I sat in the wheelchair looking at my surroundings. This was the Queen Elizabeth Military Hospital in Woolwich, South London, conveniently situated next to the Royal Artillery Garrison Headquarters where I would also be spending some time. I sat in the wheelchair in the room waiting for something to happen, I seemed to have been waiting hours on my own and I wasn't used to not having people around me and started to feel a panic that maybe they had forgotten I was here. I wheeled myself through the door and into the corridor, content to just wait there watching people go by or looking at the picture of HMS Trafalgar hanging on the wall opposite.

"Get back in your room!" a stern voice shouted. It was the Matron, or some other rank I wasn't too sure of, in her dark blue uniform. She ran over grabbing the handle on my chair and pushed me straight back into the room.

"We have to test you for any kind of infection, until then, stay here." And with that, she left.

I had had some low moments in the past month, now I regretted coming back, I felt small and insignificant, I was a pain in the arse and a problem to these people and just as I thought, I was in a country that doesn't give a shit.

A while later the same Matron came in with an older Officer, a Lieutenant Colonel.

"You are 24866218 Gunner Hutt, correct? Hello, I'm the Commanding Officer of this Hospital, I'm here to remind you that you are under arrest and while you are here you are in our custody. If you do try and leave you'll be formally arrested and spend your time in the Artillery Garrison in a cell. Do you understand?"

"Yes Sir."

"Good. I'm sure it won't come to that, we are here to get you up and about again. You're in isolation at the moment until we can check for something called MRSA which is quite infectious." The Big Boss was smiling now he had got all the uncomfortable official arrest business out of the way.

"The Nurses will take some swabs and get you some food and we'll see you in the morning. Anything else?" he was looking at the Matron.

"Could you inform my parents I'm here Sir."

The Matron spoke this time, "We've done that, and they'll be down to visit you tomorrow."

"Oh…Thank you Ma'am."

Soon after they left a Nurse came in and took swabs of all my scars and the inside of my mouth. Her black hair was pinned into a bun on the back of her head, her expression blank and cold, her grey uniform neatly pressed.

"So you're the AWOL bloke in from Bosnia," she said in a London accent.

"Yep, that's me."

"So what did you go out there in the first place for?"

"Someone's got to make a difference."

"Did they pay you much?"

"No, nothing, I didn't go there for the money."

"And this is what you got for it? You must be fucking mad!" she laughed at she was putting the swabs away.

I said nothing, but the anger was growing inside me.

"At least you won't be doing it again will you?" she said smiling.

"Fuck off."

"What?"

"Just…fuck off," I repeated, staring straight into her eyes.

The Nurse turned and went out in a hurry taking the half dozen tubes of swabs with her. I could just about take her ignorance, it was her piss-taking manner that got to me. She was so different from the Nurses in Croatia, they were caring and there was a warmth about every expression, she was cold, uncaring and had a voice that immediately grated. I already hated this place, telling me to be a good boy and not run away because I'm under arrest, the fucking petty rules, the "Yes Sir!" and "No Ma'am!" I didn't belong here with these idiots.

The door burst open and the Matron stepped in.

"Gunner Hutt, I appreciate you've been through a lot, but please do not swear at my Nurses."

"Yes Ma'am," I said, realising I was part of the system whether I liked it or not. At least the food was nicer here.

I didn't sleep much that first night back in the UK, the bed felt different, the sounds of the Hospital were quieter and I was on my own with no one snoring or groaning in pain next to me. What sleep I did have was nightmare ridden and I woke with my pillow soaked in sweat, it would take me several minutes to get my bearings and realise where I was before eventually falling asleep again. The sound of a mortar shell woke me, it screamed louder and louder, closer and closer, before I sat bolt upright, panting and sweating as I saw a blonde Nurse standing in the doorway frozen, staring at me with her hands gripping the handle of the drinks trolley tightly.

"Er…good morning…. would you like a cup of tea?" her Scottish voice trembled.

The sun shone through the patterned orange curtains and on to my bed, from my window I could see a large field surrounded by trees on the other side of the main road and a Puma helicopter sat in the middle of the field, its rotors drooping lazily downwards. I stared out of the window for most of the morning, I was a prisoner in my own room and even though I had nothing to say to the rest of the patients I missed the constant company I had been used to. It was ironic that I could spend the whole day talking to my Bosnian friends who could hardly speak English but had nothing in common with, or any desire to talk to, the people here. I realised that I was better on my own.

It was mid afternoon when I heard them come in, my parents wore plastic aprons to counter any kind of MRSA infection. They had been talking all the way down the corridor, no doubt being filled in by the Matron on my condition which she had established by looking through my notes that had been hastily translated. My Mother was all smiles as the Matron showed her to the seats at the side of my bed and my Father looked pale and tired but attempted to smile. They sat on the seats next to me, I felt embarrassed and stupid, I wanted the Matron to stay there and carry on talking.

"Half an hour, OK," the Matron said, smiling as she left.

"God, you look thin," said my Mother. The smile was now gone, replaced by a shocked and concerned expression.

I could see my Fathers blue eyes redden as they filled with tears. I didn't understand. What should I say? I had never seen my Father cry and I didn't like it because it was my fault, we were a family of few emotions. Now my Father wiped the tears that ran down his cheek and I couldn't say a word.

"I'm just glad you're alive. It's so good to see you back," he said wiping his eyes.

"I'm sorry I had you worried." The words didn't seem enough.

"Are you eating, you've got to put on some weight, are they looking after you," my Mother said. I reassured her I was OK and I explained what happened to my leg and why I had lost so much weight. My Father sat looking on holding back his tears and I tried to avoid eye contact.

"What did you go out there for? It's not your war," Mum said.

"I thought I could help."

"They're all as bad as each other," she said.

"I had to do it, I wanted to make a difference."

"Rubbish, it's nothing to do with us."

There was no point explaining my reasons why to her, she saw her son almost get himself killed so the reasons were irrelevant. We sat a while longer talking about nothing, the usual uncomfortable silences punctuating the stilted conversation. I felt a complete shit for having put them through this, though I still couldn't understand why they were so upset and was stunned by my Fathers visible show of emotion. I had no words to make them feel better and "sorry" was a bit pathetic and in truth I wasn't sorry for what I had done, only sorry for worrying them.

"Are you brushing your teeth?" Mum asked inevitably.

Another day and night spent looking out of the window in my room, the Matron on night duty had seen me at midnight, staring out on to the field, waiting for something to happen and dreading the horrors of sleep. I told her I couldn't sleep because of the dreams so she gave me a little yellow jelly-like sweet called Tamazepam.

The following day I had another couple of visitors; the Special Investigation Department of the Military Police. They were both in civilian clothes, the older man was a Captain, although judging by his accent he had come through the ranks. The other was a woman in her twenties who didn't say a single word the whole time she was there and she may as well have been invisible, then again maybe that was the point. Neither of them smiled as the man introduced them both.

"I suppose you know why we are here?" he said as his female assistant set up a tape recorder next to him. They wanted to get straight down to business which was fine with me. I had been thinking for some time how I would play this and the only way I could think of doing it was just to tell them everything and be as honest as I could. After all, what could they do to me when my leg is already my life sentence and my honesty can only go in my favour, besides, you can't get ten years in prison for being AWOL.

"...however anything you do say may be taken down and used in evidence against you in a court of law. Do you understand?"

The red light on the tape recorder was on and the machine whirred as the Officer read me my legal rights.

"Yes."

"And for the record, you do not at this stage, want legal representation present?"

I wasn't taking in the seriousness of the situation I was in, I was in the shit but at the time I hadn't got a clue, I still thought they would see me as a bloke who lost his leg; tough shit son, serves you right, now off you go. What do I need legal representation for?

"No."

I went through everything from start to finish including names, places, and numbers. From the moment I boarded the flight to Vienna to the moment I handed myself in to the Embassy in Zagreb. Every event; losing my I.D. card, joining HOS, the firefight and the killing of the Četnik, joining 106 Brigade, the village, being blown up and my evacuation. Every detail I could think of, although most of what I knew would have been common knowledge anyway, I also left some of the people out of the story and changed all the names. I left nothing else out and was completely honest, which was just as well as they cross-examined the hell out of me. After several hours of statements and questions they seemed satisfied they had everything and terminated the interview.

"Remember, you are still under arrest for being Absent Without Leave, you'll be hearing from us soon," he said as his invisible assistant packed up the recorder and sealed the cassette tapes containing my interview.

The miserable bastards didn't even say goodbye and I had given them enough information to keep MI6 busy for a couple of hours at least.

I had been in the Hospital a couple of days and seen only a handful of people and most of those only came to tell me I was under arrest and not to do anything stupid. The hours passed by looking out of the window at the field, helicopters would come and go regularly, the fat Puma or the huge twin-rotored Chinook dropping off casualties from God knows where. Some didn't even stop, the rotors chopping through the air as patients were unloaded before being waved away by ground crew. I was beginning to enjoy my solitude, it wasn't that I didn't want to talk to anyone, it was just that I had nothing to say to them, unlike my Bosnian friends. The reaction from most people so far was one of "serves you right."

"You have to spend some time in isolation, a kind of quarantine, because you have something called MRSA," the Matron explained through a mask as the Nurses wheeled my bed and me out of the room and down the corridor, their plastic aprons squeaking as they walked. I had no idea what MRSA was, not many people did in 1992, but isolation was fine with me. If I was on my own there would be even fewer people who I would have to explain or justify myself to and with the Tamazepam at night at least I'd have something to look forward to during the day.

The Isolation Ward was a large room with four beds at each corner and an array of equipment next to them, across the far wall was a window that ran the whole length of the wall, the Nurses station was a space in the corridor. I even had my own T.V. Twice a day the Nurses would come in to wash me down and dress the infection, the site of which was on the scar of my stump. I was told that MRSA "breaks down tissue" although I had no idea what that meant either, but it didn't hurt which was a bonus. The Nurses were friendlier, maybe because they spent most of their time behind a mask and plastic aprons, they always seemed in a good mood and were sorry that I would be stuck in that room on my own for God knows how long, maybe they hadn't been told I was under arrest and couldn't go anywhere if I wanted to anyway. The view from the window was of the back of the Hospital which overlooked council football pitches and a few houses, I watched grown men covered in mud play football on a freezing Sunday in December and felt envious it would never be me.

My parents came and visited me in quarantine and they too had to wear the plastic aprons and gloves. It was less uncomfortable than before, mainly because one of the senior military Doctors was with them and he explained everything in detail, as much for my benefit as for theirs. The phantom pains that I had would be with me forever, it was a case of managing to cope with them, I would be put on a course of tablets called Carbamazepine which were used in the treatment of epilepsy but were found to help with phantom limb pain. I would be fitted for a limb as soon as I had got rid of the MRSA bug then it would be up to me as to how quickly I wanted to walk, there was the Military Rehabilitation Centre in Surrey called RAF Headley Court where I would spend a couple of months learning to walk with my new limb as well as coping with everyday tasks. My parents asked lots of questions as if I wasn't even there, wanting every detail and every bit of information they could get.

"What's that scar on his chest?" Mum pointed out a dent a few inches below my left nipple which I had always assumed was from when I had chicken pox as a young child. The Doctor had a quick look at my chest and smiled.

"That is a third nipple. Apparently a sign of good luck in China!"

Fucking typical, I thought, I've got one leg and three nipples.

The days went by slowly, there was only so much you could see from one window and my leg showed no signs of getting better. It would soon be Christmas. The Lieutenant Colonel that I had seen on my first day in the Hospital came to see me.

"We often find the MRSA bug clears up outside a Hospital environment and we've spoke to your sister, she's a highly qualified Nurse in her own right, yes? She's agreed to look after you for a few weeks until the MRSA clears up. In other words you'll be going home for a while."

I wasn't sure if I was pleased or not to be going home as I didn't really want people to see me with a leg missing, I wanted my artificial one so that I wouldn't look any different. And I was also enjoying the isolation.

"A lot of people took a lot of persuading, they want to make an example of you as they think too many soldiers go off to Bosnia then come back and just get a telling off, they really wanted to throw the book at you."

"What for? I've got my punishment," I said.

"They were thinking of charging you with Attempted Murder. Like I said, they want to make an example of you."

The word "Murder" seemed to hang in the air, I had been totally honest with the Military Police, probably too honest.

"It's only because they have no evidence apart from your own statement that they can only charge you with being Absent Without Leave. Believe me when I say they tried everything to pin something on you."

"It doesn't seem very fair, Sir"

"It's the system and your part of it. You're still under arrest even though you're going home. And once your up and about with your new prosthetic leg and you've been to rehab, you will face a Court Martial."

The wankers were going to get me up and mobile again just so that they could put me on trial.

"I've said this before and I'll say it again, don't do anything silly, get yourself better, face the music, then get on with your life."

The Colonel seemed a nice guy and we talked for a while about rehab and artificial limbs and the nightmares. When he left I tried to feel positive about going home but all I could think about was what they wanted to do to me. I imagined a group of suits and high-ranking Officers and decision makers sitting around a table talking about me and what I had done and ultimately how they could punish me. They didn't know me but wanted to make an example of me because I had been a bad boy for going to another country and fighting in someone elses war. Nobody wanted to know the reasons, would they listen if I told them that the Gulf War was someone elses war? Was I being naïve again? Nobody really cared except me and all I could do was keep my mouth shut and bend over and take it. At that moment I missed Croatia, the people helped me, they knew what I had done and they cared as if I was one of their own.

Being at home actually felt good, nobody asked me the details of what I had done or why just like after the Gulf and I skipped around the house on crutches as if nothing had happened. Nobody spoke about it, maybe it was the fear of talking about a subject that might reveal some uncomfortable emotion.

"Where's the tree gone?" I had sat looking out of the window onto the garden for ages trying to think what was different.

"What?" said my Dad.

"The Willow Tree's gone." There used to be a huge Willow tree that stood at the bottom of the garden, I had climbed it, played under it and rode my bike round it as a child.

"We had to cut it down, it was getting too big."

And that was it. The tree had gone the same way as my leg, only I felt the loss of that tree. It was part of my childhood, good memories of sitting under it in the summer. Gone, all gone. I felt anger at my Father for getting rid of it, it was some kind of symbolic reference for me that I hadn't realised until it was no longer there. My sister dutifully dressed the hole in my leg that the MRSA bug had caused and after only a few days she noticed it wasn't getting bigger.

A week into my home leave I had another visitor who looked like a middle-aged schoolteacher, complete with wire rimmed glasses and leather patches on his elbows. My parents had already shown him in.

"There's someone from the Army to see you, do you want to see them?" my Mother said. My parents estimation of the Army had gone down considerably when they knew I would face a Court Martial.

"I'm from Intelligence. I'd just like to get some information about your time in Bosnia. As you know our troops are out there as part of the UN so any information you can provide will help."

If the man had been wearing a uniform or was part of the Army system I would have told him to stick it, they had all the information I gave them and used it in evidence against me. This guy however, wasn't part of the "official" system.

"I'm not taping anything, it's an informal chat just so we can get some information, from ground level so to speak." He seemed to have read my mind, he probably had read all the files relating to me anyway. In truth I wanted to talk about it to someone.

The man spread out a huge map of Yugoslavia on the dining room table and I pointed out the areas; Županja, Orašje, the villages of Lijesvojac, Domaljevac, Matiči and Vidovice. I gave him names, some of the names anyway, uniforms, roughly how many men in a Brigade and how I thought the units and Brigades were organised. As well as the plan to relieve the enclave around Brčko by retaking the Serb village. The man was writing down all the information I was giving him in shorthand, he spoke Serbo-Croat and translated stuff I didn't know the meaning of, even complimenting me on my pronunciation.

"At 106 we had weapons still in their grease, brand new."

"So arms weren't a problem then. Were they Russian?"

"No, Chinese."

The mans eyes lit up. He loved it.

"You're sure?"

"Yep, Chinese writing everywhere on the crates, I think it even said Made In China on the side."

We chatted away like old friends while he took down a few more scribbled notes.

"You glad you went?"

"Yes, I really miss the people now I'm back."

"You've been really helpful and we'll put a good word in for you, we may be back in touch if there's anything we need to clarify."

I went to my local pub with friends on a few occasions but walking around with most of your leg missing draws stares, that was a strange experience in itself, initially I wondered what the hell people were staring at and it took me a while to realise. I couldn't drink much because of the medication and if I drank too much and fell or slipped my automatic reaction would be to use my right leg to stabilise myself, but as it wasn't there I would probably land on my stump. Christmas day was a bit of a nightmare as well, the phantom pains in my non-existent foot alongside the constant electrical impulses were making my stump twitch sharply. It was Catch 22; the more I thought about the pain the worse it got but I couldn't stop thinking about the pain because it was there agonisingly pulsing and twitching. I discovered the more stressed and worried I was, the more pain I felt and if I was relaxed I could control the phantom limb pain to some extent. The stump twitching was something I had no control over, some nights it would go on for hours leaving me in tears of frustration rather than pain. Early in the New Year the MRSA had gone in time for me to return to Woolwich, it had left a deep dent in the scar across my stump. My sister was a one-woman cure for MRSA who carefully dressed the wound twice a day and never judged me for what I had done or told me off for doing what I did, her only desire was to get her little brother's leg better.

The next few weeks at Woolwich were a blur of leg measurements and being smothered in plaster casts at Dulwich Limb Fitting Centre. The waiting room at the Limb Fitting Centre was filled with an array of people with missing body parts, most of them were elderly, losing legs through poor circulation or from action in World War Two. People in their twenties and thirties with missing limbs were usually as a result of traffic accidents, especially motorbikes. The stories in the waiting room were always about what happened; an IRA bomb at a train station, the accident with a forklift truck, the fall of Singapore, Meningitis or Diabetes. It didn't take long for them to get a leg ready, the hardest thing was to get a comfortable fitting socket for the stump to rest in. Eventually the plastic socket fitted my stump perfectly, the large amount of "meat" between the end of the bone and the end surface of skin providing a natural cushion, the socket came all the way up the inside to the crease between my leg and my groin and on the outside it came up to my hip. It stayed on with the aid of a neoprene belt that fastened around my waist with Velcro. The leg itself was metal "bones" with a pneumatic knee and a slightly springy ankle all of which was covered with sculpted foam and a nylon stocking to make it look leg-shaped and skin-coloured. It could never be confused with the real thing but I wouldn't have cared if I just had the metal skeleton of a leg as long as I could walk, which they said would take a few months.

They told me to wear it a few hours a day and take it easy, but there was never any chance of that. As soon as I had the leg there was no stopping me, first with crutches, then with two walking sticks then with a single stick. I was totally focused on my single objective - to walk properly again. I would walk until I was sore, I lost count of the amount of times I tripped or stumbled or tried to put weight through the leg when my knee hadn't locked into place and gave way. People would hear me swear and turn to see me flat on the floor of the Hospital corridor, I would often get cramp in the muscles of my stump and would be unable to stretch it to relieve the pain and the socket filled up with sweat as if I was wearing a plastic shoe. The Physiotherapists wanted me to slow down when all I wanted to do was run. Physically at least, I was back. It was the best I had felt in some time and I had achieved my aim of some kind of mobility, however awkward and clumsy. It took me about three weeks to walk without a walking stick at all.

Now that I was mobile and feeling fitter all I wanted to do was get out of this Hospital and out of the Army and its system of bullshit, I was a man in a rush. The longer I stayed in that Hospital the more I hated it. At a ward inspection patients were expected to stand to attention when the Head Matron came round to do her rounds, I sat on my bed and said nothing and after a while and unless it was someone I liked, I refused to say Sir or Ma'am, it was my own small rebellion. Most of them were OK with me although I didn't care much either way. I wanted to start again and put the Army behind me and I was starting to become disillusioned and angry. I even questioned my reasons for going to fight in Bosnia, had I done the right thing? Or was it just everyone elses apathy rubbing off on me? As the weeks went by the more Bosnia seemed further away. It was my history, right or wrong, all I had to do now was get on with my future and at the minute it only stretched as far as me being kicked out of the Army, I hadn't thought about after that, more through fear than anything else.

RAF Headley Court was a huge Manor House with extensions built onto it, it stood in acres of grounds complete with football pitches and tennis courts. Inside the building was a hive of people moving from one therapy class to another, moving like ants in a line to their next destination. Most of the patients had minor injuries; muscle tears or recovering from a broken leg, occasionally a wheelchair bound patient would ride past. I was shown to the upstairs accommodation and it was here that those with more serious injuries stayed. It had wide carpeted corridors and comfortable chairs, this was the place where the people who wouldn't make a full recovery stayed; a Brain Haemorrhage, two men who had both been shot through the spine by the IRA, the man who was electrocuted, the girl who had recently come out of a coma after a car crash, the young Para who had both his legs blown off in Northern Ireland. It was a sad place full of people who had survived but only had civilian life and a disability to look forward to, in the meantime they stayed here, learning to cope. In reality they wanted to stay here as long as possible around military people and a military environment, here people understood, when they were eventually on the outside they would face their country that didn't care.

All too often one of the patients would get the dreaded letter from a loved-one which would always contain the words " I'm sorry but..." or, "...can't do this anymore..." or, "...found someone else..." it happened with a sad regularity, for some it was a relief that their partner no longer had to care for them, or even look at them now that they were physically or mentally damaged.

We would have several classes a day, which consisted of physiotherapy, P.E or occupational therapy. My Physiotherapist was a middle-aged cockney who was built like a rugby player and he showed me no mercy. He would grab my stump and massage it violently trying to desensitise the stump so it was less painful as other patients looked on in disbelief at me gritting my teeth, he was fantastic and constantly took the piss out of me as he did it. If I wasn't having a violent stump massage I would be hooked up to a TENS machine, which sent electrical impulses through my stump, again trying to desensitise the nerve endings. The Para with no legs was called Alex and was only a year older than me, he had accidentally detonated a booby trap whilst on patrol in Armagh, Northern Ireland and only realised he had done it when he was flying up in the air, it resulted in one above knee amputation and one below knee amputation, chunks of flesh were also blown off his arms. Alex was in all of my classes and for us P.E was a bit of a joke. We would try and join in just for a laugh but trying to play badminton when you're standing still or sitting in a wheelchair isn't easy. Sometimes we would just say that we didn't want to do it, the RAF staff understood most of the time unless they thought we were just being lazy in which case they would give us an almighty talking to. They can't have had an easy job trying to cope with so many disabilities and emotions and at the same time trying to get people motivated to get better. Occupational therapy taught us how to go about daily life doing normal things such as cooking or pumping up the tyre on a bike. It all seemed pretty pointless, all the things they showed us none of us had done when we were able bodied, we were all in the Army, Navy, or RAF, we weren't civilians. And besides, why the hell would I want to pump up the tyre on a bike when I can't ride the fucking thing anyway.

We filled out forms to claim Disability Living Allowance and had presentations by the British Legion, SSAFA and various other agencies that were there to help us. What the staff there couldn't do was make us think for ourselves and most of us had been in the Forces since leaving school. The Army taught me how to shave and when to do it, everything about military life is structured and done for you, all I had to do was turn up and do it and never ask why. I would be fed, clothed and paid. The Army was a ready-made family who would always be there for you unless, as in my case, you really pissed the family off.

I still felt like the outsider in that place even though I was surrounded by people in a much worse state than me. Alex was the brave Para injured in Northern Ireland whereas I was the idiot who went AWOL and decided to go to Bosnia. I kept my head down during my stay at Headley Court, I had been warned on my first day by the Commanding Officer yet again that I was still under arrest and I was just focused on getting better and stronger. I had the occasional trip to Dulwich Limb Fitting Centre for an upgrade, my first leg lasted only a month before I wore out the joints in the ankle and the foam poked out of the nylon stocking like the filling coming out of a stuffed toy. My next leg they decided, would be "low-tech" in order for it to last longer.

The Psychiatrist was Flight Lieutenant Turnbull who I recognised as the guy who dealt with the British Tornado pilots that were shot down and held in Iraq during the Gulf War. He sat back in his comfy leather chair crossing his arms, his neat grey hair parted at the side, he could have been any kind of Officer in the Forces and he didn't look like a shrink, although this was the first time I had ever seen one. He looked ahead expressionlessly and we talked for a while about how I felt and what happened, I told him that the nightmares had gone mainly due to the Tamazepam and I had no flashbacks to speak of apart from the occasional sound of a mortar, but that was so rare it didn't bother me. I didn't want to say that I was constantly angry and hated everyone and everything, so after about half an hour of me saying I think I'm OK he told me I didn't have Post Traumatic Stress Disorder. Maybe I wasn't as high profile as the Tornado pilots or maybe he just thought it served me right, but after his cold emotionless diagnosis I left his office. That was the sum total of the military's psychiatric care as far as they were concerned, I suppose that as I would be discharged and would be no further use to the Army they didn't need to look after me and after all, in a few months time I would be a civilian then it would be the NHS' problem. Besides, it wouldn't look good if a man with a mental illness was being Court Martialled would it?

18. No Requests and No Complaints

After a few months Woolwich Hospital started to feel like a Prison. I was moved to an almost empty ward and left to my own devices, isolated from the rest of the military personnel in there. The Nurses and staff kept their distance, seeing me as some kind of lost cause, a man who didn't care anymore what the Army might do to him and who was also aggressive and cold. As anybody who was able went home to recuperate whenever possible, there were sometimes a few others in the huge ward at weekends, mainly Scottish and Irish guys as the distance and expense stopped them from returning home. We would sneak in bottles of Vodka and get hammered in the Hospital, confident that the staff were elsewhere. For me though it was still a Prison and the reminders that I was still under arrest were never ending.

I just wanted it over with and the waiting was starting to get to me. I had just turned twenty in May of 1993 and it had been almost six months since my injury. It felt a lifetime away. I tried to remember everything that I had done and seen but it was all confused and jumbled, none of it seemed real, it was as if it had happened to someone else. I had no evidence of me even being in Bosnia or Croatia, no photos or friends and any proof I had was left behind, including a body part. The idealistic reasons for fighting in a foreign war were forgotten, nobody wanted to hear and I had nothing to say. I buried all the memories deep inside, that man died in Bosnia and now I thought I was someone else; a one legged ex-soldier with a jumble of strange memories which may have been dreamt and, like a soldier without a rifle, I had no real purpose. In the short time I had been back in the UK I had mentally deteriorated, maybe my coping mechanism was to shut everything and everyone out. I was a shell of a human being, content to put one foot in front of the other and slowly walk onwards with my eyes fixed to the floor, not knowing where I was going and unsure of what I had done. My only emotions were anger and hate, there was no sadness or thoughts of "poor me". I stumbled onwards to my goal of getting out of the Army because then, I thought, maybe things would get better.

I was transferred to the Royal Artillery Garrison, Woolwich, the base next to the Hospital. It was both the Headquarters of the Royal Artillery and home to 17 Training Regiment, which gave recruits too old for Junior Leaders their basic training. It was a big sprawling Victorian era base with lots of gleaming brass and marble columns and filled with soldiers in badly shaped berets trying to march in step. At the guardroom the Sergeant in charge gave me the usual lecture reminding me that I was under arrest and to behave, which always sounded more or less threatening depending on the accent it was said in. The Geordie Sergeant's accent sounded quite friendly.

"You couldn't wait to get here could you?" he said.

"No Sergeant, I was getting a bit bored," I said.

"Enjoy a few drinks at night as well I hear."

"Er...yes, how did you know?"

"My wife was the cleaner on your ward, she's told me all about you," he said with a gleam in his eye.

I remembered the cleaner, a nice woman in her forties who we used to ask to dispose of our empty Vodka bottles in return for us helping to empty the bins. She told the dirtiest jokes you've ever heard, and was one of the few people in the Hospital I liked. I'm glad that I had a laugh with her which would have made a good impression on the Sergeant who, if he wanted to, could make my stay here an absolute misery.

"Keep your head down and your mouth shut and you'll be out of here in no time."

Keeping my head down and my mouth shut was all I had been doing for the last few months.

I was put in a big empty barrack room until my Court Martial along with two other guys but ten extra bed spaces. These two had been backsquadded through injury; they had injuries that prevented them passing out this year but would be fit enough for the next intake. The three of us went to the pub opposite camp every night. The Kings Arms was one of the most bombed pubs in mainland Britain and an easy target for the IRA as every night it was full of soldiers from either the Hospital or the Artillery Garrison. Posters covered the walls warning of suspicious packages and dodgy looking people, in other words blokes with Irish accents, and being a soldier's pub it was usually full of pissed up squaddies and rough looking women, but at least we didn't have far to walk home. And I thought I'd enjoy it while I had the chance.

"You what?" I said, not knowing whether to laugh, cry or punch him in the face.

I was sat opposite my Solicitor who was due to represent me in my court martial. A slick civvy in a grey suit which matched his personality, or lack of it. With some people you instinctively "know" when your going to get on, like Terry and Ivan, but this bloke, however hard I tried, had absolutely no redeeming features whatsoever.

"Sorry but that's the way it is," he stuttered, giving me the distinct impression that he didn't want to be there.

"You want me to come across as immature and naïve so they feel sorry for me?" I said.

"You don't have to do anything, we do all the talking. It's better to do that than do some kind of revolutionary speech and really get on their tits."

"This is bullshit. I've already got a life sentence with my leg, now I have to say sorry I've been silly and act like I've been a twat just so they're nice to me?"

"Remember they wanted to charge you with murder, now you'll only be charged with desertion."

"Fucking desertion?"

"Yes, like AWOL only with no intention of coming back and handing yourself in," he said shutting his briefcase.

The more I looked at him the more I realised that in a week or so I was going to get shafted no matter what and this guy didn't give a rat's arse about me or what I had done or even if I were to spend the next twenty years in prison, he would still get paid. Nice work if you can get it. The worst thing was that I would have to play the "I've been a silly boy" card, which was exactly what they must want, humiliation on top of punishment.

"Good luck and don't worry, there's nothing to panic about, I'm sure you've been through worse," Slick Solicitor said, shaking my hand.

"There'd be no point worrying anyway, their minds are already made up about me," I said angrily.

I was issued new Army clothing in preparation for my court martial, though I made an excuse about being unable to wear boots because my artificial ankle wouldn't bend properly that way I didn't have to spend the rest of my stay here polishing them. I secretly wanted to wear the boots, wearing the rest of the green clothing made me feel good and my beret was especially smart compared to the new recruits around me, I did look a bit of an arse wearing a pair of trainers though. At the same time as they issued me with new kit, I was also charged with the loss of Army property, namely some of my stuff I had left behind in Germany when I went AWOL. Every soldier wants spare and extra equipment and a soldier going AWOL meant it was open season for some of the more unscrupulous guys of 176 Battery. Most of the kit was the usual jackets and clothing and a spare pair of boots, however the British Army Kevlar helmet cost about £80, and why the hell someone would want an extra helmet I didn't know. A total of about £200 was deducted from my wages for the loss of kit.

"You ready?" the Geordie Sergeant said as he checked my smart Number Two Dress uniform, ready for my court martial.

"Just want it over with Sarge," I said.

"You know your going to do time."

"Doesn't seem very fair though," I said pathetically

"You know the press wanted to be here."

"What?"

"Some guys from the papers have heard and they're within their rights to be there."

"Won't make any difference to me though will it?"

"They're not going to get past the gate, mate. Orders from above."

"British justice, you can't beat it," I said sarcastically.

"Careful."

In front of the huge parade ground was the building of the Royal Artillery Headquarters with its tall white marble columns and World War Two howitzers framing the massive doors. No stray leaves or litter could be seen and there wasn't a blade of grass out of place. I was escorted to a small side room along with two other soldiers who were also being court martialled; one for striking an Officer and one for being AWOL. We sat with our backs straight and hands on our knees, not daring to move or talk. A procession of Officers walked casually past the doorway, chatting and laughing as they went. There was a variety of uniforms and ranks; Officers from the Guards, the Engineers, Infantry and a female Officer from the Signals. The head man was a Lieutenant Colonel from an Irish Regiment judging by his dark green uniform and brass harps on his collars, he also brought his dog with him. The Regimental Police from the Guardroom were also in dress uniform and stood as escorts at the door, they came to attention and saluted sharply as the Officers filed past into the Courtroom. Having a court martial usually meant a spell in the Military Correction and Training Centre, the Army's purpose built prison in Colchester. I knew I wouldn't be going there as they wouldn't know what to do with me and even by the Army's standards so far, sending a disabled man to Colchester prison would be pushing it. After an age of nervous waiting the AWOL soldier went first. The Geordie Sergeant shouting drill instructions in the soldiers face, the familiar quick march at the double, the soldiers boots hammering into the floor as he marched on the spot.

"GETYOURFUCKINGKNEESUP!" the Sergeant bellowed into his ear.

"FORWARD...LEFRIGHTLEFRIGHTFLEF."

The doors to the courtroom swung open just as the soldier reached them and he marched, double time, into the courtroom full of Army Officers and civilian Solicitors, the door swinging shut behind him.

"MARK TIME...HALT!" the Sergeant could be heard inside the room.

The bullshit and the predictability of it all was depressing. Going through the motions in front of a portrait of the Queen, in boots that took hours for men to polish like glass and brass buttons that couldn't even be seen that were shining like gold. If she only knew, then again maybe she does and doesn't give a shit. After twenty minutes the Sergeant's drill voice could be heard again and the familiar hammering of boots on tiled floor at the double. The doors swung open again and the soldier quick marched into the corridor next to us closely followed by the Sergeant as the doors swung shut again.

"LEFRIGHTLEFRIGHTLEF...MARK TIME...HALT."

The soldier stood panting and sweating, mouth open gasping for breath.

"FALL OUT...right, wait in there...MOVE!"

The soldier ran into the side room and sat opposite us with arms and back straight and fists on knees, his cheeks flushed and his eyes glued to a point above our heads before casually looking round to see if he was being watched.

"That wasn't too bad...thirty days," he whispered in a Scouse accent, the sweat running down his face and dripping off his chin.

Another nervous wait and activity from the room as Officers went to the toilet and Solicitors changed over. With some dread I saw my Slick Solicitor enter the room without even seeing me. With everybody settled again there was a lull, a calmness which reminded me of the moment before the tank fired in Vidovice.

"Gunner Hutt," the Sergeant called to me.

I walked out into the corridor, no marching at the double for me.

"Just walk in, halt when I say, there's a chair for you so sit down when they tell you to. Keep your mouth shut and we'll be done in twenty minutes. Then we walk out the way we came in," he said calmly, there was no shouting in my ear. "OK?"

"Yes Sergeant," I said, trying to convince myself that this was all just superficial bullshit, but I was unprepared for what was so predictable again.

The doors swung open as I walked as smartly as I could into the large Victorian room. In front of me were around ten Officers in their colourful uniforms, in the middle was the Lieutenant Colonel from the Irish Regiment, above his head a coat of arms and the ever-present portrait of the Queen.

"Halt."

* * * *

I stop in the middle of the room, my Solicitor and his team to the right of me, more Officers, the prosecution, to the left of me. The lull again, my stomach churns, it's all just bullshit, just bullshit. I can hear a posh voice reading out the charge and my number, rank and name. Inside I'm screaming.

"Sir, yes Sir," I say.

"Be seated."

I move to the chair next to me and sit down, still in the middle of the room with my back straight and arms locked, my hands clenched into fists on my knees as I try and concentrate on the coat of arms and Queenie. All eyes are on me, I'm surrounded by people who don't know me but are about to judge me. Mouth shut, look up, remember it's all just bullshit. The prosecution Officer starts outlining the details of my offence.

For a second I wonder who it is she's talking about. She starts describing the devil, a murdering mercenary, a disgrace to Queen and Country, bringing the British Army into disrepute and putting British UN troops at risks. Is this me she's talking about? I want to scream again and tell her that it's not me. I try not to listen but I can feel everyone's eyes burn into me. Then she starts reading parts of my statement and I immediately start to crumple, she reads the sentences verbatim and it's like the final twist of the knife. It sounds like somebody posh is trying to talk in a Nuneaton accent; lots of "dunno", "ain't", "ar" instead of yes, "nah" instead of no, "int it" instead of isn't it, "like" at the end of sentences. It sounds so common and ridiculous in her educated voice as each "ain't" is pronounced perfectly. She makes me sound so stupid as well as evil.

Tears start to troll down my cheeks. I try to stay strong but there's no strength left, my eyes drop to the floor instead of the coat of arms. They've beaten me. The humiliation is complete and my personality has been ripped to shreds, why do they need to do this? Is this the example they wanted? Tears stream down my face and drop to the floor between my trainer clad feet, my fists are still clenched but my body sags, bent over, broken and hollow. Being shot in the back of the head and being buried naked in a ditch would be less humiliating. I feel like I've been mentally raped.

"Do we need a break?" asks the Lieutenant Colonel.

Looking down, I shake my head through the sobs, I don't want to recover just so they can do this all over again. The prosecution continues quoting my statement and each word is a psychological kick in the balls. Eventually she finishes and I look at her, she returns my gaze with disgust. I should be screaming at them to fuck off and just walk out, what could they do? Instead the Army has trained me to sit there, like a robot, taking it, serves you right Gunner Hutt, what did you expect Gunner Hutt? You've been a silly boy Gunner Hutt.

"Glass of water?" my Solicitor whispers to me.

I sip it slowly during the pause in proceedings, end of Round One. Papers are shuffled and the Officers discuss a brief adjournment, I shake my head at my Solicitor.

"My client would rather get on with it," he says, probably wanting to get on with it as well, he has his legal-aid money to count.

It's the first time I've been called a "client". Seconds out, Round Two. Slick Solicitor stands up, looking out of place in his grey suit against all the others in their fancy dress and shiny buttons. He does well to start with, saying how the prosecution has misrepresented me, I'm not the demon they make out. Here we go again I think to myself staring at the floor, an already broken man. He's just a young boy who wanted a bit of adventure. He was, no, is naïve, immature, and childish, not understanding the consequences of his actions. Immature and childish, well what did you expect Gunner Hutt? The tears stream down my face again, my body crumples in the chair. Stop this please. You've been a very silly boy Gunner Hutt. Please God, I've had enough. Keep your mouth shut and your head down Gunner Hutt. I try and sip the water again as Slick Solicitor informs the panel of Officers how much information I had provided Military Intelligence, how I have a lifetime of coping with a disability and how co-operative I had been for all parties involved. Another pause as impassive faces stare back or shuffle papers, uncomfortable with the sobbing of a grown man.

"I think we should have a short break at this point," says the Lieutenant Colonel. End of Round Two.

"Stand up," the Sergeant says behind me.

I uncrumple my body and raise myself of the chair, standing with head bowed as the group of Officers stand and file out of the room lead by the Lieutenant Colonel's black Labrador, a show of respect and further humiliation.

"It's nearly over now," says my Solicitor when all the Officers have left.

I stare at the coat of arms again, my tears exhausted and say nothing, what's the point?

* * * *

"About turn," says the Sergeant.

I turn and walk slowly out of the room, returning to the side room I had started from. The other two soldiers were still there, still sitting to attention.

"Don't worry about it mate, there's no firing squad anymore," the Scouser said seeing the tears in my eyes.

I looked out of the tall window onto the field and parade ground outside.

"He's taking his fucking dog for a shit," I said quietly.

I watched in disbelief as the Lieutenant Colonel walked out onto the field with his black Labrador bouncing after him, I could hear the shouts of "c'mon boy," as the Officer threw a tennis ball for his dog to chase. I thought they should be at least discussing me, deliberating my judgement and sentencing, instead we had a break so his dog could have a crap.

"This is a fucking joke. They've made their minds up about me long ago," I said.

The whole court martial was a show to make sure justice could be seen to be being done, when in actual fact somebody somewhere months ago said that this was what was going to happen.

"What did you expect?" whispered the Scouser.

"Yeah. Suppose so," what did you expect Gunner Hutt?

I don't know what I expected, certainly not to be stripped of any dignity and humiliated. It was all just bullshit, unnecessary bullshit and the person I thought I was had been torn apart. I was physically broken and now I had been mentally shattered. The past six months since my injury had been spent trying to figure out who I was, the past half hour was spent in a room of strangers telling me exactly what I was.

I stood to attention in the middle of the room again as the Officers filed past and into their seats. Their eyes were fixed on me, judgement time.

"Be seated."

The Officers sat first followed by everyone else, the room silent. This was all a pantomime, but not a very funny one. The Lieutenant Colonel spoke about putting UN lives at risk and bringing the Army into disrepute. I switched off as the tears started again, tears of frustration and anger. I wondered when he wrote this summing up.

"Stand up," the Sergeant said.

I stood up to attention and looked at the Officers, still seated, in front of me. The head man gave his sentence as his dog scratched himself.

"...Section Thirty-Seven Alpha...Desertion...The Army Act..." Words and legal bullshit came out of his mouth.

" ...Ninety days detention. Sergeant, take him away."

My body crumpled again, I had had enough and didn't know what else I could take. All the physical pain from the explosion I could cope with, phantom pain or nightmares I could learn to deal with, this was different, it was an abandonment, as if someone came into your face and said simply "I don't care", or a friend tells you that your either a murdering scumbag or immature and naïve. The anger and hate that had got me through he last few months was gone, there was nothing left inside now except the wish that I had died.

My accommodation changed from the large barrack room to the cells in the guardroom. There was a long, highly polished corridor with four steel doors on each wall and the first three on each side were single cells, just like the ones I had spent time in at 39 Regiment, the doors at the end were large eight man rooms, although one was used for storage.

"You can sleep in the end room, but at inspection you use this cell," the Sergeant said pointing out the second cell down, "I want a bed made with a bed block, so it looks like that's where you're staying. Make sure it doesn't look like you're staying in the end cell."

"Yes Sergeant." I was so glad his wife had put a good word in for me.

"Keep the place shit free and nobody will be on your case, as long as you don't do anything daft you'll be out in sixty days."

"Yes Sergeant."

"I don't want you here and you shouldn't be here, but it's tough shit. At inspection you have to say these words to the duty Officer of the day, learn them. Fill in the blanks with your information."

The Sergeant pointed to a sign on the wall above the posters about legal rights and health and safety.

"Sir, I am 24866218 Gunner Hutt S. E. of 17 Training Regiment Royal Artillery. I have been awarded ninety days detention by District Court Martial under Section 37 alpha of The Army Act 1955. I have served…days, and have…days remaining. I have no requests and no complaints. Sir."

"Good. This counts as day one of your sentence, if you do have any requests or complaints see me first and I'll try and sort them out. You'll do sixty days unless you do something stupid. Go sort your bed block out and get your shit in the end room. The duty Officer will be round at 8PM, one of the lads will shout you when it's time for food and you'll be escorted to the cookhouse. Nobody will give you any grief unless you make it happen. Do we have an understanding?"

"Yes Sergeant."

"I don't want to see you or hear you, now fuck off," he said smiling. Also glad the day was over.

The truth was that he probably didn't know what to do with me anyway, the usual Army punishment consists of a "beasting", strenuous physical exercise to the point of throwing up and they obviously couldn't do that with me. The Sergeant also knew a bit more about me thanks to his wife and shouting and bawling at me wouldn't do anything except piss me off. The humiliation of the court martial was over and I could now focus on getting through the last hurdle of the next sixty days, the last bit of bullshit.

I kept my head down and my mouth shut as usual, doing menial tasks around the guardroom, just enough to stop me getting bored but not too much or too menial that I told them to shove it. The Regimental Police were all fine and let me sit in the guardroom and watch TV with them and at the end of each shift I would have to polish the floor with the buffer. I wasn't shouted at nor did I give anyone any bother. The solitude and isolation were now things I enjoyed. The Adjutant of the Regiment did think I was his personal dogsbody, on one occasion sending his brown leather belt and his boots to the guardroom to be polished by me and I did the worst job possible without actually ruining the belt and boots. The Adjutant came down and attempted to give me a serious bollocking before the Sergeant gave him a quiet word, something along the lines of "Gunner Hutt doesn't give a shit, Sir." He didn't bother sending his stuff down again. Another of my menial tasks was to make badges. In the storage room at the end of the corridor was a badge making machine with thousands of metal discs and pieces of paper that said, "Royal Artillery - The Gunners" along with our capbadge, I would spend a whole morning making hundreds of these badges at a time whilst listening to music on my new Walkman. Cranking the handle of the machine over and over again as I sang along to the Manic Street Preachers. These badges were given out at Army shows and recruitment stalls, if only the kids knew who made them.

At 8AM and 8PM everyday it would be the same routine.

"Sir. I am 24866218 Gunner Hutt S.E. of 17 Training Regiment Royal Artillery. I have been awarded ninety days detention by District Court Martial under section 37 alpha of the Army Act 1955. I have served twelve days and have forty-eight days remaining. I have no requests and no complaints. Sir."

"Is your leg made of wood?" asked the duty Officer, an ancient-looking Sergeant Major on his last posting before retirement.

I stood in the doorway to my single cell, the bed and its bedblock immaculate behind me. Usually the Officer would listen to the words and ask me if I was OK, or what made me go to Bosnia, or if I wanted to stay in the Army, or if I regretted what I had done, the usual questions that I would politely answer and sometimes make a joke out of. Most of the Officers were friendly, there was no point in shouting.

"I'm sorry Sir?" I said, not sure if it was a genuine question or a piss take. The Geordie Sergeant behind the Officer rolled his eyes.

"It's just that I also sell cleaning products and have some brilliant polish," he went on.

"Are you serious?" I said, feeling the anger burn inside me. The Sergeant glared at me, his eyes telling me not to do anything stupid.

"It's cheaper than you can get on the high street," he said.

The Sergeant slowly shook his head at me.

"It's metal encased in foam with a nylon covering, they don't make legs out of wood anymore, Sir," I said trying to stay calm. The Sergeant quietly breathed a sigh of relief.

"Pity. You ought to think about it for when you leave the Army. You can make some money."

"I'll bear that in mind, Sir," I said through gritted teeth as they both left.

"He's a fucking twat," the Sergeant said when he returned, "tries to flog his shit to anyone and he retires in a few months. You don't want to be doing more time than you have to because of that arsehole however satisfying breaking his nose might be."

Three times a day I would be escorted to the cookhouse by one of the RPs. I would be the first one in, or if not would go to the front of the queue. I must have looked odd with my uniform of neatly pressed olive green shirt and trousers with a pair of trainers and no beret, I attempted to march but my balance was all over the place when I tried to swing my arms and I often stumbled. One particular day it had been raining and the verges were muddy and I trod on the edge of the grass and slipped on my arse in the mud, my pride and dignity in pieces yet again.

"HA HA!" came laughter from the accommodation block opposite as I stood up immediately.

"You OK mate? Wait there," the RP said to me.

The RP was about five feet tall and almost as wide and went running over to the window where he heard the laughter from, before jumping into the room.

"WHO THE FUCK WAS IT? WHO? THINK IT'S FUCKING FUNNY DO YOU? I'LL SEE YOU LATER," the RP screamed from inside the accommodation block.

Later that afternoon the Sergeant called me into the small external courtyard in the Guardroom.

"Right, some arsehole laughed at you, yes? I'm going to get him in here and give him a gobful in front of you so he feels a total prick. Is that OK with you?"

"No problem Sergeant."

I stood with my back to the wall as a skinny kid was marched into the courtyard. You can tell when someone is absolutely shitting themselves and the kid was almost in tears. There was a long pause, heightening the fear and anticipation as the Sergeant walked around the recruit, the metal on the soles of his gleaming drill boots crunching and scraping on the concrete. The Sergeant was an expert at this.

"Were you the one that laughed at him falling over?" the Sergeant said quietly.

"Yes Sergeant," said the recruit standing in the middle of the courtyard facing me.

"Disabled people funny are they?"

"No Sergeant," his voice was shaking.

"How long have you been in the Army?"

"Four months Sergeant."

"Four months. FOUR FUCKING MONTHS!" the Sergeant was going up the gears.

"Yes Sergeant," he said quietly.

"THIS ARSEHOLE HAS HAD HIS LEG BLOWN OFF IN A FUCKING WAR, IS THAT FUCKING FUNNY?"

"No Sergeant." It was almost a whisper.

"AND YOU THINK YOU CAN LAUGH AT HIM! HE'S SEEN MORE THINGS IN THE LAST YEAR THAT YOU COULD EVER DREAM ABOUT. HE'S PROBABLY KILLED MEN THAT WERE BETTER THAN YOU!" the Sergeant was in full red-faced anger mode and I was starting to feel quite proud of the way he was sticking up for me. The recruit was visibly shaking.

"I think you owe him an apology. And if you ever get your legs blown off in Northern Ireland, you fucking think about today," the Sergeant said in a low growl, going down the gears again.

"Yes Sergeant…I'm sorry mate."

"HE'S NOT YOUR FUCKING MATE! NOW FUCK OFF!"

The recruit legged it as quickly as he could and I noticed all the other RPs through the window giving the recruit an added mouthful and a kick up the arse as he went past.

"You OK?...good…now you can fuck off as well," the Sergeant said to me. "And what are you fuckers looking at?" he shouted to the other RPs who in turn gave him a round of applause.

The rest of my time there dragged on; twenty-five days and thirty five remaining, thirty seven days and twenty three remaining. I had become a permanent fixture of the guardroom, doing the cleaning and buffering the floor. The RPs treated me with respect as did the majority of the duty Officers. Every so often the Sergeants wife, the cleaner from the Hospital, would come to the guardroom bringing some cakes with her for all of us and would always wave hello to me, the worry of a Mother. I stayed quiet most of the time and tried to keep myself busy and out of view.

"Sir. I am 24866218 Gunner Hutt S.E. of 17 Training Regiment Royal Artillery. I have been awarded ninety days detention by District Court Martial under section 37 alpha of the Army Act 1955. I have served fifty-nine days and have one day remaining. I have no requests and no complaints. Sir." I said, smiling broadly at the duty Officer.

"Well done Gunner Hutt, you got through it. Now you can get on with the rest of your life," said the Officer.

"Yes Sir."

"Any plans on what you want to do?" he asked.

"Er…no sir," I hadn't thought about anything other than first learning to walk again, then getting out of the Army. I didn't know what would happen after that.

"You could consider staying in the Army, there are desk jobs."

"I don't think so Sir. I'm not a soldier anymore." As I said the words the reality hit me, how can I not be a soldier, after all it was all I knew and what I was good at, it was my vocation in life. Deep down I loved it, not so much the bullshit and pantomime of parades and regulation, but the Gulf and Bosnia had become addictive. The adrenaline and fear, life and death, the black and white with no grey areas. There was a clarity that I craved, a madness that I was part of.

The following day I thanked the Sergeant and his RP staff for having me as a guest and promised to buy them all a pint whenever I saw them next.

Being a free man however, was a sudden comedown. I handed my almost new Army equipment back in after only a couple of months before visiting the Commanding Officer to organise my paperwork. There was a constant round of signatures and documents until I could go home and I didn't know what I was signing for most of the time; medical cards, the Official Secrets Act, apparently meaningless records for this that and the other.

"On your release you have some more forms that shows prospective employers what you did in the Army as well as your disciplinary record. As you went AWOL you are rated Fair, which isn't exactly exemplary but neither is it unsatisfactory."

"OK Sir."

"Now. We could Dishonourably Discharge you, in which case you'd be out the door with sweet F.A. However, the Army has decided to be nice to you and kick you out on medical grounds," the Officer looked at the notes in front of him, " Queens Regs 1975 Paragraph 9.387; Ceasing to fulfil Army Medical Standards."

"Er…OK Sir."

"That's not all Gunner Hutt. Oh no. Being medically discharge also means you get a special prize. An Army Pension for the rest of your life. In other words we're giving you some money every month until you die."

"Oh…OK Sir," I said, slightly bewildered by everything.

"Good. Any plans?"

"Haven't really thought about it yet Sir."

"According to your records you were a good soldier, outstanding during the Gulf War but somewhere along the line it all went wrong. You can go forward from here and start your life again. Try and consider this an opportunity for a new beginning instead of the end."

I tried to take everyones words on board but it all became a jumble of well meaning advice. The Army offered me a resettlement course, a chance to learn a skill, usually something in the construction industry or IT but I was focused on my goal of walking out those gates and not turning back, my Prison sentence was over with and my life could start again. I was back in my previous mindset of putting up all the mental barriers by keeping my head down and my mouth shut. I was in a race to get out and stupidly didn't take up their offer of a resettlement course or get in touch with the services they offered or speak to the British Legion and BLESMA, the British Limbless Ex-Servicemen's Association. They sent me home for a few months, which felt like being on leave and as they were still paying me I partied like I had to go back to Germany for another year.

In September 1993 I returned to Woolwich Barracks to be officially discharged by signing more paperwork and rechecking my details for my Army Pension.

"Hutt!" the Geordie Sergeant shouted from the Guardroom as I walked towards the gate.

"Hello Sarge."

"It won't be easy being a civvy, mate."

"I'll be OK Sarge. No problem."

"Just keep your head together and move on, don't waste your chances."

It was more well meaning advice that went in one ear and out the other.

"Sure Sarge, and thanks for everything."

"You're still in the Army until midnight tonight. If you stick two fingers up, shout Fuck the Army or show us your arse when you're outside these gates we can still arrest you."

"I wouldn't do that, even though I'm tempted."

"I know. Now fuck off and I don't want to see you again."

After four years and seventy-two days service in the British Army, not including my time spent Absent Without Leave, I was officially no longer a soldier.

It didn't feel like it though.

I returned home to Nuneaton and my parents and more well meaning advice that I didn't hear. I spent the rest of the time in the pub or visiting my civvy friends in Universities up and down the country, my world revolved around alcohol and it was like being on leave but never knowing when it would end. I was waiting for someone to tell me what to do, I didn't want the advice I just needed a kick up the arse or for someone to shout at me, telling me what to do.

I had felt my mood swings worsen in Army prison, now the constant alcohol that had replaced the Tamazepam made them even more extreme and I started staying in bed until midday before going to the pub when it opened and drinking all day. At night the nightmares were still there; Bomber Jacket and Beardy walking towards me, my bullets missing as they laughed at me.

I would often catch myself staring quietly into space for hours at a time, sometimes I didn't know where I was and on one occasion heard the sound of mortars falling nearby as I walked through Nuneaton town centre. My friends were excellent but they had their own lives, jobs and student work to do. They couldn't spend all their time getting drunk with a bitter ex-soldier. I was confused and my emotions were everywhere; one minute I was elated and manic, the next silent and angry, the drink masked all the feelings but at the same time made them worse. My mental walls were up and nobody could get in, nor could anything get out.

Job Centres are dirty, depressing places. Full of people who have been forgotten about who are dealt with by people who didn't care. I wasn't used to this. A thousand forms to fill out about who I was and what I could or couldn't do, the nature of my disability, do I tell them I think I'm mental? The woman at the desk looked like she had seen a million people like me before, I was a name and national insurance number, a statistic.

"So, Mister Hutt..."

It was the first time anyone had called me Mister.

"OK...if you could just sign there...and there."

I noticed I was shaking, I felt small and worthless.

"Excellent. So, what kind of job are you looking for Mister Hutt?"

"Erm...I don't really know."

"OK that's fine. What kind of things can you do?" she said emphasising the word "can".

I had to think for a while, genuinely searching my mind for any kind of skills I had. I realised I couldn't actually do anything.

"Er...I can fire a rocket launcher," I said smiling, hoping she had a sense of humour.

There was a moments hesitation as the bored woman looked up without smiling from the pile of forms on the desk in front of her.

"Yes...well...there's not much call for that in Nuneaton," she sighed.

19. Scars

I'm sitting on the floor of my room surrounded by broken glass and ripped pictures and posters. The empty bottles are at my feet, I find that Whisky or Vodka have the quickest desired effect. Clothes spill out of drawers, it stinks in here of sweat and stale alcohol, Depeche Mode sing that they're "clean" before the tape ends with a snap from the stereo that lies upended on the floor. I can see dried spots of blood on the carpet.

* * * *

I had to move out of my parents house to save them from this. I couldn't control my mood swings and drinking, I had tried to keep up the pretence of a public and a private face; to my friends and family I was still just an ex-soldier looking for work, quietly trying to get on the first rung of the ladder while coping with a disability. Behind that mask was a man slowly imploding and by mid 1994, nine months after being discharged from the Army and almost two years since my injury in Bosnia, I was in a downward spiral of drink, drugs, self harm and mental illness. I had just turned 21 years old. I had moved into a flat with one of my best friends girlfriends, we had nothing in common but she needed someone to help pay the bills and I needed my own space to destroy myself. I stayed in my room most of the time. Solitude and alcohol my only comfort.

* * * *

I can see the empty white plastic cylinder of the bottle of paracetamol, a bargain at £1.99 for a hundred tablets. I'm in a haze and don't know what's real anymore, I'm sure that my memories of a war were parts of a film I must have watched or a weird dream I remembered. I can taste the Whiskey in my mouth again. I can see crusty dried blood, paint? No, it's blood, smeared on my arms reminding me of one of those dreams I have that I don't understand. I cut deep enough for me to bleed, the violent act strangely satisfying. I don't understand anything anymore. My body convulses and my insides cramp. I can taste the chemicals from the paracetamol. I vomit the chemical cocktail powerfully onto the floor next to me, it's a river of Whiskey and semi-digested tablets, the taste and smell make me vomit again. I continue to retch and heave until there is nothing inside me anymore.

* * * *

I still continued to exist behind a mask, keeping up an appearance that everything is fine in my world. In reality every moment outdoors was spent in terror; scanning hedgerows for snipers, watching my own footsteps for signs of mines and tripwires. I once even dived into a ditch when I heard a car backfire. I spent my time drinking with friends and travelling all over the midlands following Nuneaton Boroughs exploits in non-league football. Watching a football match on a cold winters day in Redditch, or Corby, or some other nameless Midlands town gave me some much-needed distraction from my internal confusion, my friends were around me so I felt safe. I was still the party animal, the money saved from my time at Woolwich along with unemployment benefit and disability living allowance meant the world was my oyster.

I grew my hair long in the clichéd way every ex-soldier does and shaved intermittently, the discipline was now gone. I had no focus and there was nothing to aim for anymore, all I wanted to do is get through tomorrow, then the next day. The days on my own were spent in my self-imposed solitary confinement watching ultra-violent Japanese Manga and drinking steadily. I would go to bed at night wondering what kind of day I will have when I wake up, often I hope I don't wake up. They were now divided into "good" and "bad" days, on my good days I can take on the world, on my bad days all I want to do is hide. I started smoking, which was once my pet hate and I also smoked drugs and occasionally take LSD and Amphetamines. Everyday I had something, I'm either pissed or stoned or just generally off my head. It's like the first few days after my injury, I never know if I'm awake and it's real or I'm asleep and dreaming.

* * * *

Exhausted from the vomiting I eventually pass out again before waking up some hours later in the darkness. The stench of chemical vomit makes me gag as I crawl over to the light switch. It looks like I've been burgled but nothing taken, just needlessly vandalised and ransacked, reminding me of a place I once was. My

Gulf War medals, mounted and framed by my parents for me for Christmas lay on the bed, the glass smashed from where I put my fist into it, all the other framed pictures are the same, some of the photos have been ripped and there is a line at chest height that runs horizontally around the room on every wall continuously where I have dragged a Stanley knife through every poster. I look at my knuckles and see slivers of glass still embedded in the dried black blood. It's not the first time I've done this. Shaking, I put the stereo back on the table and play the Depeche Mode tape again before picking up the larger pieces of glass and slowly starting to tidy up, ready for the next time.

* * * *

I'm unhappy so I start drinking, then get angry and smash the room up, then I feel despair and take the tablets but I never get the balance of tablets to alcohol right and my body rejects it. I sometimes find myself standing by the very edge of a busy road or on the train station platform thinking; "If I just take one step forward…" I always thought God had kept me alive for a reason; the time I left HOS and the time in Vidovice, Terry's magazine pouch saving me from the rifle grenade, the medic stopping the bleeding from the mortar wound, I didn't want to die and was saved. Now I feel abandoned and there is nobody left to save me. People who say suicide is the easy way out have never been in a position to consider it and after several unnoticed attempts to kill myself I was exhausted mentally and physically, even wondering if God was keeping me alive as some kind of punishment. I plotted a graph for a week to see how many good days to bad days I had and if anything triggered them off but the line was just a sharp zigzag, with no two days the same, one day up the next day down. At that point I knew I needed help and eventually I went to see a Doctor, hoping for another kind of tablet to make it all better.

"Have you heard about Post Traumatic Stress Disorder?" said the Doctor.

You can tell when someone is worried by their body language and expression, the serious tone of their voice. This Doctor was genuinely concerned about me and it felt strange, this hadn't happened since Croatia.

"Yes, they said at Headley Court that I didn't have it."

The Doctor let out a sigh with an almost imperceptible shake of the head.

"Right. PTSD can occur at any time, there are veterans of World War Two who only now, years later, experience any symptoms."

"OK."

"Given everything you have told me, I have absolutely no doubt you are suffering from PTSD."

"Are there some tablets then, to help me think straight?"

"It's not that easy I'm afraid. I'll give you tablets called Prozac to help the depression and mood swings, I'll also get a counsellor from the Community Mental Health Team to get in touch."

"Mental Health?"

"It doesn't mean your mad, PTSD is a perfectly normal reaction to an extremely abnormal situation. Remember, you're not on your own and there are people to help, however it may take time, after all this is the NHS," the Doctor looked at me in his serious manner. "If you feel you can't go on, phone the CMHT or come and see me. Just take time to stop and think."

The Prozac worked for a while, for a month or two I felt as if I was somehow more than normal, going around smiling contentedly like a Stepford Wife as I awaited the call from the Mental Health team. The tablets turned me into something I had never been, a happy little zombie, smiling even though in reality everything was actually shit. Whether it was a side effect of the medication or, more likely, the drink and drugs I continued to take, I smashed my room up and binned the tablets, much preferring the unstable and unpredictable version of myself. The Mental Health Team eventually phoned to arrange an appointment but I told them I was better now and wouldn't require their services, though I would keep their number just in case.

In truth who could ever understand? My friends and the others around me were starting to finish University and trying to land graduate jobs. For them long-term girlfriends and long-term career plans were just around the corner, the property ladder, a company car, an expensive wedding and children with names like Olivia awaited them. I on the other hand was starting all over again.

I somehow managed to cope, keeping all the memories and nightmares locked inside until at some point they would come out in a violent drink and drug-fuelled explosion behind closed doors. I learned to drive an automatic car and bought a sky blue Vauxhall Astra and I also enrolled at college at the end of 1994 to do a Higher Education Certificate, a years full-time study with other mature students which was a stepping stone to University. Education provided a much-needed direction and I found I really enjoyed learning. I told people I had lost my leg in a motorcycle accident as it usually avoided any awkward questions and in reality the war felt a million miles away. I often wrote to Terry and Ivan, who were now back in Bristol and Dublin respectively, Ivan also having being injured a few months after me. Their letters and photos were my link to my own memories that I constantly tried to bury opening their letters was like opening old wounds and unlocking the past. I wanted to be normal, although I had no knowledge of what normal was. I had joined the Army as soon as I left school and in the five years since then I had been in two wars and almost died countless times. I reasoned that to be normal was to have the long-term girlfriend and the mortgage and the highly paid job with company car and possibly even children called Olivia. I started to try and focus on who I thought I should be, someone just like everyone else and lock away the person I was.

With my new found semi-stable persona I managed to get a girlfriend who I eventually moved in with, renting a small house in Nuneaton. We were happy, I was at college and applying to go to University to do a degree in Politics, Economics and Russian Language starting in September 1995. She had graduated and was on the first rung of the highly paid career ladder, her parents were also quite posh and didn't know what to make of me. I kept up the pretence of the motorcycle accident resulting in my leg being amputated and tried to be like every one else. I started to regularly go to the Gym. It was a thin veneer of reality and an act that I believed, as there was nothing else for me to hold on to.

Underneath in my subconscious the madness and memories simmered away waiting for the moment to explode again. I did the mature grown up thing and started seeing a counsellor in mid 1995 as I could feel myself slipping again. The counsellor talked about all kinds of seemingly unrelated shit, my childhood, my school, was I bullied in the Army? Of course I wasn't bullied you stupid cow, I've been in a couple of wars and seen some bad shit - maybe that's the root of my problem. The woman twiddled with the beads around her neck as she attempted to hypnotise me so I could relive one of the moments in Bosnia, not exactly the thing I wanted. She didn't understand. Still nobody did.

Maybe I thought that to be like everyone else you needed money and at the same time I craved the feelings that I had experienced in Bosnia. My short-lived criminal career was about to start, the pressure cooker was about to explode. I never really thought I could get away with trying to blackmail a large superstore and I'd never really done anything that criminal. It was my cry for help, my self-destruct button being pressed and my chance to escape from my pretend life without being found in a pool of my own blood. I had been at University only a couple of months but found myself surrounded by eighteen year olds and although I was only twenty-two I felt like an old man. There were few mature students here and the structure of learning was too relaxed, Economics was too hard, Politics was dull and only learning Russian Language interested me. I was also skint now that I was a student and my disability benefits were stopped as I no longer fitted the Governments criteria of "disabled", although if I had sat on my arse in a wheelchair and said I couldn't walk, rather than try and keep myself fit and active I would have ticked all the boxes.

These aren't excuses for doing the most stupid thing I have ever done and the thing I most regret but it was these little things that kept chipping away at the locks in my mind, until eventually the locks broke and the stuff I had kept inside came flooding out.

During November 1995 I sent several letters to a large superstore over the period of a few weeks threatening to poison food unless money was left at a certain place and they would confirm via the local papers personal ads, copying a Dirty Harry film where something similar occurred. I knew the police would be informed and I knew they would be waiting. When the day came for them to drop the money off, I stopped and thought, I could just stop and forget it and they would never know or I could go and pick up the money and walk into the waiting police. Obviously I went for the latter.

The West Midlands Regional Crime Squad called it "Operation Prancer", I assume all of their operations during the festive season are named after one of Santa's reindeers. Nobody was ever hurt or in danger but they had mobilised at least twenty Officers and based themselves at Bedworth Police Station, near Nuneaton. I was totally honest from the start during the initial twenty-four hours of questioning. I should have learned from my time being interviewed by the Military Police as when the Officers realised I had fought in Bosnia they immediately assumed I was some kind of big fish, a "Mercenary", the crime was well planned, almost military they said, is there a gang? Suddenly in their eyes I was a bad guy from a James Bond film, not the average junkie that they usually dealt with.

After the first twenty-four hours they gradually realised that I was on my own and I was just a screwed up ex-soldier, screwed up ex-soldiers though are still dangerous and I had committed a serious offence. I was transferred from Bedworth Police station to Nuneaton Station in handcuffs to appear before the Magistrate. The cells were like those in the Army except dirtier and graffiti covered and as I waited in the silence of the cell wrapped in a blanket now aware that the facade that was my life had been shattered, I felt strangely relieved.

There was an underground tunnel that linked the police station to the magistrates court, and at the end of that tunnel behind floor to ceiling bars stood my parents and girlfriend.

"I'm so sorry," I said, bursting into tears.

I never knew what to say, it was always "sorry" but that didn't quite seem to ever cover it. I could hardly say that it was better than committing suicide. My girlfriend cried. My Fathers face had the familiar look of exhaustion, or exasperation. His eyes were red rimmed again, this time though there was an air of disappointment, a sense that he couldn't be put through this again.

"You'll get through it," my girlfriend said, sobbing.

"What were you thinking, why didn't you talk to someone?" said my ever-practical mother.

"I tried Mum, I really did," I said.

"Lets just get through this," said my Dad.

"I'm sorry I've let you down again."

"Don't say that," my girlfriend said.

My Father looked to the ceiling and I wanted to be a million miles away from there. My mind was as battered and scarred as my body and again I had no fight left.

The magistrate remanded me in custody despite my Father offering bail money by remortgaging the house. The seriousness of the offence along with the prosecutions belief that I would have so many contacts abroad that I could easily disappear made sure I would stay behind bars. I was sent that afternoon to HMP Blakenhurst near Redditch to await trial.

On arrival at the Prison I was photographed and processed by Prison Officers that had already heard of my imminent arrival. Most were ex-military themselves and wanted to find out about me. I was determined not to live up to their stereotypical idea of some kind of hard-core psychopath mercenary, the James Bond bad guy that the Police also initially thought I was. I wasn't going to make their lives difficult, after all they could make my life inside infinitely worse and I made an effort to answer all the questions they asked, even joking about my leg when being strip-searched. Another place and another uniform and serial number, this time I was Prisoner MK1357. Hutt, Simon.

It wasn't the Prison system or the Officers that bothered me, it was the other inmates. I fitted in with the regimes and discipline, that was easy and I quite liked it, my early assessment was that most of the other "cons" had drug habits and Prison for them was an occupational hazard, a few months inside for petty offences committed in order to feed a heroin habit before being released for a further few months to do the same again. My experience of men using hard drugs was HOS, the unpredictable and dangerous, scum who would always be looking out for themselves. I was determined to do my own thing in Prison, keeping my head down and my mouth shut was good advice here and it had worked for me so far in Army

Prisons. I was friendly to the "screws" but not overly so as I didn't want the other cons to think I was some kind of informant. The inmates of this Prison were mostly all on remand; in custody and awaiting trial and sentencing, some had been tried and sentenced and awaited shipment to other long term Prisons. There was a grading system of offenders, initially everyone was a category "C" Prisoner, for shorter punishments such as driving offences or burglaries, Prisoners could be downgraded to a "D" category and go to an Open Prison. Category "A" was reserved for terrorists, some lifers, armed robbers and serial escapees, "B" category was less dangerous armed robbers, lifers and me. I mixed with the armed robbers and murderers more than the petty offenders, it was the petty offenders that were predominantly drug addicts and guys in their early twenties who acted like teenagers, their short-term sentences meaning they had less to lose. The rest were usually older and had the possibility of a long stretch in Prison to look forward to and they, like me, didn't want their time spent inside to be a constant battle with the screws or the young dickheads that would be in and out of the Prison several times whilst you awaited trial.

Keeping my head down and mouth shut worked as I moved through the Prison regimes of basic then standard and onto the "enhanced" regime. A few more privileges such as an extra hour out of the cell, although I had the rarity of a single cell thanks to my disability and I craved its solitude. People on the enhanced regime were drug tested regularly and the majority on the enhanced wing were long-term Prisoners. My Solicitors and Barrister were confident that I would get a two-year stretch by playing on my experiences of war and my PTSD. It was an all too familiar story of playing the naïve little boy to the Psychologists when they assessed me prior to my trial. Yes, it was a cry for help and I knew that I had been falling apart mentally during the last year. I also knew that the only way to defend me was to play the ex-soldier with PTSD card against the prosecutions assertion that I was an evil master criminal.

The trial at Warwick Crown Court was in early 1996, a Victorian courtroom with oak panelling and the ever present royal crest on the wall, the Judge looked as old as the room itself and looked ridiculous in his red gown and horsehair wig. It was the bullshit of tradition all over again. I pleaded guilty of course and like the Court Martial three years before, the prosecution tore me apart, the ancient Judge Harrison-Hall even commenting that I "joined a neo-fascist organisation" in Bosnia as he looked over his half moon spectacles. At that point I knew he had already made his mind up, it was a familiar story. My defence couldn't respond and there was an air of resignation over the courtroom as I sighed and looked to the floor realising that I had been too honest in my statements and everything I had said had been used against me. I didn't care anymore.

"Despite what you have been through and the problems you have, the crime you have committed far outweighs them. And I have no other option to give you a custodial sentence, with the condition that you have some kind of treatment for your PTSD in Prison," said the Judge looking like he was about to fall asleep.

That was nice of him, I thought. As he droned on I stood watching a pretty blond clerk who sat between myself and the elderly Judge opposite, this time I was numb to what was going on. There were no tears or frustration, I just wanted to get back to my cell.

"Seven years." And with that his hammer fell and I smiled at the blond clerk.

My parents visited me in the cells below the courthouse and I told them not to worry and that I would be fine, my Solicitor assuring them that we would appeal at the unfairly harsh sentencing and after six months already spent inside I was already getting used to it. Back at Blakenhurst Prison staff and Doctors interviewed me to see if I was going to kill myself or generally go mental at the thought of the seven years stretching out in front of me. I was OK, I just wanted to be alone again.

Seven years. The screws couldn't believe it either but then again after six months here they knew me, as did most of the other cons. Seven years. You get that for armed robbery or manslaughter and you get less for rape.

The screws checked me constantly that night as it's routine for anyone getting a long stretch to be on "suicide watch". The first opportunity for release would be parole at the halfway point of my sentence, if I misbehaved or used drugs I'd be out at the two-thirds mark, if I were to act like a total arsehole I could do the full seven. I was determined to be out on parole at the first attempt and having done six months already on remand I now had another three whole years in Prison, I aimed to be out in June 1999 aged 26.

Time spent in Prison is like driving on the motorway, the brain switches off and you can't remember having driven the last ten miles. Every day in Prison is the same, a constant routine interrupted occasionally by memorable incidents; the sex offender being caught and having boiling water thrown over him, the guy being battered over a drug debt, the rest was just motorway driving. One memorable, and possibly life changing incident, was seeing the Prison Doctor for the first time shortly after sentencing.

"What is it?" said the bored little Asian Doctor who had probably seen thousands of men pass through here asking for Methadone or painkillers, most of them wasters and junkies.

"As part of my conditions for parole the Judge said I had to have some kind of counselling for Post Traumatic Stress Disorder caused by my time in the Military," I said being as polite as I could. The Male Nurse in the room smiled at the thought of having a real patient.

"For what?" the Doctor said not looking up from the files in front of him.

"PTSD, Post Traumatic Stress Disorder. I was in the Gulf and Bosnia, had my leg amputated out there."

"PTSD."

"Yes, it's probably all in my file there."

"I don't believe in it."

"What?"

"PTSD. I don't believe in it. It does not exist."

"You don't believe in it?" I could see the male Nurse behind the Doctor look to the floor shaking his head.

"No. Is there anything else?

"You don't believe in it?" I repeated.

"No. Is there anything else? "

"Er...no," I said. I didn't quite understand. It was one of those moments where you think, "did he really just say that?" I was suddenly confused and stood to leave, the male Nurse followed me out the door.

"Sorry mate," he said, as I left the medical centre thinking of all the things I should have said and where this would leave me in three years time when I saw the parole board.

Back in my cell I realised that this so called Doctor was just like all the other fucking idiots, content to do their own thing and get paid without actually having to care. I smiled to myself, realizing that I wasn't like him, because good or bad, I cared. I remembered the faces of the Doctors and Nurses in Croatia, I remembered the faces of the man I shot and the face of the medic as he clamped his hand on my bleeding artery. This Doctor has already forgotten me and obviously cared even less. I never wanted to be like him, I want to care, it makes me who I am.

At about the same time as my chat with the Asian Doctor my Father was diagnosed as having Cancer. Any relative with Cancer is a nightmare, but being in Prison while my family had to go through it all was even worse. My family weren't sure whether to tell me or not, but I could tell something was wrong on one of their regular visits to the Prison and they eventually told me that he had Cancer of the bladder which may have spread. For the next two years my Father would have constant chemotherapy as well as various internal organs removed to stop the Cancer spreading. In the meantime I had to sit in a concrete room and wait for the next three years. The thought of my Fathers illness made me angry at myself and more determined to survive Prison and get out at the earliest opportunity, I had put him and my family through hell and not once had he turned his back on me or told me that I was an arsehole.

I began to read anything and everything, even getting a job in the Prison Library. I read books about meditation, yoga and religion, I wanted some answers, or at least something I could latch onto to keep me focused and stop me going totally crazy or wanting to use hard drugs. On one occasion I even went to Catholic Mass, which turned me off organised religion for good. I knew that if I wanted to survive I had to do it myself and began every night to meditate. I hadn't been able to sleep properly since the Gulf and usually used alcohol or drugs to help but I couldn't do that here. I taught myself to sit on the bed in my cell for hours relaxing and clearing my mind of the constant rattle of memories and dreams. I had also been good at art at school and rediscovered my talent for drawing and painting, the painting, like the meditation, would clear my mind for hours at a time and I would do watercolour portraits from photos for five phone cards (£10), and I had a constant stream of work as the other cons always wanted something meaningful to give their wives and girlfriends, the painting focused me as much as my nightly meditation did. For the first time I could actually cope, I had a mechanism to deal with the PTSD and the nightmares and although I knew the nightmares and depression would be with me forever, I also knew I could get out the other side.

The days and months ticked away monotonously and the system didn't quite know what to do with me as the Prison service doesn't cater for the disabled, no other Prison wanted me and it was too early for me to go to an Open Prison as a Category "D" Prisoner. So I was stuck at HMP Blakenhurst, a remand Prison, watching the same faces come and go for two whole years. My time there was spent working in the Prison library, a cushy number that fed my appetite for books and was close to the art rooms and education department. The civilian staff were polite and talked to us like we were human beings, there was a better class of scum in the education block. Due to the high turnover of Prisoners, as soon as they were sentenced they would be off to "proper" Prisons like HMP Featherstone in Wolverhampton, Winson Green in Birmingham and lifers would go to HMP Long Lartin near Leicester.

Eventually, after two years at HMP Blakenhurst I was being transferred to HMP Ashwell near Oakham, Leicestershire. It was now 1998 and I was 25.

The move coincided with my Fathers Cancer going into remission, after two years of chemotherapy and numerous operations they had finally got on top of the disease. My Father looked like he hadn't lost a hair on his head and still ran his TV rentals business with the aid of my Mother and Brother, although the TV business was harder as technology had moved on from valves and circuit boards to microchips and manufacturers warranties. For the last two years I had learnt to meditate and paint, I also found that Prison itself was easy as I was already totally institutionalized. With the Prison move and my Father beating Cancer, finally things were looking up. I also started applying to local colleges to study an Art Foundation Course starting in September 1999, if the Parole Board saw that I had a course to go onto upon release it would go in my favour.

HMP Ashwell was like an Army base but with a huge fence and barbed wire all around the perimeter. All the rooms were single and had windows without bars on, the doors were made of wood and we even had our own keys. Most of the cons here were coming to the end of their sentences and were either awaiting release or an eventual transfer to an Open Prison. The screws were public sector Prison Officers, unlike the security guards at Blakenhurst, which was a private Prison, for the most part the screws here were coming to the end of their service and approaching retirement. The atmosphere was relaxed, Ashwell was a good Prison with plenty to offer if you wanted it and if you didn't you could always go back to a Prison with its steel doors, three men to a cell and twenty two hour lock-up and obviously no one wanted that.

I went through the stages of standard, basic and eventually the enhanced regime and also got my favourite job of Librarian back. At the end of 1998 I could see light at the end of the tunnel as there were only seven months to go until my parole date, I had a place at college confirmed and the idea was that I would help out with Dad's business. I read, meditated and painted, that was my therapy and it worked better than alcohol, drugs or some well-meaning stranger trying to hypnotise me. I had regular visits from family and friends although conversation was difficult as every day was the same. My girlfriend I was with when I was arrested had visited me every week and although it was apparent early on that our relationship was over, she still visited me as a friend. My other friends would often visit, on one occasion even Terry and Farmer Joe came to see me.

"It's come back," my Mother said.

"What?"

"The Cancer has come back."

"I though they had got rid of it." I had wondered why my Father hadn't been for so long but didn't really want to know the answer.

"They did... it's spreading quicker this time though," my Mum struggled to get her words out.

"OK...they can treat it again though can't they?" I said hopefully.

"They said they'd try," my Mum's words tailed off and we changed the subject.

The Cancer did spread quickly, racing rapidly around his body and I was stuck in here, selfishly happy that I couldn't see the Cancer eat away at my Father. It soon spread up his spine and into his brain. I was glad I didn't witness any of this but I never believed that my Dad wouldn't make it, not now that I was almost free again, a better, if not changed man. The screws were helpful and sympathetic, everybody knows somebody who has gone through this.

"Hi Dad," I said to him as he walked into the visitors centre with my Mother's arm around him, guiding him to the seat.

"How are you doing? Soon be out then," he said smiling.

He still looked the same with his thick grey hair and broad shoulders, his light blue eyes were watery and bright.

"Your Dad really wanted to come today," said my Mum, her voice shaky.

I didn't want to understand what she meant, it was just a normal visit by my parents, I'll be out soon and the Cancer will be gone we'll all be back to normal.

"Good to see you, how are you feeling?" I said.

"Not bad, a bit tired," he smiled.

We made smalltalk without ever mentioning the Cancer, I noticed that he kept repeating the same sentences and asking the same questions that I had already given the answers to. I made sure I didn't cry although I wanted to, I could see in his eyes that he was still in there, the spark that made him who he was. He knew what was happening. He knew he had to come today and I knew why he had to come. This was it, this was to be the last goodbye but I couldn't bring myself to say it. Neither could he. Eventually the visit came to an end after repeated conversations about nothing in particular.

"You'll be OK Dad, don't worry I'll be out soon."

"I know," he said smiling.

"I'll see you next month then," I said trying in vain to convince myself as my Mother escorted him to the door.

He turned and nodded smiling. It was the last time I saw the spark.

Back in my cell I broke down, thinking of all the things I should have said and done in the visit. I wanted so much for him to hang on if only for a couple more months to see me a free man, how I had turned my life around, just one more chance for me to say goodbye and I'm sorry for all the fucking shit I put you through, you didn't deserve any of it.

A few weeks later the screws knocked on my door late at night.

"We've had a phone call about your Dad," said the Officer.

"Fuck it," I said.

"They don't think he'll make it through the night. We've arranged for you to go and see him for an hour."

"Thanks."

I didn't really want to see him lying on a Hospital bed, it just wasn't him. The Hospital in Birmingham looked like a dirty depressing place and as we got nearer and nearer to the ward the less I wanted to be there. My Brother, Sister and Mother surrounded his bed as the screws took off my handcuffs, tears already streaming down my face.

His chest wheezed for air and his hair looked messy, drips emptied fluid into his arms. In the space of a few weeks since I had seen him last he had become thin and pale. I noticed he didn't have his teeth in. I couldn't remember the last time I saw my Father without his teeth in and felt angry, he was a proud man, stocky and broad shouldered and here we were looking at him without his teeth in, I was intruding on his privacy. It wasn't him there though, I could tell the spark was gone, replaced by the evil shitty disease. My Dad was already dead. This was just his body. After an hour of uncomfortable and sad conversation with the family, I kissed him on the forehead and left, glad to be out of there.

My Father lived for another week, his brief moments of lucidity making it all the more painful for those witnessing it. Eventually though he died, I didn't feel any shock at the final moment, I was relieved that it was over, my Dad would never want to hang on like that without any dignity and putting his family through the pain of his deterioration. I was angry with myself for not saying sorry or goodbye, but then again maybe he knew. I was escorted to the funeral in handcuffs and the black trousers and clip on tie of a borrowed Prison Officers uniform. It was early 1999 and I was almost 26.

The next few months felt like an eternity, waiting for news from the parole board about my release. I knew they would have to have a damn good reason to turn me down as during my time inside I had never been in trouble or used drugs, I had managed to deal with my "demons", I had a place in college studying Art and to top it all my Dad had just died. Eventually the news finally came and in June they told me I would be released the following month on parole. I would have to report to the probation offices in Nuneaton on a weekly basis and would be subject to recall for the next year and a half, I would also have to declare my conviction whenever asked as it would never be "spent" or wiped from my record, failure to do so was a criminal offence.

In July 1999, aged 26 and after three and a half years in Prison I was a free man. I didn't feel elated in any way, there was more of a sadness that my Dad wasn't here to greet me and the thought that I had wasted three and a half years of my life. It was my girlfriend that came to pick me up, we smiled and hugged awkwardly in the warm July sunshine as I looked at the world that wasn't surrounded by a fence or wall.

"Look...you know...things are..." she stuttered to find the right words.

"It's OK, I know what you mean and you don't have to say it," I said, relieved at not having the pressure of a relationship to deal with.

"We'll still be friends though." Tears were in her eyes, she was probably just as relieved at not having to pick up the pieces of my life again.

"Of course."

We stopped at McDonalds on the way home though their salty fries and greasy burgers were not something my stomach was used to after almost four years of overcooked, tasteless and generally unhealthy slop. We drove on in silence as I looked at the country that had carried on without me, the cars looking so different, almost space-age. Signs for Nuneaton started to appear, places and pubs I recognised. It wasn't like returning from the Gulf, this time there was no excitement or anticipation, I was just glad to be back.

Home was a very empty place, the large detached house of my childhood now only contained my Mother and I. There wasn't a house full of my civvy friends to greet me or yellow ribbons and I thankfully wasn't filmed as I walked up the drive. My Sister had gone back to Canberra, Australia where she now lived and my Brother had his own family with two young children to look after. My girlfriend was no longer my girlfriend and eventually as the weeks went on without the routine of prison visits we drifted apart and gradually saw less and less of each other until we both realised we were going in different directions and sadly stopped making the effort. My Father's TV rental business had been sold and the sheds and garage, once floor to ceiling with dusty televisions, were empty.

I had been in the Army or Prison for about eight of the last ten years and before that I was at school. I had "institutionalised" written all over me. Now though I was determined not to make the same mistakes I had before, I could now just about deal with the PTSD and didn't see the need to be someone I wasn't. This was who I was, tough shit. For the first time I looked forward to the future and was determined to make the past part of me rather than burying the memories, however painful.

20. Picking Up the Pieces

I went to college to study Art in the September following my release and applied to countless jobs, but having a criminal record on top of a disability and no skills made sure that my fresh start wasn't easy. So I had no choice but to stop telling prospective employers that I had a criminal record.

I stayed at college full time for a few months before realising that being around the eighteen year olds again was driving me mad, I could feel it was becoming trigger to my PTSD so I changed to a two-year part time course. Here there were plenty of mature students and as it was part time the course was less intense, I was enjoying it at last. At the same time I got a job in a factory grinding down the welding on huge metal cabinets; a dirty, sweaty job which required full breathing apparatus to be worn at all times due to the metal particles that hung in the air covering everything in a grey, gritty dust. I quite enjoyed the hard work and I enjoyed the money, late on in 2000 I worked the nightshift for extra money, the solitude of the nightshift I also found appealing. By that time however, the Art course had moved into the latter stages which included writing an essay on some dull artist or other. The nightshift, along with trying to maintain the college course that I was no longer enjoying meant something had to give and as I was no longer enjoying the course I gave it up. I still enjoyed my art and spent hours in the now empty shed that served as a makeshift studio, painting and enjoying my isolation.

Redundancy at the factory soon followed and I took it voluntarily as most of the other workers had families, whereas I just had myself. I took the few thousand they gave me and picked up a gambling habit. Gambling isn't bad as, say, a crack cocaine habit but it is just as destructive and addictive. Once the money was gone though I looked for help. I drifted from job to job never staying long enough to make an impression but long enough to get bored and walk out before I punched someone and the job centre didn't quite know what to do with me either. I still went out to get drunk at weekends with my friends although we were all now almost thirty and they had their long term girlfriends and long term jobs, while I was yet again starting from scratch and at the same time trying to hold it all together. Going to a Nuneaton nightclub was like going to New York when I was seventeen years of age, now though the place looked just what it was; shabby and full of drunks and vomit, women in short skirts watched fights spill out into taxi ranks and kebab shops with a depressingly monotonous regularity. I met girls through my friends and often wondered what they saw in me until I realised when they started to become distant that it was because they thought I was "a bit of rough", whereas someone who paints, reads poetry and sometimes listens to classical music (a habit I picked up in prison) just didn't float their boat.

One night in the "Zanzibar" nightclub in Nuneaton I met a girl with a beautiful smile, I was drunkenly slurring as she sipped water and pretended to look interested.

"OK. I like you, but before we go further you ought to know I've got an artificial leg." I always said that to avoid any future embarrassment.

"Yeah."

"And a criminal record," I laughed.

"So what? I have two kids and a council house," she said raising her eyebrows at me.

I'd never met anyone like her; she took the piss out of me if she thought I was being an arse and told me my taste in music was "shit", she liked hardcore dance music, I listened to the Fields of the Nephilim, but we would make each other laugh until we cried. She hated football, didn't "get" my paintings and preferred soaps to documentaries, we had absolutely nothing in common which for some reason made us closer. She didn't care what I had done in the past, she just saw something in the person I was. A year after we met we moved in together and it was strange coming into a ready-made family but it forced me to see the other priorities, luckily though the two young boys were fantastic and accepted me into their lives immediately. In March 2004 we were married, one of the children was my best man and the other gave the Bride away. I had a job as a manager of Betting Shops (I obviously didn't tell them I had a criminal record) and managed to stay for several years despite working long hours for little money. Exactly nine months after our honeymoon my daughter was born and another eighteen months later in 2006 my son was born. It was the happiest I had ever felt.

It's only in the last few years that I have started telling people that I lost my leg in Bosnia rather than a motorbike accident and until I started this book I have always thought that I was part of Croatia and Bosnia's past, not its present. During the writing of this book I have made many friends and returned to Croatia in November 2008 with the Association of Foreign Volunteers of the Homeland War.

Returning to Croatia was one of the most moving things I have done. My memories of seeing a country torn by war, its overgrown unharvested fields, sandbagged windows and bullet scarred buildings were gone. Croatia is now a vibrant country, its children don't remember the war but are always reminded.

I met Ivan at Luton airport, his long pony-tailed hair was now gone and he wore an eye-patch which covered his missing eye; removed thanks to a rifle grenade in December 1992. His soft, calming voice was the same and it was strange to think that last time we had seen each other was in the Hospital ward at Slavonski Brod. I met others I also remembered; Nico the Dutchman from HOS now lived in Croatia, he was so different from how I remembered him but war does that to people, he was quiet, well mannered, though slightly weak and pathetic, very different from the Nico of my nightmares. I also met the English volunteer that visited me briefly in Hospital in Zagreb who had a similar injury to mine, he was Rod Morgan and said the guilt of saying I would be OK stayed with him for a long time, we talked for some time how I actually wanted my leg removed and we both agreed that I now walked better than he did!

The drinks flowed and war stories were told in Pero's Bar in Vinkovci, where we stayed for the five day trip. Thirty or forty foreign veterans of the war, one from as far away as Australia, letting their guards down with their comrades who had seen and done the same as they had all those years ago, finally talking and laughing about it. There was also a serious side to our reunion, the remembrance of soldiers lost. Services were held in Ovčara, near Vukovar where soldiers were executed after the fall of the City. At the Vukovar remembrance parade itself, attended by all of Croatia's dignitaries, we marched through the town where shattered, bullet riddled buildings that serve as a memorial stand next to modern glass and steel shopping malls. I remembered the TV pictures I saw all those years ago of the men in beards and greatcoats marching through this city, making me so angry. Finally there was our service in Vinkovci town centre for our own fallen comrades. Prayers were read and the names of dead foreigners were read out, the names of men gone but not forgotten, at least by us anyway. It was only then that I realised how far I had come, maybe it was the same for all the others, we could so easily have been one of the names read out.

I didn't visit Bosnia and the places I had fought, Bosnia is still a divided country. Although I have seen film of the village of Vidovice where I was injured, it has all been rebuilt with children's playgrounds and modern flats, not the nightmarish memories I had of it. I'll go one day, but one step at a time. I left Croatia a happy man, not just the last chapter closed and ghosts put to rest but also friends made, friends that had seen and done it just as I had and also had to cope with the invisible scars of war. I will be returning, though not because I need to as I did in 2008.

I can now look back at all the things I have been through and seen and done, how close I was to death on so many occasions and sometimes wonder how or why I'm still here. I've looked back on my life and I now realise I wouldn't change anything. Being a Father myself I now see what I put my parents through, although given the choice I would still go to Bosnia, even prison probably saved me from myself. I still have PTSD and I have good days and bad days; I still have trouble sleeping, there is depression, nightmares about Beardy and Bomber Jacket and I can suddenly click into a combat ready, high-alert mode, although I haven't dived headfirst into a muddy ditch since that day in 1994. My wife is patient and doesn't ask the awkward questions and on my bad days she gives me space to get through it without judgement. My group of Army friends and veterans are also there to help, as I am for them. The difference now is that I can deal with it, one look at the children or a phone call to a veteran friend like Terry, Ivan or Pete and I can drag myself through it, knowing that I have to come out the other side.

I like to think I stood up for what I thought was right in fighting in someone else's war and in doing so I have left my mark on the world. The only problem is the mark it has left on me, but I manage, quietly. I no longer feel that I made a mistake in fighting in Bosnia, it is now something I am proud of. While others watched atrocities on TV, I wanted to do something about it and almost gave my life for it.

Most of the foreign volunteers went out there for the same reasons I did, to make a difference in the only way they knew how.

"We would rather die on our feet than live on our knees"

– Emiliano Zapata.

Epilogue

The Allies launched "Gulf War Two" in 2003 with the aim of toppling Saddam Hussein with the since disproved motive that he had "weapons of mass destruction". The MLRS of 39 Regiment again took part, however it was no five-day war. Gulf War Two was part of the Americans "Global War on Terror" following Al-Qaeda's attacks on the Twin Towers. Afghanistan; home of Al-Qaeda and the Taleban, was invaded in 2001 and to date hundreds of British soldiers have died in the two war zones. British Military casualties are now treated in the NHS' Selly Oak Hospital, as The Queen Elizabeth Military Hospital, Woolwich was closed down in the mid-nineties and reopened a few years later as an NHS Hospital.

The war in Bosnia ended in 1995, but at the end of 1992 soon after I left, fighting broke out in the southern sector of Bosnia between the HVO and ABiH, who up until that point had been allies against the Serbs. The arms embargo meant the only place Bosnia could turn to was east to the Islamic world for money and weapons. And a flood of hard-line Muslims from Afghanistan and Iran replaced the tolerant Muslim volunteers of the likes of Mahmood and Murat that we met whilst at HOS, in some places Bosnia became a training ground for Al-Qaeda. Often war crimes were committed and the Serbs no longer looked like the "bad guys" anymore, undoing all the hard work the HVO and Muslims had done in the North and confirming the outsiders view of everyone killing everyone else. The fighting was violent and atrocities were committed on all sides, I was glad I had no part of it. Serbs still continued to shell civilians in the streets of Sarajevo and Gornji Vakuf and to "ethnically cleanse" villages. The most famous of which was Srebrenica where many thousands of people went missing after the UN troops let the Serbs into the so called "safe haven", but to most outsiders these were just another horrific series of acts in a dirty war.

In 1995 NATO began using air strikes in on the Serbs primarily because of the Serb attitude and their treatment towards the largely ineffectual UN troops. Before the Dayton Peace Agreement was put into place the Croats and Muslims (now at peace again) launched two massive offensives in Operations "Blijesak" (flash) and "Oluja" (storm) and regained the majority of the land they had previously lost to the Serbs, who themselves had been suffering from UN sanctions and war fatigue for some time.

Today Croatia is pushing to get into the EU and Bosnia is a loosely united country consisting of the Croat/Muslim Federation and the Republika Srpska, who despite constant tension, manage to carry on together. Most of the main war criminals have been handed over to the international tribunal in the Hague, however the main perpetrators of the war; Slobodan Milosević, the Serbian leader, died in custody during his lengthy trial and Radovan Karadzić, the first leader of Republika Srpska has only recently been handed over whilst his military commander Ratko Mladić, is still at large.

For every soldier "Killed in Action" there are usually another three or four that are injured, sometimes severely, these are the ones that aren't featured in the News bulletins. They, like many others, take their scars into civilian life and the country that doesn't care. Physical disabilities can be patched up and coped with but it's the invisible scars that are harder to treat. However, RAF Headley Court, the military rehabilitation centre is still open and run by the Armed forces but it's after Headley Court where the difficulties begin. The treatment of PTSD is a growing concern due to the numbers suffering, usually in silence, as our Army does constant tours of Afghanistan, but it's a low priority for the already overstretched NHS. There are some excellent counsellors that work for local Mental Health Teams, but they too are under funded and over employed. It is only the charity "Combat Stress" that is dedicated to soldiers suffering PTSD. They rely on donations, not Government funding to keep its residential homes open to anyone that may be suffering.

It's only recently that I've tried to research the events and the people I knew, for most of the time I had been trying to bury all the memories and move on. Some of the following information is third or fourth hand as well as, in some cases, ten or fifteen years old.

The Battle - The village we were meant to be retaking was Kopanica, which overlooked the vital supply line that the Serbs needed to move heavy equipment to Brčko. With just two hundred men 105 (Modrica) Brigade HVO had initially held Kopanica but had been pinned down for three days under heavy and constant attack by the Serbs. With no reinforcements forthcoming Commander Pero (The short, fat guy with the Brandy at Vidovice) gave the order to withdraw from the town in order to save what was left of his Brigade. It was these tired and battered men that we saw in Vidovice. A few months after our failed attack it was 101 (Bosanski Brod) Brigade HVO that retook the village, inflicting heavy casualties on the Serbs and in turn saving the town of Brčko.

Pete (The Gulf) - Pete, upon receiving my postcard that I posted from the airport, immediately went AWOL with the intention of joining me but was arrested before he could get to the airport. Pete went on to serve another ten years in the Army, doing all kinds of Commando courses and serving all over the world rising to the rank of Bombardier. He left to become a Paramedic then in 2006 became a Police Officer. He was stabbed and almost killed after apprehending a burglar in Bedworth, Warwickshire, resulting in bravery awards and commendations. The only person who could go to all the Worlds war zones then gets stabbed in a town near Nuneaton.

Terry - The porn in Terry's bag took some explaining away to Croatian customs but he eventually made it home OK. He went on to University and returned to Croatia as a freelance photojournalist on many occasions after the war, as well as reporting in other eastern European countries. Terry has now distanced himself from the war and its people, preferring to look forwards rather than backwards. He is now happy, like me, to stay at home and raise his family.

Ivan - Ivan organised the "Free Crusaders" into a very professional unit using his combat experience. More foreigners joined but it didn't last. In an operation in the village of Lepnica, Ivan was injured by a tromblon, the shrapnel of which hit Ivan in the eye, destroying it and part of his skull. He only just survived but eventually returned despite his injuries to the Free Crusaders, which was falling apart without him. 106 HVO wanted to discharge Ivan from the Army there and then but Ivan refused and stayed in Croatia and Bosnia until finally being discharged from military service at the end of the war in 1995. He now lives back in Ireland with his Croatian wife and young family.

Peter (Van Ekeren) - After Ivan was hit, Peter had no choice but to go to the front. He panicked and refused as he had apparently lost his nerve well before. He got drunk and admitted to the squad that he was terrified, which was why he had avoided line and patrol duty. Under his leadership things went from bad to worse and combat operations ceased after Ivan was injured. Thereafter the dodgy business he had been engaged in behind our lines became all the more obvious and serious and eventually the Unit left Posavina because relations between Peter and High Command (to whom the Unit were directly answerable) had degenerated to such a bad degree. Peter eventually found himself in Kosovo fighting with the Kosovo Liberation Army, as many volunteers did after the war in Bosnia ended in 1995. The myth of Peter lives on; some say that he survived and now lives back in Holland, others say that he was killed in a hotel near the border of Albania and Kosovo, not by the Serbs, but in a shoot-out with other foreign volunteers and local police after attempting to smuggle weapons out of the country. Knowing Peter, the latter theory is probably true.

Smiley - Smiley did not leave Posavina with the rest, choosing instead to rejoin 104 HVO with a line platoon. One night, when on sentry duty, he saw someone coming forward from the direction of the Serb positions and called a warning three times, eventually firing when he didn't receive an answer. Then, with others of his unit, moved out into no-mans land to investigate. They found out that the guy was a member of the same platoon, from two bunkers down the line - a Muslim and a war hero. He had gone forward and doubled back apparently to check out Smiley's reactions. It was the last thing he ever did. He died in Smiley's arms - and messed Smiley up in the process. Smiley was last seen in Orašje, just before Christmas 1994. He spent most of his days with his nose in a bottle - thinking that one of the local Muslims would certainly kill him for what he'd done, even though he'd been exonerated of responsibility by his commanders. He tried to get back into 104 HVO but couldn't and decided instead to go home. There has been no word since.

Farmer Joe - When the group went their separate ways after losing faith in Peter, Joe went home to Arizona. Peter and Joe were drinking, smoking and arguing buddies and Peter letting the team down affected Joe. Joe worked as casual farm labour in the US, saving enough money to travel and often coming back to visit Terry and Ivan and on one occasion visiting me in Prison. Farmer Joe sadly died of alcohol poisoning in January 2010, he had no relatives and was penniless, but given a military funeral by the American Legion veterans association. A sad end to a great warrior.

The Three Germans - Rommel, Gustav and Norbert stayed with what was left of the group and fought in Lepnica with Ivan. Gustav was suffering severe PTSD and on more than one occasion had to be physically disarmed. They eventually went their separate ways and the Germans went south to Mostar. During fighting in the town, their position suffered a direct hit from a tank or artillery round with all of them inside. Rommel was killed instantly, Gustav lost an arm and Norbert lost both his legs.

Marco Tigrić - Marco still lives and works in Domaljevac with his wife and young family.

The "Free Crusaders" - The Crusaders became the "Special Operations Group" for 106 Brigade and therefore the whole of the Posavina enclave from Bok, in the West, to Vidovice and Kopanica, in the East. The unit was later transferred to Tolisa, under the command of the 4th Operations Zone. The "Standing Order" from 4th OZ Command was that all new "foreign" recruits that crossed the

Sava were to be directed to Tolisa, and the Free Crusaders. After Peter's involvement with the hierarchy the unit, by now almost 20 to 30 strong, left Posavina in late December and moved south, engaging in combat in various sections of the line. The Unit broke up some months later.

There isn't an exact figure of foreign volunteers that fought for Croatia and Bosnia with the HV, HVO or HOS. The current approximate figure, according to the Veterans Organisation USDDR, is around 450 confirmed identities. Some stayed for years and saw little action but received the paperwork and documentation from the government such as the "Zagreb Commandos" that Peter pointed out at Zagreb Station, many volunteers stayed on after the war and have become part of the community, especially in parts of Slavonia, Eastern Croatia and the Posavina area where they fought. Some volunteers stayed for a few months or weeks and fought hard before returning home with nothing but memories. Others didn't survive and are buried in plots throughout Bosnia and Croatia; in many cases a nickname and a nationality written on a wooden cross is their only identity.

Glossary

'66	British Army's version of the Zolya.
ABiH	Armija Bosnia I Hercegovina- Army of Bosnia and Hercegovina. (The Bosnian Muslim Army.)
AK-47	The Worlds most popular rifle first made by the Soviets in 1947.
APC	Armoured Personnel Carrier.
AFV	Armoured Fighting Vehicle.
AWOL	Absent Without Leave.
BCP	Battery Command Post.
BACP	Battery Ammunition Control Post.
Battery	Usually six guns and their associated support.
Beasting	Punishment usually in the form of strenuous physical exercise.
Bergen	Large military backpack.
Bomblet	Small explosive device contained within an MLRS missile.
Challenger	British Army's main battle tank.
Četnik	Serb ultra-nationalist paramilitary.
Civvy	Civilian, non-military.
CMHT	Community Mental Health Team.
CO	Commanding Officer.
Con	Convict - inmate of a civilian prison.
FDC	Fire Direction Centre.
FV-432	The name of the British Army's APC.

HMP	Her Majesties Prison.
HOS	Hrvatske Obrambene Snage- Croatian Defence Forces.(Croatian nationalist militia.)
HQ	Headquarters.
HVO	Hrvatsko Vijece Obrane - Croatian Army Council. (The Croat / Bosnian Army.)
HV	Hrvatska Vojska - Croatian Army.
JNA	Yugoslav National Army- Serb regular Army.
Kalashnikov	An AK-47.
KIA	Killed in Action.
Lifer	Prisoner with a life sentence.
MG-42	Belt-fed heavy machine gun, developed by WW2 Germany and still in use today.
MLRS	Multiple Launch Rocket System.
Mine	Passive explosive device, detonated by pressure or movement.
Mortar	Portable short range Artillery equipment used by the Infantry.
MP	Military Police.
NBC	Nuclear, Biological and Chemical warfare.
NCO	Non-Commissioned Officer.
NIG	New Intake Gunner.
OP	Observation Post.
Parole	Early release from a long-term prison sentence for good behaviour.
PTSD	Post Traumatic Stress Disorder.
QMS	Quarter Master Sergeant. The NCO in charge of stores and supplies.

RA	Royal Artillery.
REME	Royal Electrical and Mechanical Engineers.
RP	Regimental Police.
RPG	Rocket Propelled Grenade.
RRF	Royal Regiment of Fusiliers.
RSM	Regimental Sergeant Major. Highest ranking NCO in a Regiment/Battalion.
Screw	Civilian Prison Officer.
Sitrep	Situation Report. A radio term for an information update
Sloppo	Slop Jockey- Catering Corps soldier.
SLR	Self Loading Rifle.
SMIS	Sergeant Major Instructor in Signals.
Srpski	Serbian. (Srpska – Serbia).
Stretch	Prison sentence (i.e. a seven year stretch).
Tracer	Phosphorous tipped bullet that burns as it flies.
Tromblon	Croatian rifle-launched grenade.
UNPROFOR	United Nations Protection Force.
USDDR	Udruga Stranih Dragovoljaca Domovinski Rata - Association of Foreign Volunteers of the Homeland War.
Warrior	British Army's newer APC, replacing the FV-432 in the nineties.
Webbing	Soldiers personal load carrying equipment.
Zolya	Croatian disposable shoulder launched rocket.

Lightning Source UK Ltd.
Milton Keynes UK
29 April 2010

153504UK00001B/27/P